Guide to

COUN

of Arizona, New Mexico, and Texas

The "Guide to the Recommended Country Inns" Series

"The guidebooks in this new series of recommended country inns are sure winners. Personal visits have ensured accurate and scene-setting descriptions. These beckon the discriminating traveler to a variety of interesting lodgings."
—*Norman Strasma, publisher of* Inn Review *newsletter*

The "Guide to the Recommended Country Inns" series is designed for the discriminating traveler who seeks the best in unique accommodations away from home.

From hundreds of inns personally visited and evaluated by the author, only the finest are described here. The inclusion of an inn is purely a personal decision on the part of the author; no one can pay or be paid to be in a Globe Pequot inn guide.

Organized for easy reference, these guides point you to just the kind of accommodations you are looking for: Comprehensive indexes by category provide listings of inns for romantic getaways, inns for the sports-minded, inns that serve gourmet meals . . . and more. State maps help you pinpoint the location of each inn, and detailed driving directions tell you how to get there.

Use these guidebooks with confidence. Allow each author to share his or her selections with you and then discover for yourself the country inn experience.

Editions available:

Guide to the Recommended Country Inns of
New England • Mid-Atlantic States and Chesapeake Region
South • Midwest • Arizona, New Mexico, and Texas
Rocky Mountain Region • West Coast

Guide to the Recommended
COUNTRY INNS
of Arizona, New Mexico, and Texas

by Eleanor Morris
illustrated by Bill Taylor Jr.

A Voyager Book

Chester, Connecticut 06412

Library of Congress Cataloging-in-Publication Data

Morris, Eleanor (date)
  Guide to the recommended country inns of Arizona, New Mexico,
and Texas.

  ("Guide to the recommended country inns" series) (A Voyager book)
  Includes indexes.
  1. Hotels, taverns, etc.—Texas—Guide-books.
2. Hotels, taverns, etc.—Arizona—Guide-books.
3. Hotels, taverns, etc.—New Mexico—Guide-books.
I. Title. II. Series.
TX907.M66 1987   647′.947901   87-8541
ISBN 0-87106-836-2

Manufactured in the United States of America
First Edition/First Printing

Contents

Indexes

How This Guide Is Arranged

Inns are arranged by states in the following sections: Arizona, New Mexico, and Texas. Because it is so large, Texas is divided into five geographical areas: North Texas, East Texas, Central Texas, Gulf Coast/Border Texas, and West Texas.

At the beginning of each section is a map and an index to the inns in that section, listed alphabetically by town. At the back of the guide is a complete index to all the inns in the book, listed alphabetically by name. Additional indexes list inns by special categories.

Abbreviations:

AP: American Plan. Room with all meals.

EP: European Plan. Room without meals.

MAP: Modified American Plan. Room with breakfast and dinner.

E: A personal comment from Eleanor.

The ☛ ☛ inserted now and then in the text are a way of calling attention to something outstanding, unusual, or special about an inn; it is not a rating.

There is no charge of any kind to an inn to be mentioned in this guide. The inclusion is a personal decision on the part of the author, who visited each inn, as well as many others that were not included. Please address any questions or comments to Eleanor Morris, The Globe Pequot Press, Box Q, Chester, Connecticut 06412.

Caveats and Considerations
of Country Inning

Webster's Dictionary says that an inn is a hotel, usually a small one. *Thorndike Barnhart* says that an inn is a public house for lodging and caring for travelers. Taking that larger view, you'll find in this guide a unique and eclectic selection of fine and fun places to lodge in the great Southwest. This is big country, with an incredible diversity of terrain presenting a wide variety of ecological systems. Like the land, from the mossy reaches of East Texas's Piney Woods to the arid deserts of southwestern Arizona, all manner and sizes of inns open their doors to the traveler eager for lodging that is not cloned from another in the next town.

Inns range from romantic Victorian cottages to rustic dude ranches, from small, intimate European-style hotels to larger ones that somehow manage to retain that same feeling of intimacy. Lodges sequestered in the mountains, mansions restored to original grandeur, log cabins (with modern conveniences), or luxury resorts with personalized attention—all await the traveler who wants something different to explore.

Some lodgings may disappoint you, but most likely never the innkeeper, for what makes the inn, comfort aside, is the innkeeper, who will treat you like a favorite member of the family at best and an honored guest at least. Innkeepers are gregarious, friendly, interested in you, and often quite interesting themselves. They range from retired stockbroker to ex-restaurateur, from educator to carpenter, from nurse to rancher. Without exception, every innkeeper in this book to whom I posed the question "Why are you doing this?" answered, "The people. We love the people."

"The people" is you, the traveler, and here are some caveats that will smooth your path to better and more beautiful inn experiences:

Rates: I have listed the range from low to high at the time I visited, realizing that it's up to you to decide how many in your party and what level of accommodation you wish. However, rates change without notice, sometimes overnight, so I cannot promise that there will be no surprises; always check beforehand. The rates given do not include taxes.

Reservations/Deposits: These are uniformly required, and if you do not show up and the room is not rented otherwise, you will most likely be charged. Expect to pay a deposit or use a credit card.

Minimum Stay: I have noted this wherever necessary, but most inns in this guide have no such restrictions. Check when you make your reservation, though, because policies change. Often during slow times minimum stay can be negotiable.

Credit Cards: Most inns accept credit cards. The few that do not are so noted in the text.

Children: Children are permitted, even welcomed, in many of these Southwest inns. Those that do not, or that impose restrictions, are listed in an index at the back of the guide as well as in the text.

Pets: A surprising number of inns are prepared to deal with pets, with some restrictions, and I have listed them in an index at the back of the guide as well as in the text.

Food: I have noted which inns serve food, whether included in the rates as in a bed and breakfast inn or whether there is restaurant service on the premises. Where there is not, most of your innkeepers will have an assortment of menus on hand for your perusal and are happy to make recommendations.

BYOB: It is usually perfectly all right to bring your own bottle, especially to an inn that has no bar or lounge facilities. Often the innkeeper will provide set-ups of ice and mixes, and many serve wine where licensing laws permit.

Smoking: Many inns, in Texas particularly, have restrictions as to where, when, and if their guests may smoke. This information appears in the text.

King, Queen, Double, or Twin: If you have a preference, always ask when you make your reservation.

Television and Telephones: I have not listed where these are available, assuming that, like me, you want to get away from it all when you go "inning." Many inns have both located in the common rooms, others in guest rooms. You have only to ask.

Air Conditioning/Heating: I have not listed these amenities because almost without exception they are taken for granted in the Southwest if climate warrants. But when in doubt, always ask beforehand.

Wheelchair Access: So few inns have this facility that I have not listed it. Please inquire when you make reservations.

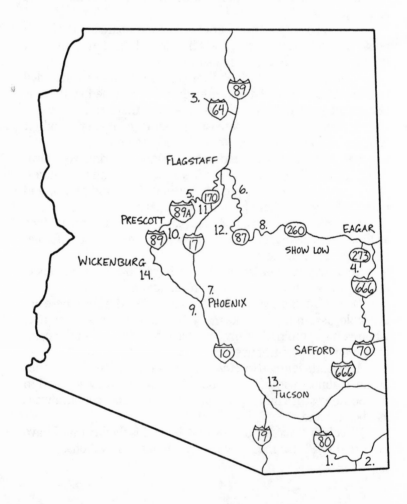

Arizona

Numbers on map refer to towns numbered below.

Bisbee Grand Hotel
Bisbee, Arizona
85603

Innkeepers: Joan Bailey and Isidro Chavez
Address/Telephone: 61 East Main Street; (602) 432–5055
Rooms: 12, including 3 suites with private bath; others share hall baths. Rooms have wash basins.
Rates: $49 to $125, including continental breakfast and champagne on arrival. Pets permitted by prior arrangement. American Express, MasterCard, Visa accepted.
Open: All year.
Facilities and Activities: Saloon, antique shop, ballroom-conference room. Historic Bisbee, Copper Queen and Lavender Pit Tours, Theater in the Gulch.

Watching the sunset, or the rainbow after it rains, over the mountains facing the balcony of this small elegant hotel is only one of its pleasures. Exotic luxury abounds at the ☛ posh, treasure-filled Grand Hotel. I climbed the red-carpeted stairs, leading from the Main Street entrance to the second floor lobby and found myself in a world I certainly never expected in the quaint and charming Old West mining town of Bisbee.

"The owner, Nell Peel, collected these antiques for thirty years," Joan says. What's more, if you like any of them, you can take them home with you—they're for sale! Every piece has a discreetly placed tag with a code number keyed to the catalogue price.

It's no coincidence that there's an antique shop on the first floor. Nell Peel moved herself and her antique shop here from Scottsdale in 1974. Also on the main floor is the hotel's 🖛 old-fashioned Victorian parlor, where you can play the antique piano if you're careful. The adjacent Grand Bar's thirty-five-foot bar came from Wyatt Earp's Oriental Bar by way of the Wells Fargo Museum.

🖛 The storefront windows on the street are a gas, containing live-looking figures of Orientals and cowboys playing poker, kibitzed by a fancy Western madam.

The three suites are extravaganzas, excitingly imaginative. The Oriental suite is unashamedly opulent, with walls covered in black-and-gold fabric depicting Chinese scenes. The brass bed is adorned with onyx and alabaster; bronze dragon vases and black lacquer vie with choice collectibles.

The Arizona Suite is a plethora of cowhide: hooves, horns, and stuffed heads, muted by hand-woven draperies and carpet. The Victorian Suite is splendid with burgundy velvet, more than sixty yards of it in the bed canopy alone.

Breakfast is simple: orange juice, coffee, and Danish. But for dinner, the excellent restaurant of the Copper Queen Hotel is just a few minutes' walk away.

The innkeepers work both the inn and the antique shop. "I like keeping in touch with people, as well as the everyday changing excitement. Never are two days alike," Isidro says as he unloads a truckful of beautiful antiques for both shop and inn.

"That's right," Joan adds. "We treat our guests very special, with all the grace and elegance of the best of a Victorian mining town. We're different from a boarding house," she says firmly.

How to get there: From Highway 80 East take Tombstone Canyon Road for approximately 2½ miles until it becomes Main Street. You can't miss the Bisbee Grand on your left.

The Bisbee Inn
Bisbee, Arizona
85603

Innkeepers: Zenia Estrada and Norma Kiddwell
Address/Telephone: 45 OK Street; (602) 432–5131
Rooms: 17, all with washbasins; share 5 shower rooms and 7 restrooms.
Rates: $22 to $49, including all-you-can-eat breakfast. No pets.
    MasterCard and Visa accepted.
Open: All year.
Facilities and Activities: TV room, laundry facilities; wine served after
    5:00 P.M. Brewery Gulch, Copper Queen Mine Tour, Lavender Pit
    Mine Tour, Bisbee Mining Museum.

   This historic inn first opened its doors in 1917 as the LaMore
Hotel, overlooking Brewery Gulch, then a wild boomtown street.
Owners Joy and John Timbers kept the mining hotel's spartan
but comfortable Victorian atmosphere when they undertook the
certified historic restoration. I like the spare but clean look that
solid light oak, lace curtains, and brass bedsteads can give.
They're real, too—the brass beds and oak furniture are ☛ the
original hotel pieces, in excellent condition. In the closets I found
flowered and plain flannel robes, hanging for guest use—a
thoughtful touch.
   Both lounge and dining rooms are homey. Three rooms, the

center one a small atrium, form the dining area. Look up and you'll see a set of stairs and a wrought-iron balcony under the skylight. Lace cloths are on the tables, with places marked by pretty ruffled mats.

Breakfast, made in quantity by Zenia, consists of three kinds of juice, fruit salad, whole wheat bread made by Joy, scrambled or fried eggs, bacon, pancakes, potatoes, waffles, or French toast. "All you can eat," says Zenia, "and sometimes quiche, too!"

☛ An enthusiastic innkeeper, Zenia says she enjoys talking to guests while she's busy making breakfast. "Being around people, talking with them and hearing their different accents, especially foreign ones—I love to hear about their countries or their states."

The entire crew gets into the innkeeping act. "When we have a full house, Joy [who teaches] comes up after school. She and John take part, help cook breakfast—we all work together." It's the kind of place where guests like Roger (the "elderly live-in gentleman who does tours" is how Zenia describes him—I didn't get to meet him) often help Norma serve wine to other guests in the evenings. The social hour can take place wherever you like—in the dining room, in the TV room, out on the porch, or even in your room if by chance you want to be alone.

All the crew will recommend good Bisbee eateries, and the Timbers also own the Plaza, a restaurant in the Warren area of Bisbee. (The town is really three small towns strung out along the copper mountains. Get an area map, brochures, and a walking-tour map from the chamber of commerce on Commerce Street.)

How to get there: From Highway 80 take the business exit into the heart of Old Bisbee and go straight up the hill, which is OK Street. The inn is 200 yards up the steep and narrow street, and there's parking to the right just beyond the inn building.

Copper Queen Hotel
Bisbee, Arizona
85603

Innkeepers: Virginia and Richard Hort
Address/Telephone: 11 Howell Avenue (mailing address: P.O. Drawer
    CQ); (602) 432–2216
Rooms: 43; all with private bath.
Rates: $30 to $71. No pets. MasterCard, Visa accepted.
Open: All year.
Facilities and Activities: Restaurant, lounge, outdoor café, swimming
    pool. Copper Queen Mine Tour, Theater in the Gulch, Coronada
    Trail, hiking and rock hunting.

Copper fortunes built the beautiful old Copper Queen, and
innkeepers Virginia and Richard Hort feel fortunate to own this
historical treasure.

"She's an old love, a gracious old lady," Virginia says of the
hotel built shortly after the turn of the century.

Antiques furnish many of the rooms, which vary from high-
ceilinged large quarters to cozy little nests. The upper floors, both
halls and rooms, are a burst of flecked-red wallpaper and red
shag carpet. Both dining room and saloon are restored to their
original rustic form of Western–Mining Town elegance. The saloon has a juke box and pool table and a small card room off to

one side with a window wall so you can kibitz the game without distracting the players.

"It's a funky old bar, and people have a lot of fun here," Virginia reports. "This bar is like some of the locals' living room— they come every evening to have a glass of beer or wine." On nights the saloon doesn't offer entertainment, local musicians play its piano or bring their own instruments.

I loved the huge oil painting in the bar; it shows Lily Langtry and Eros reclining on a chaise longue with a Cavalier on horse-back in the background. "When she came to Bisbee, she sang at the Opera House," Virginia told me.

The hotel's past also includes Teddy Roosevelt and "Black Jack" Pershing, who was sent to comb the nearby hills for Pancho Villa. (He didn't find him.) When the hotel was built, Bisbee was the largest copper-mining town in the world. You can tour the Copper Queen Mine (no longer in operation) and take wonderful photos of the hills, a blazing rust orange color from the ore.

Food is served outside on the veranda as well as in the res-taurant. As Virginia says, "Our weather here is super." I espe-cially enjoyed the breakfast special "Queen's Favorite," a savory mix of scrambled eggs, sautéed spinach, ground beef and Parmesan cheese. For lunch I recommend poulard à la Reine, thin crêpes wrapped around chunks of chicken and mushrooms in wine sauce, served with the inn's special frozen fruit salad.

☞ Gourmet dinner specials include roast duck à l'orange, veal Mornay or chicken Imperial. Bisbee may be a mining ghost town, but the Copper Queen Hotel is right up to the minute!

How to get there: From I–10 drive into Bisbee, taking Howell (not Tombstone Canyon Road), and you'll see the hotel (you can't miss it). Streets are narrow, winding, and one-way, so drive by the hotel and on up to the public parking lot at the YWCA at the end of the street.

The Inn at Castle Rock
Bisbee, Arizona
85603

Innkeepers: Dorothy Pearl and Jim Babcock
Address/Telephone: 112 Tombstone Canyon Road (mailing address: P.O. Box 1161); (602) 432–7195
Rooms: 12; 10 with private bath (including 4 suites).
Rates: $23 to $36, including breakfast. Children and pets welcome. MasterCard, Visa accepted.
Open: All year.
Facilities and Activities: Bisbee is busy: National Bicycle Races, March; Renaissance Fair, June; Poetry Festival, August; Art Show, September and October; Historic Home Tour, November; Christmas Fair, December.

"We believe strongly in providing inexpensive lodging on the European idea," says Dorothy. Both she and Jim are ☛ well-traveled people who are interested in meeting other travelers. "What's nice is when strangers, an entire cross-section of people, sit around a table and interact," she added. I found it easy to interact in the informal Southwestern atmosphere here at Castle Rock. Jim, an artist, has decorated all the woodwork with designs painted in bright colors, and his unique touch is everywhere. "This is really a labor of love," says Dorothy.

Every room is different. I was fascinated by the Arabian Nights Room, with its ☛ ceiling of draped India print fabric. The walls of the Micronesia Room are covered with grass mats. The Inn at Castle Rock is definitely for adventurous people.

The inn faces the famous landmark Castle Rock, rising steeply up from the road. The steep hillside in back of the inn is planted by Jim with all sorts of greenery—yucca, pampas grass, roses, and fruit trees—making a vertical Garden of Eden. He has built wood walkways so that guests can enjoy the hillside.

The inn is full of architectural surprises. The huge A-frame lounge atop the roof has a fireplace, books and games and toys for children, and two rattan swings hanging in mid-air. I climbed up by conventional steps, but there's also a circular stairway that leads up from the dining room.

Down in the lowest level, with picture windows facing the rock and just over a deep run-off for flash floods from the mountains, there's another lounge. ☛ This one has an even more unusual surprise—an original mine shaft!

"Now it's a spring-fed well," Dorothy says, indicating the ladder leading down in case rescue is needed. (The well is kept covered when children are near.)

Breakfast in this unusual inn consists of juice, fruit, cereal, toast and muffins, coffee, milk, and tea served on an Italian Provincial dining set with cane-back chairs.

There are also porches and gardens that offer tempting places to sit. I found the Inn at Castle Rock a lot of fun.

How to get there: From Highway 80 take the exit into downtown Bisbee. Turn left at the stop sign onto Main, which becomes Tombstone Canyon Road. The inn is on the left, 2½ blocks from town center.

The Gadsden Hotel
Douglas, Arizona
85607

Innkeeper: Marjorie Madsen
Address/Telephone: 1046 G Avenue; (602) 364–4481
Rooms: 160; all with private bath (including suites).
Rates: $25 to $85. No pets. All major credit cards accepted.
Open: All year.
Facilities and Activities: Restaurant, lounge, and coffee shop. Pool, tennis, and golf privileges at the Douglas Country Club; bird watching.

From the outside the Gadsden Hotel doesn't look like much—it's a big mint green cement block. But my mouth dropped open when I went inside. Shades of ancient splendor! A ☛ solid white Italian marble stairway sweeps down into a lobby whose pink marble pillars, topped with gold pediments, hold up a ceiling glowing with the light from ☛ two signed Tiffany skylights. The entire back wall of the stair landing is ☛ a stained-glass mural of a complete Sonora Desert scene.

What's all this opulence doing in an Arizona border town almost at the end of the road? Well, The Gadsden is a majestic memory of the extravagances of the early boomtown days when mining and cattle barons were making money hand over fist. They wanted Douglas to have the most beautiful hotel the West had ever seen. They succeeded beyond their wildest dreams, and they named the hotel after James Gadsden, the man who was responsible for the territory's becoming a part of the United States.

The hotel went through many vicissitudes until Marjorie Madsen and her husband, Russell, came along to create a warm and wonderful place amid all the grandeur. People come to eat, to bird-watch, and ☛ to have their names engraved on the walls of the bar. "It's a Gadsden tradition," Marjorie says. "Will Rogers' brand is on the wall of the Saddle and Spur, and for five dollars you can have yours, too. Of course, [the actual engraving] costs more than that today, but we still charge the same, and you'd be surprised the folks who want it done."

The restaurant's Mexican food is so good that Mexican dignitaries come across the border to eat. Prime rib is a specialty, too: this is beef country. Often the lobby is full of ranchers' big hats, Marjorie told me, "and they keep them on when they eat," she says with a laugh. The restaurant packs lunches for the many bird watchers who stay at the inn. One woman threw her arms around Marjorie, crying, "I have ninety new birds on my list!" I can see why guests throw their arms around her—the minute you meet her you can tell she is a warm and generous person.

Rooms are comfortable, which is all that matters here when you consider the rest of this hotel's glories.

How to get there: Highway 80 becomes the town's main G Avenue, so you can't miss the hotel if you try.

.

El Tovar Hotel
Grand Canyon Village, Arizona
86023

Innkeeper: Bill Bohannon
Address/Telephone: Grand Canyon National Park Lodges, P.O. Box 699;
(602) 638–2631
Rooms: 78, including suites; all with private bath.
Rates: $85 to $200. No pets. All major credit cards accepted.
Open: All year.
Facilities and Activities: Restaurant, mezzanine food service, cocktail
lounge, gift shop. In Grand Canyon National Park, with tours of
both south and north rim of the canyon, both mule and horseback
trips, day hikes and walks, Colorado River trips through the
canyon.

Not only is the Grand Canyon awesome, I found the famous
El Tovar Hotel to be quite a special sight, too. Opened in 1905,
the hotel, built of native boulders and Oregon pine, is a wonderfully majestic mix of Norwegian villa and Swiss chalet. Heavy
and rugged, it blends right into the canyon scenery. It was named
El Tovar in honor of Spanish explorer Pedro de Tovar, who led
the first expedition into this country in 1540.

Nothing was spared to make the El Tovar one of the great
hotels of its time. "We extend genuine hospitality and the utmost

courtesy to the new hotel's guests" was the byword back in 1905. It remains the byword of El Tovar's staff to this day.

The hotel's two-story lobby, surrounded by the Spanish balustrades of the mezzanine, has walls and rafters tinted a soft black. Hunting trophies hang from the timber walls, Navajo rugs add the warmth of color, and copper hurricane lamps add soft light around the stone fireplace.

Rooms, in warm earth tones, are large and comfortably furnished. Many have beds with brass headboards, and all have the luxury of thick, plush bath towels. I wanted one of the suites on the hotel's four corners, each with a good-sized porch. Though it was misting, I went outside to look out over ☞ the magnificent view of the Grand Canyon; the inn is that close.

The restaurant, with Indian murals decorating the walls, offers sophisticated food, from cheese blintzes at breakfast to chicken in champagne at dinner. On the mezzanine, light soups, salads, and sandwiches are served afternoons and a continental breakfast in the morning for inn guests only.

Although the innkeeper was out during my visit, I found the staff exceptionally friendly and helpful. It was stimulating being in such an outpost of civilization on the absolute brink of the canyon's raw beauty.

How to get there: From Flagstaff take Highway 180 north; it becomes Highway 64 and goes directly into the park. Directions to the hotel are clearly marked.

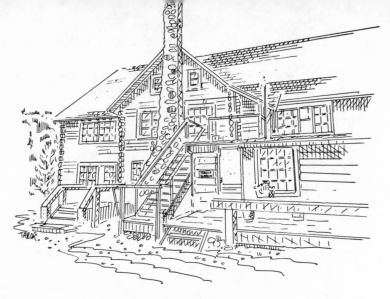

Greer Lodge
Greer, Arizona
85927

Innkeepers: Brenda Forman and Michael Rodgess
Address/Telephone: P.O. Box 241; (602) 735–7515
Rooms: 10, plus 1 cabin; all with private bath.
Rates: $59 to $68, MAP. (Breakfast and dinner.) Cabin suites, $68 to
$205. Two-night minimum on weekends, three nights on holidays.
No pets. American Express, MasterCard, Visa accepted.
Open: All year.
Facilities and Activities: Restaurant (closed Wednesdays for lunch),
bar, stocked trout pond, hiking, bird watching.

Here's a great place for communing with nature. While we
were touring the inn grounds, Michael shouted, "Quick! Get
your camera!" He had spotted a blue heron, and off he ran. I ran
too, but I wasn't fast enough.

"Never mind," Michael said. "During dinner you'll see the
owl zooming down and buzzing the pond, catching his dinner. If
he doesn't get a fish he'll get a duck. I've seen him pull a full-
sized duck out of the water."

Such is the view from Greer Lodge's magnificent two-story-
tall 🖝 greenhouse dining room at the back of the inn, all glass
with an indoor stream and waterfall and plants everywhere. The

room overlooks the pond and the pine-covered mountains in the distance.

"Brenda and I enjoy the beauty of the White Mountains a lot, and we really love it when our guests rave about how wonderful it is up here in Greer," Michael says.

The inn's spacious, comfortable rooms also have windows with views. The lounge has two stories, too, with a balcony that surrounds it like a catwalk. The large sitting area up there overlooks the skylights of the restaurant and bar as well as the beautiful scenery; down below is a massive stone fireplace and comfortable lounging furniture.

Homemade soups are wonderful here, as was the French Dip sandwich I had for lunch. Fresh homemade rolls are served with meals; and for dinner I recommend the New Zealand chicken stuffed with garlic, egg, and ham, served with wild rice, buttered broccoli, and carrots, and topped off with fresh blueberry pie.

After dinner (or maybe early in the morning?), sit on the back porch and just throw your line into the stream feeding the pond.

 Sitting out on the sun deck facing the pond, I see fish jumping up out of the water—rainbow and German brown trout, Michael tells me. Horses graze in the meadows in the distance. The hurly-burly of the city is far, far away.

How to get there: Greer is at the end of Highway 373, a short road that runs south from Highway 260 between Eagar and Indian Pine. The inn is at the end of the road on the left.

ॐ

E: *Three dogs—Kona the Samoyed, Kelly the Heinz 57, and Butkis the yellow Labrador—greet guests. But it's Butkis the "rock hound" that everybody comes to see. He'll even go under water to fetch a rock. "Wonderful for kids, keeps 'em busy all day!" says Michael.*

Molly Butler Lodge
Greer, Arizona
85927

Innkeepers: Sue and Jake Jacobs and Terry Richardson
Address/Telephone: Box 134; (602) 735–7226
Rooms: 10, plus 6 cabins; all with private bath.
Rates: $22.50 to $35 for rooms, $45 to $60 for cabins, two-night minimum on weekends, three nights on holidays. Pets permitted. MasterCard, Visa accepted.
Open: Usually closed from Thanksgiving to the Friday before Christmas, but check (changes every year).
Facilities and Activities: Restaurant and bar. Hunting, fishing, horseback riding, hiking, skiing.

Molly Butler is Arizona's oldest guest lodge, serving fabulous food since 1910, when Butler's Lodge put out a sign advertising "regular meals." Rooms numbered five to twelve in the Long House have plaques on their doors commemorating early settlers. The one on number six marks the Ellen Greer Room, "A Pioneer of the Valley, 1884." Rooms are rustic, as befits the ambience of this rugged little mountain village.

I loved being in a log house, which is what the lodge is. There are ☞ cozy fireplaces everywhere—it gets chilly in these mountains. I sank into one of the two curved sofas around the sunken fireplace in the lounge, under the large elk rack and the mounted javelina (wild pig), mule deer, and antelope heads. A huge elk head hangs on the Indian Room wall—this place is a hunter's paradise.

It's also a people place, according to Terry, who hails from back East. "I like people," she says. "It all boils down to people. I like the people here better than back East!"

Two of the three dining rooms have fireplaces, too. The piano in the lounge is "for anyone who wants to play," Terry says, and the bar has a pool table and a television set. Coffee is served here as well as stronger stuff, and it's a popular hangout for some of the local Greer characters as well as the guests. During my visit a cheese salesman came by, and nothing would do but that we all taste his samples to help Terry make up her mind what to order.

Chef Stephen Cooksley likes it here, too, having brought his gourmet talents with him from elsewhere. ☞ People drive up from Phoenix just for his broccoli-cheese soup, and I loved the trout Amandine sautéed in butter and sherry. The mud pie of coffee ice cream in a chocolate-cookie crust, covered with fudge topping and mountains of whipped cream, offered no hardship either.

How to get there: Greer is at the end of Highway 373, which runs south from Highway 260 between Eagar and Indian Pine. The inn will be on your right as you enter the village.

White Mountain Lodge
Greer, Arizona
85927

Innkeepers: Sophie and Russ Majesky
Address/Telephone: P.O. Box 139; (602) 735–7568
Rooms: 9; 2 with private bath, 2 with connecting bath, 5 with shared
bath.
Rates: $27 to $35, continental breakfast included. Pets by prior arrange-
ment. MasterCard, Visa accepted.
Open: All year.
Facilities and Activities: Dinner by prior arrangement. Fishing, hunt-
ing, downhill and cross-country skiing at Sunrise Ski Area 13 miles
away.

I loved Russ's answer when I asked why he liked being an
innkeeper after supervising in Tucson's main post office. Not
only did he say that both he and Sophie like caring for people and
that, although a lot of work, it is enjoyable, he added energeti-
cally, "and—I gotta have something to do!"

Both he and Sophie have found plenty to do in their inn
in ☞ the oldest building in Greer. It began as a farmhouse, built
in 1892 by one of the first Mormon families to settle here. The
Majeskys have preserved a wonderful landmark in a cozy and
comfortable way. Russ, who likes working with wood, did much

of the reconstruction, and Sophie decorated the rooms with talent she is just beginning to realize. With a Masters Degree in nursing, she is now "doing art," as Russ puts it. Every Tuesday morning she's off to Show Low, a town almost fifty miles away, for an 8:30 A.M. painting class three hours long.

The enclosed front porch and the main lodge room are comfortably furnished, and the word *cozy* keeps returning to my mind. ☞ The feeling is of warmth and interest in guests—genuine hospitality. "We've never charged a single cent for a cup of coffee in the seven years we've been in business," Russ says.

Breakfast, of juice, coffee, toast, and jam, is served in the family dining room, and a full breakfast is available for a nominal fee. Enjoying breakfast with other guests, the Majeskys believe, "provides spontaneity in talk and in striking up friendships while at the lodge." And in their experience they find that such friendships often are ongoing.

Sophie cooks dinners for groups but otherwise sends guests to the Molly Butler Lodge, Greer Lodge, or the new Green Mountain Shadows Restaurant and Bar for steaks or fried chicken. She and Russ like to drive the seventeen miles to Springerville, where the Safire Restaurant or the Piñon Tree offer prime rib or special fried chicken.

Behind the lodge, the farm's original log cattle barn is still standing, and energetic Russ has plans to restore it as an art gallery and craft shop. By the time you get there, I bet he'll have done it already!

How to get there: Greer is at the end of Highway 373, south off Highway 260 between Eagar and Indian Pine. The inn will be on your left as you enter the village.

The Miner's Roost
Jerome, Arizona
86331

Innkeepers: Betty and George Daech
Address/Telephone: 309 Main Street; (602) 634–5094
Rooms: 6; 1 with private bath, others share 2 baths.
Rates: $30 to $35 weekdays, $50 to $55 weekends, breakfast included on weekends. No children or pets. MasterCard, Visa accepted.
Open: All year.
Facilities and Activities: Restaurant, bar. Jerome State Park, Douglas Mansion, Gold King Mine Tour. Shops, arts, and crafts in historic buildings.

The Miner's Roost is atop Betty's Ore House Restaurant and Bar, so like everybody else, I entered through the restaurant. The first thing George did was offer me a drink from the bar. "Hotel guests have been driving a long way," he says, which is pretty understanding of him, to say the least. The drive up to Jerome, whether you're heading west from Sedona or east from Prescott, is sort of an endurance contest up Mingus Mountain. ☛ Jerome is stacked up the mountain like a Swiss village in the Alps.

The ex–copper mining town is now a boom town for tourists, and the Miner's Roost Hotel is a fun place to stay. The second-floor rooms were originally intended as offices, but Betty and

George have turned them into Victorian treasures. Miss Kitty's Room is named after a seamstress, and Jennie Banter's Room commemorates Jerome's leading madam. Her photograph is framed on the wall, and there's ☞ an old Victrola that still plays.

The parlor has a fireplace, a skylight, and a jar of candy for your sweet tooth. There's always coffee on, or you can have it downstairs in the restaurant.

"George and I know how we like to be treated," Betty says. "We were pleasantly surprised by British and Dutch bed and breakfasts when we traveled; it was a positive experience for us." Going through Jerome, they saw the view, "which was beautiful, and the town was friendly, so we decided to stay."

George loves to talk with people, Betty says. He'll sit for hours with hotel guests, getting to know them. They feel they've made a lot of friends. "The hotel and bar are a lot of fun. The restaurant, well, that's a lot of work," George says with a smile.

Betty's Ore House is becoming famous for three things: big, half-pound "build your own" hamburgers, deep-dish fruit cobblers, and homemade soups. I had a bowl of chicken soup that was more solid white-meat chicken than broth, and I'm told the Spanish meatball soup is extraordinary, too.

How to get there: Take Highway 89A up the mountain until you wind around on to Jerome's Main Street. There's parking on the bluff across the street from the hotel.

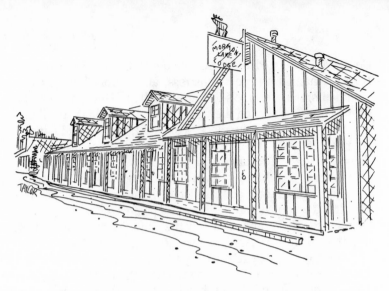

Mormon Lake Lodge
Mormon Lake, Arizona
86038

Innkeeper: Jim McCann
Address/Telephone: P.O. Box 12; (602) 774–0462 or 364–2227
Rooms: 7 cabins, including 2 two-bedroom cabins with kitchens.
Rates: $30 winter, $40 summer. Children and pets welcome. American
  Express, MasterCard, Visa accepted.
Open: All year.
Facilities and Activities: Restaurant, general store, service station. Boat-
  ing, fishing, horseback riding, stagecoach rides, cross-country ski-
  ing.

Although I found it charming, I almost decided to leave Mormon Lake Lodge out of this book when Jim McCann told me that
the water in the cabins gets turned off in the winter! (Because
the pipes freeze.) But he convinced me to include his establish-
ment by proving that such a lack of water was no deterrent to the
enjoyment of Mormon Lake—the lodge is full, both winter and
summer. I leave it up to you when to come.

When the lodge was built in 1924, all guest rooms were
upstairs, above the restaurant and lounge. The building burned
in the same decade, however, and when it was rebuilt, the upper

floor was reserved for dining and meeting rooms, leaving the cabins for lodging.

The small settlement of Mormon Lake was established in 1878 when Mormon settlers brought dairy cattle to the area and began producing butter and cheese. Today Mormon Lake is a premium hunting ground for deer, elk, antelope, turkey, bear, and goose. And when snow comes, there are ☛ sixty-seven miles of groomed cross-country skiing trails. Then, everyone gathers around the firewood stove in the bar, or the big fireplace in the lobby, before toting cans of water to their cabins. (Every cabin has a portable toilet in the rear for winter use, as indoor ones are in use from May 15 to October 15 only.)

Summer, the water supply is normal, and people come to enjoy the lake, the good food, and country-western dances on Friday and Saturday nights. Jim says the restaurant's ☛ steaks, broiled over mountain oak, are famous "coast to coast." I don't know about that, but the cup of chili I had at lunch warmed the cockles of my heart.

Years ago, local ranchers had a branding party, burning their brands into the lodge's log walls. (Maybe that's how the early fire started!) There are antiques, too, like old school desks, safes, and sewing machines around the lobby, and the restaurant has cozy red-checked tablecloths and savory odors.

"I love the area," Jim says. "It's pristine wilderness with variable weather conditions. We can have a lot of snow but it can be warm enough to ski in your shirtsleeves."

He wants to keep it that way. "People from Phoenix come up and mess up my wilderness," he complains. But he softens it with a laugh. All the same, if you go, don't mess with Mormon Lake!

How to get there: Mormon Lake is south of Flagstaff, off Lake Mary Road. Turn west when you see the Mormon Lake sign. The lake road circles the lake, and the inn will be on the east side of the road as you come through the village.

Hermosa Resort
Paradise Valley, Arizona
85253

Innkeeper: Harold Frey
Address/Telephone: 5532 North Palo Cristi Road; (602) 955–8614
Rooms: 35 villas; some with kitchen, all with private bath.
Rates: December 1 to April 30, $125 to $350; May 1 to June 30, $75 to
$225; July 1 to August 1, $50 to $150; September 1 to November
30, $75 to $225. No pets. American Express, MasterCard, Visa accepted.
Open: All year.
Facilities and Activities: Restaurant, bar, swimming pool, Jacuzzis, tennis courts, putting green. Jogging, horseback riding, golf privileges
at nearby club.

In 1930, western artist Lon Megaree chose this lovely spot
for his studio/home. Over the years, it changed from an exclusive
guest ranch to the resort hideaway it is today.

Six-and-a-half acres are hidden behind a pink adobe wall—
almost all I could see were greenery and flowers. In among the
palms and the yucca and the manicured lawns are scattered pink
adobe cottages, from *casas* with a wet bar to two-bedroom villas
with full kitchen, dining room, and living area.

My "standard" room opened off a covered walkway dripping

24

with flowering shrubs. The combination bedroom/sitting room had a kitchenette with a breakfast bar, a fireplace, and a private patio, and the décor was both elegant and warm.

The grounds are a joy to walk around. ☞ Cool Spanish fountains sparkle in front of the main lodge building, which contains the restaurant and lounge. During my visit a fire burned cozily in the restaurant fireplace, for the evenings were turning chilly. Innkeeper Harold acts as cordial dining-room host on Friday and Saturday evenings, welcoming guests and seating them for dinner.

Dinner was whiskey chicken: boneless chicken breast flamed in a whiskey sauce with heavy cream, julienne ham, and mushrooms. Delicious! (Veal Oscar is another fabulous dinner choice.)

Afterwards I paid a visit to the inn pets, a pair of doves in a cage in the lounge. The lounge is known locally in Paradise Valley as a jazz hot spot, with ☞ musical celebrities performing informally.

"The piano, flügelhorn, a drummer, saxist, violinist, bassist . . . they just wander on," says Peter Eickelberg, on duty at either desk or lounge. "I don't know how long it'll last, but it's been going on for quite a while."

There's a Happy Hour from 4:00 P.M. until 6:00 P.M., with beverages and hors d'oeuvres served each evening in the lounge. Though so successfully hidden away, Hermosa Resort is in the center of a fine residential neighborhood, just a mile or two away from great shopping at Paradise Valley Mall or Biltmore Fashion Park.

How to get there: Drive north on Thirty-second Street to Stanford Drive, then east to North Palo Cristi. The inn is on the northwest corner of the two streets, with its entrance on North Palo Cristi.

Kohl's Ranch Resort
Payson, Arizona
85541

Innkeeper: Corrine "Corky" Barker
Address/Telephone: Highway 260; (602) 478–4211
Rooms: 41, all with private bath; 8 cabins.
Rates: $58 to $98, including dinner. No pets. American Express, MasterCard, Visa accepted.
Open: All year.
Facilities and Activities: Restaurant, saloon, dance hall, pool, gift shop, video-game room; fishing, horseback riding. Zane Grey Cabin and Museum 5 miles away.

"We are in the hospitality business, and ☛ our guests are number one" is what Corky tells her staff at Kohl's. The lodge, a long, low L-shaped building with a two-story A-frame center, is a casual, rustic place; it lies along the banks of a stream and affords ☛ a refreshing view of the Mongollon Rim, a canyon cut in the rock below Coconino and Sitgreaves national forests. The countryside is dotted with lakes and streams for fishing and boating around the largest stand of Ponderosa Pine in the world.

Kohl's is on Tonto Creek, and the cabins are located on its banks. ☛ "Everybody who stays here wants to stay in a cabin," Corky says. "But we have only eight, so we've tried to give our newly decorated lodge rooms the effect of being in a cabin." I think they've succeeded: My room had a stone fireplace, a log wall, and plank-patterned carpet! Even the bath was outdoorsy, with plank-patterned vinyl on the floor and shower walls.

Kohl's Ranch is more than one hundred years old and has associations with Zane Grey, whose cabin is a favorite tourist destination. The lodge's huge A-frame lobby has a giant stone fireplace studded with amethyst geodes and copper rock. The open center stairway leads to the balcony gift shop.

People drive up from Phoenix—about eighty-five miles away—to eat in the Zane Grey Dining Room with its wall that's a replica of an old Western hotel front. Stained-glass windows reveal scenes of the old hotel's "interior." The salad bar was fresh, and the fixins' were so tasty I ate too much and had to groan when my entrée of Kohl's famous barbecue arrived. It was more than I could eat, a plateful more suited to a lumberjack or a hunter than to a writer short on exercise!

Between Corky and the friendly folks at the front desk, I really enjoyed my stay at Kohl's. I wasn't expecting the early frost that covered my car the following morning, but I got expert help in getting thawed out.

"To keep Kohl's friendly, bright, and clean is our main goal," says Corkey.

How to get there: The lodge is on Highway 260, 17 miles west of Payson.

Hotel San Carlos
Phoenix, Arizona
85004

Innkeeper: Chuck McBurney
Address/Telephone: 202 North Central Avenue; (602) 253–4121
Rooms: 84; all with private bath.
Rates: $60 to $70, including continental breakfast, tea and cakes in the lobby at 3:00 P.M., and bedtime snack at 9:00 P.M. No pets. All major credit cards accepted.
Open: All year.
Facilities and Activities: Indoor heated pool, valet parking, delicatessen. Close to Phoenix Art Museum and Heard Museum.

Here's another delightful small hotel with the notion of European service and style. "We're a mingling place, not one of the big plastic hotels," Chuck says. "We want to do things to make our guests welcome." ☞ I certainly soaked up the warm and helpful atmosphere when I stayed at the San Carlos. My room was furnished in traditional mahogany in a color scheme of teal blue and maroon with soft yellow walls.

"You're on the yellow floor," the cordial desk clerk said. "Each floor is a different color." Other floors have antique-white French Provincial furniture, and all rooms have lots of large mirrors, which are always a plus with me.

The lovely renovated lobby is all mirrors, too, as well as Austrian crystal chandeliers, which take a week to clean!

"We focus on the lobby to draw our guests together," Chuck says. Morning Danish and other assorted breads, coffee, and tea are served from 7:00 A.M. to 11:00 A.M.; tea and coffee appear at three, "or whenever a guest wants either," Chuck says.

The San Carlos is a seven-story historic landmark in downtown Phoenix. Built in 1927, it was one of the first buildings in the city to install air conditioning, and the original unit is still in operation, as are the steam-heat radiators.

The hotel restaurant is not open, but future plans that call for more renovation include food service. Meanwhile, the Purple Cow Deli at the corner of the lobby offers casual dining. The 🖝 heated pool is open round the clock if you want a midnight swim. There are two meeting rooms that can accommodate up to a hundred people, and often the San Carlos gets the overflow from the big Hilton down the block.

"Conventioneers say, 'We're so happy we were put here,'" Chuck says. "At first they're dubious, but not after they come. They like our warmth, our time-frame, they tell us."

How to get there: From the Maricopa Freeway (connecting I–10 and I–17), take Central north to Monroe. The hotel is on the northwest corner.

Hassayampa Inn
Prescott, Arizona
86310

Innkeeper: Denise Milam
Address/Telephone: 122 East Gurley Street; (602) 778–9434
Rooms: 67; all with private bath.
Rates: $40 to $120 seasonal. No pets. All major credit cards accepted.
Open: All year.
Facilities and Activities: Restaurant, lounge, ice cream shop, bakery
 shop, spa, gym. First world-class rodeo in July, bluegrass festival in
 August, antique car rally in September, Christmas parade in De-
 cember.

The Hassayampa Inn is named for a stream to which miners
flocked when gold was discovered in Prescott. Doesn't that pre-
pare you for a truly rustic inn? It did me, so I was surprised when
I discovered more than miner's gold at the inn. In the first place,
it's a hotel; and in the second place, an extremely elegant one.

Built in 1927 with money raised in stock sales to local citizens (Mayor Morris Goldwater—uncle of former senator Barry
Goldwater—proclaimed June 26, 1925, Hotel Day), the Hassayampa was northern Arizona's "Grand Hotel" for more than
three decades. Placed on the National Register of Historic Places
and restored in 1985, the Hassayampa is a marvelous tribute to

the art-deco excitement of the Jazz Age combined with features of the Spanish-influenced Southwest.

☞ Original frescos on the lobby ceiling, seeming as fresh as the day they were done, are painted between polished wooden beams. Spanish chairs and brocade sofas define sitting areas grouped around large Bukhara, Heriz, and Kerman Persian rugs. Potted palms frame graceful wall arches, and on the grand piano rests a sculpture by a prize-winning artist.

I found guests sitting around the lobby, having cocktails or resisting the temptations of the Ice Cream Bar and Bakery Shoppe with their delicacies from the Hassayampa's own ovens. The elegant Peacock Room has beautiful etched and beveled glass and an exciting menu. "Diners rave about our swordfish," Denise says. I raved about the veal fettuccini and the peacock lady etched on the dining room doors.

"Everybody always is so impressed with the inn, which makes my job so pleasant," Denise says.

How I loved the elevators, anachronistically run by uniformed bellmen: "Watch your step, please!" More than half the guest rooms still have original Castilian walnut furniture, inlaid with tiles, refinished, and restored to the state it was in when ☞ Will Rogers and Clark Gable slept here.

How to get there: The inn is on the corner of Marina and Gurley streets in the heart of Prescott. Take Highway 69 from I–17 if you're coming from Phoenix, 86A if from Flagstaff. They both cross Gurley in the center of town.

E: *Many places make the claim of "a step back in time," but the Hassayampa really delivers!*

Hotel Vendome
Prescott, Arizona
86301

Innkeepers: Janie Stamp and Ginny Tordrup
Address/Telephone: 230 South Cortez Street; (602) 776–0900
Rooms: 17 rooms, plus 4 suites; all with private bath.
Rates: $35 to $65 winter, $45 to $80 summer, including continental
    breakfast. Small pets "that don't bark" are permitted. All major credit
    cards accepted.
Open: All year.
Facilities and Activities: Wine and beer bar. Within walking distance of
    Courthouse Square, Whiskey Row, and downtown Prescott.

The charming Hotel Vendome, namesake of the Place
Vendome in Paris, began life in a simpler way, as a boarding
house for miners. It next became a home for unfortunate tuber-
culosis victims before the days of penicillin.

Today the small hotel has been reborn, and in a manner that
lives up to its name. I found the lobby to be a warm and cozy
sitting room, with simple white walls and dark woodwork setting
off comfortable blue lounging furniture grouped around blue rugs
over the polished wood floor. Bright yellow chrysanthemums
strike a cheery note.

Janie, who says she likes "to meet and talk to people," told me an amusing inn ghost story, and I still don't know whether it was tongue in cheek or not, but it was fun to hear.

Breakfast of juice, coffee, tea, and fresh doughnuts is spread out on the cherry-wood bar off in a corner of the lobby. During other hours of the day, there's a nice little menu of beer, wine, soft drinks, and snacks like nuts and cheeses and crackers. For other meals Janie says, "I have a stack of menus, and I send guests everywhere there's good food."

Guest rooms are small, but they're charmingly furnished, from the wood and cane-paneled ceiling fans to the blue-and-tan small-patterned carpet on the floor. Everything is on a smaller scale. Blue blinds cover the windows and tiny-patterned blue spreads match the wing-chair fabric; all are coordinated with the white-and-blue wallpaper behind the beds. Bedside lamps follow the same color and decorating motif, as do the bathrooms, with matching wallpaper and deep blue tile. My ☛ footed tub was completely encircled, the white curtain, stamped with the elegant Hotel Vendome logo, ensuring a cozy shower.

How to get there: South Cortez Street crosses Highway 69 (East Gurley Street), and the hotel is in the second block south.

∽

E: *I love such* ☛ *old-fashioned touches as the inn's antique "enunciator panel"—wood studded with call buttons connected to each room—on the wall behind the front desk.*

Prescott Pines Inn
Prescott, Arizona
86301

Innkeepers: Terry and Riley Young and daughter Kim
Address/Telephone: 901 White Spar Road; (602) 445–7270
Rooms: 12; all with private bath, some with kitchenettes; A-frame cabin
  sleeps 8.
Rates: $47 to $85, $85 to $150 for cabin, full breakfast included. Pets by
  prior arrangement. Smoking in designated areas. American Express,
  MasterCard, Visa accepted.
Open: All year.
Facilities and Activities: Kitchenettes have microwave ovens; patio with
  barbecue grill. Baby cribs, baby-sitting. Arts-and-crafts fair each
  summer weekend; hiking trails.

"We're not a motel; we're your home away from home,"
Terry and Riley say, and they proceed to prove it by the kind
of ☞ services you often count on family and friends for, like
airport pickup, reservations at restaurants, car rental, and even
appointments with realtors if you're thinking of moving to
Prescott! You'll get special attention on birthdays and anniversaries. "I've even brought in lobster dinners from restaurants," Terry
says with a laugh.
  You'll find flowers and wine in your room, games can be

checked out or can be played in the lobby, and daughter Kim is available for expert baby-sitting. It's no wonder that a lot of guests are repeaters. "We have people who come back, who send us gifts, who even pitch in and help with the work!" Terry says as I rise, feeling like I am at home, to clear off my breakfast dishes (which Kim snatched from me before I could).

Terry rightfully brags about her cinnamon rolls—they are as good as those grandma used to make, all crunchy caramel and nuts outside, soft yeast dough inside. Complementing them were the scrambled eggs with ham served with salsa on the side, cantaloupe and peaches, and orange juice, coffee, or tea.

Riley does custom woodworking, and between the two of them (Terry is an interior designer), they have created a bright and comfortable inn. I like the combination of casual country and Victorian décor they have evolved. Both the ☞ grandfather clock and the breakfast buffet are works of Riley's hands. Another interesting piece is the high desk the Youngs stand behind to register guests: It's a late-1880s railroad-station ticket desk that Terry inherited from her grandfather. "He was a station master in Dexter, Iowa, and when they closed the station, he bought it."

Inn grounds, though covering an acre of pine-covered land on the edge of Prescott National Forest, are just minutes from downtown Prescott.

How to get there: White Spar Road is highway 89 south, just as you come into Prescott from the south. The inn will be on your right. There's a sign, and parking is available right in front of the inn.

Garland's Oak Creek Lodge
Sedona, Arizona
86336

Innkeepers: Mary and Gary Garland
Address/Telephone: P.O. Box 152; (602) 282–3343
Rooms: 15 cabins; all with private bath.
Rates: $98 to $115 MAP. No pets. MasterCard, Visa accepted.
Open: April 1 to November 15.
Facilities and Activities: Private creek for swimming and fishing. Golf
   and tennis nearby, hiking, horseback riding, bicycling.

To reach Garland's I had to turn onto a small unpaved road
down a hill and over a stream. The stream was Oak Creek, one of
the prettiest spots in Arizona, a state full of pretty spots. Thick
greenery enveloped me, insulating me from the rushing highway
sounds.

"We feel we're in a very nice place," Gary Garland says mod-
estly, "and we want to share it with our guests. It's an escape for
us, and we hope it's an escape for them."

On the far side of the creek, in utter privacy, Garland's com-
bines the beauty of wilderness with all the comfort and familiar-
ity of "back home." Vegetables grow in the garden, and fruits
come from the orchards. 🖝 "Wild blackberries are real fun," inn
helper Shelly Duebler told me. "Everybody picks them in sea-

son." Everybody eats the jam, too, on the inn's delicious home-made bread and rolls.

Meals are served family style in the cathedral-ceiling, rock-walled dining room. Breakfast of *huevos rancheros* came not only with fresh-squeezed orange juice but also apple juice pressed from fruit grown in the apple orchard. I wasn't surprised, although I was impressed, to see Mary Garland's collection of ribbons from the Coconino County Fair hanging in the entryway.

Dinner of smoky-squash soup, chili-cheese bread, orange-tarragon salad and Cornish game hen Southwest style, served with a mélange of carrots, cauliflower, and zucchini, was complemented by an excellent Riesling wine. "You have to try Garland's apple tart," Shelly insisted, and was I ever glad I did! It was caramely, crunchy, and superb, unlike any other apple tart I've ever tasted. My tea was served in a hand-thrown pottery pot and mug that I would have loved to take home.

Most of the cozy cabins have fireplaces. Number four has a porch practically hanging over the creek—you can imagine the spectacular view. Little flowered Austrian shades at the windows are the kind of touches that make this rustic retreat special. "We're professional but not formal: That's what people like about our place," says Shelly.

The home-grown, homemade food is no deterrent, either!

How to get there: The lodge is eight miles north of Sedona off Highway 89A.

✳

E: *Ossa, the furry black dog, usually stays up on the hill, but he knows when it's going to rain. "We think it's not," Shelly says, "but when we see him come down from the hill . . . well, he's usually right!"*

Graham's
Bed & Breakfast Inn
Sedona, Arizona
86336

Innkeepers: Marni and Bill Graham
Address/Telephone: 150 Circle Canyon Drive (mailing address: P.O. Box 912); (602) 284–1425
Rooms: 5; all with private bath.
Rates: $70 to $95, including full breakfast. Children older than 12 welcome. No pets. Smoking outside on porch or balcony.
Open: All year.
Facilities and Activities: Pool and spa. Tennis, golf, racquetball nearby. Horseback riding, jeep rides, hiking. Indian ruins.

This lovely inn is located in the heart of Arizona's Red Rock Country, surrounded by jagged stratas of bright orange rock jutting dramatically up to the blue, blue sky. The inn, smooth and square and white, makes a cool contrast to its surroundings.

Marni and Bill can't say enough about ☛ the beauty of the countryside, and I agree with them—it is extraordinary.

"I wouldn't trade places with anyone in the world," Marni says, adding, "as long as Bill and I are doing this together." She and Bill recruited the talents of a California-trained designer, and their inn is outstanding. Each room has a name with a theme to match. The Heritage Room is red, white, and blue; the San Francisco Suite is all peach and pale blue; and the Garden Room, white with green and red geranium-flowered wallpaper, has white wicker furniture. The Southwest Suite . . . well, I could go on and on.

Bill was sales manager of a food company; Marni, a legal secretary; and with three daughters grown, they were in a position to make a dramatic change. They also wanted to work together. "We both like the openness of the countryside," Bill says. "But meeting people is the high point. Bed and breakfast people are gregarious. Innkeeping restores your faith in human nature— people are really pretty nice!"

Late afternoons Marni puts out wine, fruit juice, nibbles like salted almonds, cheese and crackers, cream cheese with chutney, and often—a Pennsylvania custom—pretzels dipped in horseradish mustard. "People sit around, get to know each other," she says.

A breakfast specialty is cheese Strata, perhaps inspired by the scenery! Meat, cheese, cubed bread soaked in milk, and mustard are baked slowly and eaten in a hurry! With it are fruit juices, fruit bowl with yogurt, and plenty of good hot coffee or tea. Then you're really fortified for the outdoors. ☛ Bill stands ready with National Forest Service maps of hiking trails so you can enjoy the beautiful Red Rock Country.

How to get there: Canyon Circle Drive circles off Bellrock Boulevard, which is in the south Sedona suburb of the Village of Oak Creek. From Highway 179 turn west at the intersection that has a convenience store and a service station on the right—that will be Bellrock Boulevard. Canyon Circle Drive and the inn will be on your right about a block down the road.

L'Auberge de Sedona
Sedona, Arizona
86336

Innkeeper: Eric Umstattd
Address/Telephone: 301 Little Lane (mailing address: P.O. Box B); (602) 282–1661
Rooms: 20 in inn, 32 in cabins; all with private bath.
Rates: $115 inn rooms; $200 to $375, MAP, for cabins. No pets. All major credit cards accepted.
Open: All year.
Facilities and Activities: Restaurant, two bars, two pools, whirlpool, gift shop. Old town Sedona and Tlaquepaque with shops and art galleries.

L'Auberge de Sedona has a French name for a reason: ☛ It's patterned after a luxurious French country inn. Rooms are decorated with Souleiado fabrics, and the furnishings are imported from Provence, France. Room 547 (it's on the third floor—there are only three floors to the inn) has a sophisticated color scheme of bronze, black, and brick red. The doors to the balcony are at an angle, and I enjoyed the lovely view of Oak Creek. Nice touches are the matching fabric shower curtains and individual dried-flower wreaths on each door.

Both inn rooms and cottages have ☛ beautifully canopied

beds imported from France, purple wisteria climbs on each balcony, and although choices on the dinner menu are printed in English, the categories under Le Diner are listed as Hors d'Oeuvres, Soupe du Jour, Les Salades, Les Entrées, Les Desserts, and Café, Thé, Lait, Décafiné. Happily, these are all terms most guests will understand, and it adds a pleasant French fillip to the inn atmosphere.

The restaurant is open to the public as well as inn guests, and it enjoys a fine reputation—it certainly was crowded during my visit. The prix fixe dinner was a difficult choice between either tournedos of beef with a burgundy truffles sauce and green asparagus or roasted roulade of veal with rosemary sherry sauce and papaya. Such dishes as shrimp and avocado omelette at breakfast also add to the inn's gourmet reputation.

The three-story lobby has two fireplaces and lots of comfortable sitting space, with meeting rooms opening off the center area. "This is a marvelous place, and we'll be back," I overheard from more than one guest checking out.

The Tlaquepaque arts-and-crafts village just up the road from L'Auberge was designed in authentic Spanish-Colonial style. In Mexico its name means "the best of everything," and the village is full of plazas with splashing fountains and shops selling works by talented artisans.

How to get there: Little Lane is off Highway 89A, one block north of Highway 179. Turn east and follow the lane down the hill to the inn, where it dead-ends.

Strawberry Lodge
Strawberry, Arizona
85544

Innkeepers: Jan and Richard Turner
Address/Telephone: Rt. 1, Box 331; (602) 476–3333
Rooms: 12; all with private bath.
Rates: $27 to $35. Pets permitted. No credit cards accepted.
Open: All year.
Facilities and Activities: Restaurant, barbecue patio. Fishing, hunting, horseback riding, hiking.

☛ I knew this was a happy place the minute I walked in the door. If it hadn't been the vibrations telling me so, it would have been the happy voices in the crowded restaurant, which is where everybody enters the lodge, although there's a perfectly good entrance at the inn lounge.

Jan and Richard, at the time a chemical engineer, drove through Strawberry on a holiday when their kids were young. "Wouldn't this be a heavenly place to live!" Jan said. She and Richard were both weary of his constant traveling while she stayed home with the children. It seemed like fate, then, when they saw "a little two-line squib about a hunting lodge for sale." Richard is a Zane Grey fan (Grey wrote about this Mongollon Ridge area), and that cinched it: They became innkeepers.

The lodge was so neglected it was a big challenge. "My husband, who had never done rock work in his life, built all the fireplaces," Jan told me. Each room has one, and each is different. Richard used all-native materials in remodeling the inn, learning how to do it himself. Rooms are rustic but warm and comfortable, with wood-paneled walls and nice touches like co-ordinated print wallpaper in the bathrooms.

For her part, Jan learned how to cook for crowds. "I was known for my pie crusts, but not in such quantity!" she says with a laugh. "Some people go through life with talents they never develop. I'd never cooked for anyone but my family, so it was a dramatic thing for me." ☞ Now the lodge is famous for her pies as well as all the other good food.

The entire family pitched in to make the inn the great place that it is. As a Christmas present for her folks one year, daughter Cindy made a set of hand-carved tiles for each shower.

The restaurant is packed during open hours. "This is the best meal I've had since I left home," customers constantly tell Jan. The "kaffeeklatsch table" next to the fire is filled with regulars, and their wives join them at 3:00 P.M. They're always sold out of the Saturday night prime rib and apple pie. "We have never compromised with quality," Jan says firmly.

How to get there: Strawberry is on Highway 87, and the inn will be on your right just as you drive into the town from the south.

 confite

E: *I was dying to know how the town got its name. "The original settlers found this whole valley a mass of wild strawberries—at least that's the story," Jan says. Now the only strawberries are at happy Strawberry Lodge.*

Arizona Inn
Tucson, Arizona
85716

Innkeeper: Robert Minerich
Address/Telephone: 2200 East Elm Street; (602) 325–1541
Rooms: 85; all with private bath.
Rates: 3 seasons: summer $52 to $105, fall $68 to $115, winter $88 to
$130 and up. MAP and FAP upon request. Pets by prior arrange-
ment. American Express, MasterCard, Visa accepted.
Open: All year.
Facilities and Activities: Restaurant, lounge, swimming pool, bar; ten-
nis courts, putting green. Nearby golf and horseback riding. Arizona-
Sonora Desert Museum; Tucson Museum of Art.

This cluster of Spanish-Indian adobe buildings hidden along
winding pathways is not what I expected when I drove up to the
Arizona Inn. The large main building has ☛ high pink adobe
walls that seem to enclose the grounds like loving arms. Inside,
manicured lawns and lovely gardens spread a sort of hush over
the desert property. "Desert" makes it sound deserted, but the
inn is actually in the middle of Tucson. You'd never know it,
though, since everything's so quiet and, well, hushed.

The Arizona Inn has an unusual history. It's the inspiration
of a New York socialite of the 1920s who found herself widowed

in Arizona. Her name was Isabella Greenway, and one of her interests lay in giving disabled veterans an opportunity to work.

She opened the Arizona Hut, where the veterans produced "everything that goes into a house except carpets, stoves, and refrigerators." But the Depression left her with a warehouse full of furniture and no buyers.

So she opened the Arizona Inn. "Mrs. Greenway was into what she called 'private spaces,' " says Patricia Boysen, in charge of public relations for the inn. Each *casita*, hidden from its neighbor, is reached by a winding path shaded by green and flowering shrubs. Each has a secluded patio and is ☛ furnished in a wonderful combination of both veteran-made furniture and articles from Isabella Greenway's home.

Mrs. Greenway was into service, too, and the inn is famous for its coddling of guests.

"If anyone wants anything, they see me—that includes anything—and I take care of it. But actually, anyone in the inn will help," Patricia says. "They *love* to help. We don't like to pass people along—the inn is a very personalized place."

I believe it. I passed what appeared to be a mailbox as I was walking into the entrance. A bellman was just wheeling in an empty cart. "Nope, that's not a mailbox; just give your letter to me, and I'll see that it gets right out," he said, and I hadn't even signed in as a guest yet.

How to get there: Take Speedway exit off I–10 to Campbell, north on Campbell to Elm, and east on Elm two blocks.

✸

E: *I haven't even mentioned the marvelous food. The extensive menu is international in flavor, and you sweet-tooth travelers must seriously consider the Arizona Inn pecan pie!*

Hacienda del Sol
Tucson, Arizona
85718

Innkeeper: Frank Fine
Address/Telephone: Hacienda del Sol Road; (602) 299–1501
Rooms: 24, plus 23 *casitas;* all with private bath.
Rates: $60 to 300, MAP, FAP, EP, with special weekly and monthly
    rates. Pets by prior arrangement. American Express, MasterCard,
    Visa accepted.
Open: All year.
Facilities and Activities: Restaurant, lounge, swimming pool, Jacuzzi;
    tennis, putting green, stables. Horseback riding, jogging, fishing,
    hiking, volley ball; informative lectures.

"We don't have a concierge; we have an activities director,
one who'll get you up out of your chair," promises innkeeper
Frank. "We're totally involved with our guests."

You can stay a night, a week, or a month at Hacienda del Sol
and not run out of things to do. Mainly, the great outdoors is the
attraction, for the ranch is 2,800 feet up into the Catalina foothills
north of Tucson. "We go horseback riding, fishing, we study the
desert wildlife," Frank says. "After all, we are in the West."

Picnic tables are set out all over the grounds, and guests are encouraged to go view the desert life: roadrunners, quail, and jack rabbits.

Bird watching is big; food is put out for birds and the fish in the pools; hummingbird nectar attracts those tiny winged creatures. ☞ During the daily cocktail hour, guests are regaled with fresh information delivered by experts from the University of Arizona or other area facilities.

I was impressed by lectures on Southwestern history and the old pueblos of Tucson. Other evening activities included excursions to Sabino Canyon, visits to the Arizona-Sonora Living Desert Museum, and tours of Old Tucson.

The restaurant is 4-star, with a ☞ gorgeous view from wide glass windows. Local people, too, come to dine from a menu that changes daily, with everything fresh made and fresh baked, but inn guests are always taken care of first. In the gourmet dining room, food is cooked at table by tuxedo-clad waiters; this, in the middle of the desert.

Spanish is the motif, with some of the rooms having hand-painted furniture. Everyone gathers in the cheerful living room, with fire blazing away in the adobe fireplace, or meets in the library to read or play a quiet game of cards.

The party set gathers at Casa Feliz—"happy house"—for cocktails, dancing, and fellowship.

"Comfort, service, wonderful food—and our nonstop program of activities—are our keynote of quality," says Frank, as he enthusiastically goes off to make sure that everything is running smoothly at Hacienda del Sol.

How to get there: From I–10 take Prince Road east to Campbell Road. Drive north on Campbell Road to Skyline, east on Skyline to Hacienda del Sol Road, then south to inn sign on the right. About ½ mile of unpaved road leads to the inn; follow the arrows.

La Madera
Ranch and Resort
Tucson, Arizona
85749

Innkeeper: Mel Roach
Address/Telephone: 9061 East Woodland Road; (602) 749–2773
Rooms: 13; all with private bath.
Rates: $29 to $59, including continental breakfast; $64 to $119 AP,
　　winters only. Pets by prior arrangement. MasterCard, Visa accepted.
Open: All year.
Facilities and Activities: Restaurant, honor bar, heated pool, Jacuzzi;
　　tennis court, bicycles, shuffleboard, and horseshoes. Scenic drive
　　up Mt. Lemmon, ski chair lift open all year, hiking Sabine Canyon,
　　trolley to Seven Falls waterfall.

　　"Because of our small size, we keep a family atmosphere,"
says Mel of La Madera, hidden away in the hills north of Tucson
yet only minutes from town. "We keep it a 'welcome-home' kind
of place." La Madera is certainly hospitable, with such courtesies
as the "honor bar" to make you feel right at home. The bar is set
up in a small room alongside the dining room, and you can help
yourself to whatever you want whenever you want it. The only
catch is that you're on your honor to keep track of what you drink.

"Our whole objective is to make you feel right at home," Mel says. "We're very casual, just like the honor-bar kind of thing."

I felt at home in the large lounge, with one sofa facing the picture window and another facing the fireplace. Books are stacked in a niche by the fireplace as well as in a long, low glassed-in bookcase. Television shows I could ignore, but who could resist the old Bette Davis and Humphrey Bogart movies on the VCR?

Breakfast is juice and coffee, fresh fruit in season, and usually homemade cinnamon rolls. You can order eggs and pancakes off an additional menu, and there's always coffee on in the morning in the card room. Here, an antique poker table is the scene of wild Trivial Pursuit games, bridge, chess, backgammon, and, yes, even poker.

The restaurant serves such fine fare as broiled prime rib "La Madera" (red and green peppers sautéed with mushrooms and garlic), shrimp Diane, and pasta Primavera. The public can dine by reservation, but ☛ inn guests "always have priority," says Mel.

Rooms are bright and cheerful if not luxurious and are spread out in cottages around the tree- and flower-filled grounds. ☛ The Jacuzzi is lit at night, and some very happy people were enjoying a good soak.

How to get there: From I–10 take Grant exit east to Tanque Verde Road, turn north, and go past Bear Canyon and Mt. Lemmon signposts. Just beyond, turn east on Woodland Drive and proceed for half a mile. The inn will be on your right.

The Lodge on the Desert
Tucson, Arizona
85733

Innkeeper: Schuyler W. Lininger
Address/Telephone: 306 North Alvernon Way; (602) 325–3366
Rooms: 40; all with private bath.
Rates: $38 to $106 EP, seasonal, including continental breakfast. AP and MAP available. Pets by prior arrangement. All major credit cards accepted.
Open: All year.
Facilities and Activities: Restaurant, lounge, pool, croquet court, shuffleboard, darts, ping-pong, library. Golf, tennis, and racquetball facilities nearby.

Schuyler Lininger has a title, Patron Grande, and he's the second generation keeper of this inn, which has been in his family more than fifty years.

"There are not many small inns left, and we are one of the few left that are family owned with hands-on family operation," he says with regret. "We're a different breed of cat, taking a proprietary interest in our guests."

Schuyler, for example, introduces guests to one another "so everybody doesn't feel like a stranger when they come in. Then, if you want to be alone, you can, but at least you're not walking into a cold atmosphere."

The Lodge on the Desert is unique in many ways, and one of them is that it's not on the desert, at least not any longer: It's in the heart of the city. But behind its adobe walls is an oasis of peace and quiet. Once inside, you seldom hear city noises.

The main lodge is the property's original Mexican ranch house. Schuyler knows every inch of it from his childhood. When he was younger he left the family place for a while, thinking he wanted a career in the East, but he found he couldn't stay away for long.

There are lovely old Mexican tiles in the walls, books, and comfortable furniture in front of the fireplace. I noticed the chess game set up on a table alongside the long porch. That always impresses me, perhaps because I never learned to play!

The inn has grown to a sprawling collection of large Spanish-style *casas,* many with fireplaces and almost all with corner windows. They're grouped charmingly around intimate patios that open onto the green oasis of the grounds.

I had trouble discovering the difference between standard, deluxe, and luxurious rooms, as they all looked gorgeous to me, each bright and cheerful with Spanish or Southwest furniture.

The restaurant has both a summer and a winter menu, and the food is very good. I recommend the delicious poached silver salmon with lemon butter or the veal Parmigiana with fettucini, and you should finish up with the mocha torte. Breads are home-made, as is the ice cream—try the coffee-raisin or the honey-vanilla. Two five-star restaurants nearby that the lodge recommends are the Tack Room and the Palomino.

How to get there: The Lodge is east of I–10 on the northeast corner of Alvernon and Broadway.

E: *"We have a very intimate relationship with our guests,"* Schuyler says. *"Long before manager cocktail parties became popular, we did them. We take guests out on picnics, too."* No wonder inn fanciers prefer such lodgings to impersonal hotels!

Tanque Verde Ranch
Tucson, Arizona
85748

Innkeepers: Lesley and Bob Cote
Address/Telephone: Route 8, Box 66; (602) 296–6275
Rooms: 58, including 13 suites; all with private bath.
Rates: $129 to $159 low season, $159 to $209 high season, AP, including horseback riding. No pets. American Express accepted.
Open: All year.
Facilities and Activities: Indoor and outdoor pools, tennis, horseback riding, health spa, shuffleboard, and horseshoes; children's playground.

Bob Cote calls his ranch a country inn—with horses. "Country inns are a lifestyle all to themselves," he told me. "Actually, I was an educator for many years, and this type of work is not much different. You're involved twenty-four hours, total involvement, the whole focus of your being. It's a complete pattern of life." Bob loves it: He glows, which should give you an idea of life on this ranch. You'll glow, too!

In addition to all the other exercise, a hundred horses are ready to be saddled at any time. Evenings, listen to enrichment lectures. "We always have an evening activity to pique peoples' interest in the Southwest, so that they'll want to return," Bob confesses. "After that, we can't keep them awake. We've tried. If you do my program, you can't stay up!"

Discussions are on Cochina and Hopi Indian legends or "rattlesnake talk" or desert animals, plants, and flowers. That, after a dinner of roast leg of veal with celery-and-olive dressing, broiled filet of ocean perch with creole sauce, or baked Hawaiian pork chops, guarantees you the soundest sleep of your life.

"We have three choices every meal," Bob says, pointing out that they're four-star in a well-known travel guide.

Lunch-buffet choices during my visit were Spanish lamb stew, broiled cod with Bearnaise sauce, and the Black Forest sandwich of roast beef and Swiss cheese grilled on rye bread. I love soups, and the inn's cream of celery-almond soup was four star with me.

Most of the luxurious guest rooms have fireplaces; all have private patios.

The ranch has a colorful history. It was built in 1862 on a Spanish land grant and is one of the oldest in America being used as a guest facility. Bob told me that the original owner is rumored to have been hanged in his own parlor because he would not tell bandits where his money was. "The second owner played William Tell and missed," Bob added. "He was sent to jail!"

How to get there: Take Speedway exit off I–10 and drive to the absolute end. The road goes through town and out toward the mountains, so don't give up—it dead ends at the unpaved road on the left leading to the ranch. There's a sign.

❀

E: *For the extra-peppy, the Dog House Bar is a popular spot. You have to bring your own liquor, but you get a locker to keep it in.*

Flying E Ranch
Wickenburg, Arizona
85358

Innkeeper: Vi Wellik
Address/Telephone: Box EEE; (602) 694–2690
Rooms: 14; all with private bath.
Rates: $70 to $130, AP; children: infant to 2, $20; 3 to 6, $30, 7 to 12,
$40; 12 and older, $50, two-day minimum. No pets. No credit cards.
(Horseback riding extra.)
Open: November 6 to May 1.
Facilities and Activities: Pool, sauna, spa; horseback riding, tennis court,
volley ball, basketball. Occasional square dances.

Innkeeper Vi Wellik and her husband came to the Flying E
Ranch in 1948 and 1949 as guests. It took them eight years to
make the transition from guests to owners, but not very long to
make the Flying E a popular spot. "We tried to think of everything to make guests comfortable," she told me. I was impressed
with the results. Rooms are not only inviting, with picture windows and comfortable ranch furniture, they are absolutely
immaculate. ☞ There are even electric blankets for chilly evenings, and every room has a sink and refrigerator, though there's
not any need—the food in the dining room is as good as grandmother's. Breakfast is served to individual order, but lunch and

dinner are family-style service. The coffee pot in the dining room is always on, and the cookie jar is always full.

The ranch has no cocktail bar, but every evening Vi hosts a happy hour in the saloon, providing set ups and ice (bring your own bottle) and snacks like nuts and mushroom dip with chips.

"I enjoy people," Vi says. "We have guests who come from all over the world. Last summer guests from Switzerland spent six weeks."

Activities besides horseback riding and swimming include hayrides, dude rodeos dubbed "dudeos," boot races for the kids, and even britches branding (not with a hot iron!). Breakfast cookouts, lunch rides to scenic spots, and chuck-wagon cookouts are regular events; and if you don't ride horses, you'll still get to the site.

Horses are not included in the tariff, however. One ride a day runs $12; two per day, $18; and an unlimited number per week, $90. If you need lessons, the wranglers are there to help.

Vi is widowed now and runs the ranch with the help of a dedicated staff, some of whom have been with her since she bought the ranch in 1952. "If you like people, it's a very rewarding experience," she says.

How to get there: From the stoplight at the center of Wickenburg, take Highway 60 west through the underpass. After you pass the new Safeway store on your left, you'll see a large Flying E sign, also to your left. The ranch is a short way down the unpaved road, across the cattle guard.

Kay Bar El Ranch
Wickenburg, Arizona
85358

Innkeeper: Judith Nash
Address/Telephone: Box 2480; (602) 684–7593
Rooms: 10; all with private bath.
Rates: $80 to $155, AP. No pets. MasterCard, Visa accepted.
Open: October 15 through May 1.
Facilities and Activities: Bar, pool, horseback riding, shuffleboard, other
   yard games. Tennis, golf. Museums, art galleries, Western and jew-
   elry stores in nearby Wickenburg.

"We don't have sophisticated pursuits—this is a dude ranch,"
Jane says. "About the most excitement we generate in the evenings is a hot game of Trivial Pursuit. This is not a big night-life
place, and that's the way we like it!" The fireplace blazes 'most
every night in the lounge—or the "Great Hall," as one guest calls
it—and everybody relaxes with books, magazines, television, or
the piano in this huge but homey room. The well-stocked bar
operates on the honor system.

Sometimes there are dances and cookouts. Mostly, though,
there's horseback riding, swimming, loafing—and eating. "We're
known for our food," Jane says. ☛ Chef Jackie Brown has been
written up in *Gourmet* magazine. "We have only one seating for

each meal, and when we ring the bell, they better show up—and believe me, they do!"

Dinner during my visit was mouth-watering: chicken breasts with cream-wine sauce and artichokes, mixed wild and white rice, and famous Kay Bar El pie, a citrus chiffon confection. Hardly the stuff by which chuckwagons are known! When the inn has just a small group of guests, they like to eat in the staff dining room, watching the birds outside and smelling the good cooking smells.

"We've tried to get everybody to sleep late on Sunday mornings," Jane confesses, "but they're here at seven, their noses pressed against the door!"

The ranch's adobe buildings cluster in a little valley along the Hassayampa River. Low hills lead to scenic trails under a cloudless cerulean sky. The ranch is ☛ the second-oldest dude ranch in the state and the oldest in the neighborhood.

It's a family operation, too, down to the appliquéd Western motifs on all the towels, done by Jane's sister Jan Martin. Even the linens are printed with a western scene, and furniture is original Western furniture from Monterey, California, circa 1920.

Out on the grounds there's a huge salt cedar tree and the largest saguaro cactus I've ever seen. Jane says it's 300 years old. Often there are golden dogs on the grounds, too. "We raise Golden Retrievers, and periodically we have puppies. Kittens, too." You'll even see a pet cow, given to a staff member by an inn guest. "It depends what kind of mood she's in," Jane says, "whether or not she'll come up and talk to guests."

How to get there: Turn right off Highway 60 to Highway 89/93 at the only stop light at Wickenburg. The ranch will be on your right two miles north. There's a sign that leads down the unpaved road to the entrance.

Wickenburg Inn
Wickenburg, Arizona
85358

Innkeeper: Lefty Brinkman
Address/Telephone: P.O. Box P; (602) 684–7811
Rooms: 47 (6 in lodge, 41 *casitas*); all with private bath.
Rates: $100 to $250, AP; minimum stay 2 nights, 4 to 7 nights during
    holiday periods. Caters to children. Pets by prior arrangement.
    Smoking discouraged. All major credit cards accepted.
Open: All year.
Facilities and Activities: Restaurant open to public by reservation. Pool,
    spa, tennis, horseback riding, archery, arts and crafts, children's
    activities.

    Try to begin your two-night-or-more stay at the Wickenburg
Inn on a Sunday night. That's Lefty's get-acquainted-party night.
"We get them started immediately, there's so much to do," says
Lefty, who positively radiates energy, health, and good humor.
The inn is definitely an outdoorsy place, with enough activities
going on daily to fill a cruise ship. But the rusticity is smoothed
with a fine layer of ☛ luxurious attentions, like wine, fruit basket, and welcome card upon arrival and nightly turndown with a
mint upon your pillow. "We try to pamper our guests," Lefty says.
    Located on 4,700 acres of Sonora Desert, the inn is a popular

tennis and riding ranch. Dozens of trails are tended by wranglers who might let you gallop your horse a little. More unusual is ☞ the resident naturalist, who implements the inn program of wildlife preservation and natural history. On the grounds is the Desert Caballeros Western Museum, dedicated in 1975 by then-Governor Raul Castro.

Casitas and rooms are cozy, with the former having wet bars, fireplaces, small refrigerators, and stoves. But what guests would want to eat in their rooms? "Our chef is a master with soups; they're dynamite," Lefty says. "And our desserts are more filled with calories than they ought to be!" Which did not stop me from trying out all the flavors on the homemade-cookie tray, as well as a hefty taste of the mud pie.

Food is served buffet style, and the chicken à la king I helped myself to at lunch was topped with the fluffiest biscuits I've eaten in a long time. "I go through the dining room seeing if everything is OK," Lefty told me as several guests came up to say goodbye and rave about their stay. When I commented on this, he remarked that his staff have their heads on straight and enjoy what they're doing. But their inspiration surely comes from the innkeeper himself. "My motto to them is that they should 'touch' each guest each day in one form or another, get them in a tennis game . . . !"

How to get there: On Highway 89 from Wickenburg, turn right four miles past the "Wickenburg Inn" sign high on a hill to your right. The road to the inn will be on your right, marked by an orange-and-green sign.

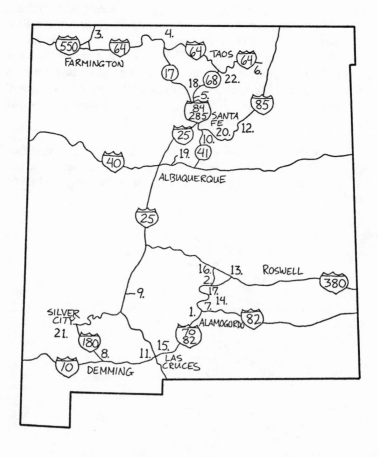

New Mexico

Numbers on map refer to towns numbered below.

D & D's
Bed and Breakfast
Alamogordo, New Mexico
88310

Innkeeper: Dottie Dunn
Address/Telephone: 1115 Indiana Avenue; (505) 434–5402 or 437–0981
Rooms: 4 share full bath upstairs and down.
Rates: $25 to $35, continental breakfast included. No pets. Smoking in
   designated areas only. MasterCard, Visa accepted. (Special weekly
   rates available.)
Open: All year.
Facilities and Activities: Alamogordo Space Center and White Sands
   National Monument; one-half block from main shopping area.

When the railroads came to Alamagordo in 1898, the first
engineer built the first private residence in town, the Ackley
House. It stayed in the same family until the mid-1970s. The
Baptist Church bought the property next, and then Dottie Dunn
acquired it and has turned it into Alamogordo's only bed and
breakfast inn.

The Ackley House is registered with the historical society in
Santa Fe. As Dottie says, you step "into ☞ the charm of yester-
year, with ☞ yesterday's prices."

For such a modest price I found four lovely, spacious bedrooms, with queen-sized beds covered with spreads in decorator fabrics. Draperies matched, and the furniture, an eclectic mix, added to the charm. There's also a comfortable, small sitting area upstairs.

Downstairs, guests have the use of a library (with television as well as books), reception room, dining room, and kitchen. Although restaurants are within walking distance, Dottie says many of her guests prefer to cook. However, she has a list of recommended establishments in case they don't.

Breakfast is a simple one of juice and coffee and some sort of roll. "Sometimes I bake cinnamon rolls," says Dottie, who is in the real estate business just a few blocks away, "and sometimes I go out and get fresh doughnuts to serve." Like many innkeepers of the Southwest, she offers catering to small groups.

There are two attractions in the Alamogordo area that are worth spending several days touring: the Alamogordo Space Center and White Sands National Monument. The space complex is composed of the Hall of Fame and the Tombaugh Space Instruction Center, which contains one of the few Omnimax Theaters in the world. Here the world's largest projector, 70mm film, a forty-foot wrap-around screen, and a six-channel audio system surround the audience with breathtaking realism.

White Sands National Monument is a 230-square-mile desert of pure gypsum, so luminous that it can be seen by astronauts far out in space. There's a 16-mile driving tour called "Heart of the Dunes," and park rangers provide an interesting variety of programs at the visitors center.

Children are welcome at the inn, Dottie says, "as long as they're old enough to navigate the stairs," and there's a nice yard in back for them to play in.

How to get there: Coming into town on Highway 70, turn east (toward the mountains) on 10th, the main east/west street, to Indiana. Turn left on Indiana, and the inn will be on your left.

La Junta
Alto, New Mexico
88312

Innkeepers: Katherine and Robert Finley
Address/Telephone: Box 139; (505) 336–4361
Rooms: 6 in the main lodge share 3 baths; 8 cabins, all with private bath.
Rates: $70 to $250. Smoking is permitted "but not encouraged." No
credit cards accepted.
Open: All year.
Facilities and Activities: Meals catered by request. Cabins have kitch-
ens, barbecue pits, and picnic tables. Ski Apache area is 1.4 miles
from inn; Ruidoso and horse-racing, 6 miles.

La Junta is up in the Capitan Mountains, with ☛ a view of
Sierra Madre, in an atmosphere in harmony with the natural
surroundings of forest, mountain, and sky, an atmosphere of
wonderful peace and quiet. The inn, at an elevation of
7,600 feet, rests on seven acres of ponderosa pine, piñon, and
Douglas fir. The Finleys have owned the property for more than
twenty years, and now, retired professors both, they have come
into their own.

Katherine taught English for thirty-five years, and Bob taught
biology, both at Louisiana University of the Southwest in
Lafayette. ☛ They brought a lot of Louisiana with them. Cabins

are named for Louisiana parishes; both cabins and lodge rooms are furnished in Cajun country décor, and croissants and café au lait are standard offerings.

And they love what they're doing. Bob challenges newcomers to horseshoes outside or to pool or bridge in the large game room. "We have a good time," he says. "Oh, it ties a fellow down, but we enjoy it. We've caught the second generation now."

Katherine wanted to show me the "family album" of other guests. She takes the pictures, they write a note, and it all gets pasted in the book. Everybody, including me, wants to come back for the ☛ holiday champagne parties.

"You can smell the wassail from Thanksgiving through Easter, the whole ski season," she says with a laugh. Another hospitable touch is the ☛ pot of soup or gumbo, on the fire for late-night feasting.

Family dogs Racey and Hans are on hand to welcome newcomers, and they always remember the old. Hans is a lady, and when I questioned her name, I got the expected answer: "We didn't know she was when we got her!"

How to get there: La Junta is six miles north of Ruidoso on Highway 37. One-quarter mile past the Ski Apache Road, turn left on the unpaved road and follow the arrows one mile.

Aztec Residence Hotel
Aztec, New Mexico
87410

Innkeeper: Mabel Lester
Address/Telephone: 300 South Main Street; (505) 334–3452
Rooms: 9; all with private bath, 5 with kitchenette.
Rates: $20, daily; $55 to $70, weekly. No children. No pets. No credit
   cards.
Open: All year.
Facilities and Activities: Aztec and other ruins, Aztec Museum; fishing,
   boating on Navajo Lake 20 miles away, skiing.

This quaint little hotel sits on the main street of Aztec, which
was named all-American City in 1963 by the National Municipal
League in conjunction with *Look* magazine. Mabel, engaged in
the real estate business, has lived in Aztec since 1953, and she
became innkeeper quite by accident.

"Everyone says that every time I buy a place, I always fix it
up, restoring that area of town as well," she told me. "When I had
this property listed for sale, I got so involved with the prospective
buyer, discussing what we could do with it, that when they didn't
buy it, I did!"

The front door is an eye-catcher with stained-glass panels,
and the pine paneling in the reception hall is a nice touch. Mabel

restored a lot of the hotel's old furniture, and each bedroom has a period brass bed (two in the twin-bed rooms). There's a small lounge area upstairs, with books and magazines for guests to read.

Interesting to see are the ☛ photographs hung in the hall showing different eras. First, there is a surrey in front of the entrance; next, an early automobile; so you can see that the Aztec Hotel has been around for some time. Mabel has the abstract of title, dated 1878.

☛ There are thirty-eight Aztec buildings on the State Register, Mabel says. The town received a Main Street–project grant in September 1986.

The Aztec Ruins, a National Monument just minutes away, are a mystery. About A.D. 1106, Indians built one of the largest pre-Spanish pueblos, a massive 500-room apartment complex. No one knows why it was abandoned (about 1300), and fear of the ghosts of the "Old People" kept Navajos and Apaches away.

The inn does not serve any meals, but if you want to dine out (as opposed to cooking in your kitchenette), Mabel warmly recommends an international assortment of nearby restaurants. "There's the Chinese House Restaurant, Becky's Restaurant (Mexican), and, at the end of Main, the Aztec is a general restaurant and very popular."

Aztec's climate is beautiful year round, with just two or three little snows. "It's all up in the mountains," Mabel says, and of course this delights the skiers.

Two very happy fishermen were staying at the hotel during my visit. They come regularly for the fishing and were able to show me quite a catch, which they kept fresh for dinner in their kitchenette refrigerators.

How to get there: Highway 44 North becomes Main Street in Aztec. The inn will be on your right when you reach the 300 block.

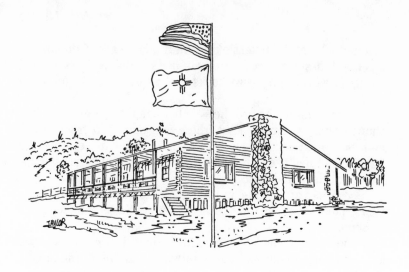

Oso Ranch and Lodge, Inc.
Chama, New Mexico
87520

Innkeepers: Jessie and Benny Salazar
Address/Telephone: P.O. Box 808; (505) 756–2954
Rooms: 6; all with private bath.
Rates: $100 to $135, seasonal, including three meals and open bar.
  Children and pets by prior arrangement. American Express,
  MasterCard, Visa accepted.
Open: All year.
Facilities and Activities: Hunting, fishing, horseback riding, hiking,
  cross-country skiing, snowmobiling, overnight pack trips. Cumbres
  & Toltec Scenic Railroad.

Ah, wilderness. Where the deer come down and feed at night.
Where coyotes and eagles can be sighted. Where the mountain
air is crisp and clear, the sky an incredible blue. Where snow-
capped peaks and momentous sunsets are the norm.

"Right here you have the feeling of being isolated," says
Benny, "but we're only five minutes from town." Oso Ranch, two
miles south of the small town of Chama, is a ☛ perfect place for
sportsmen and nature lovers. The log lodge has a huge activities
room with hunting trophies not only over the mantel, but hung
from the rafters, too. The biggest trophies personify the inn's

name. *Oso*, Benny tells me, means "bear" in Spanish, and there are several stuffed ones in the room.

You'll also find Western and Indian art and a Western-history library, as well as a piano, game and pool tables, and a wide-screen television. "Some folks just like to relax around the big fireplace," Benny says.

Good, wholesome food is served at tables at one end of the big room, food like Jesse's rich pecan rolls along with fried potatoes and ham and eggs for breakfast, homemade chili for lunch (or a packed lunch if you'll be out enjoying nature), and maybe roast beef, potato salad, carrots and corn, homemade bread, and banana pudding for a hearty dinner.

The six guest rooms are down a hall off the big room. ☛ Each door is completely covered with a scene made from colored leather, a unique, innovative idea that makes it easy to find which room is yours. It'll be large and comfortable, too, with twin or king beds and ☛ a mountain view from the window.

No license is required to fish in the ranch lakes, personally stocked with rainbow trout by Benny. For a small fee you can have a lesson in fly fishing, if, like me, you've never done it before. Hunting? There's bear, cougar, elk, and deer in them thar hills. Then it's back home to the warmth and welcome offered by the Salazars.

"It's just like having friends come to visit," Benny says. "People leave here elated."

How to get there: From Highway 84 turn west on Seco Drive (about two miles south of Chama) and drive one-half mile to the end, over the river and up to the lodge.

Hacienda Rancho de Chimayo
Chimayo, New Mexico
87522

Innkeepers: Florence and Arturo Jarramejo
Address/Telephone: P.O. Box 11; (505) 351–2222
Rooms: 7; all with private bath.
Rates: $49 to $76, continental breakfast included. Children 4 and older.
No pets. MasterCard, Visa accepted.
Open: All year except January.
Facilities and Activities: Restaurant (closed in January). Nearby 1850s
Church of San Tuario, the "Lourdes of the U.S." Weavers' shops
famous for rugs, jackets, cushions.

Chimayo is a very small town with an interesting history
bound up in both the Hacienda Rancho de Chimayo and, just
across the road, the Restaurante Rancho de Chimayo,
serving native New Mexican cuisine. Both belong to a family
that has lived in Chimayo since the 1700s and can trace its roots
to the first Spanish settlers.

In the 1880s two brothers, Hermenegildo and Epifanio
Jaramillo, built family homes facing each other across the road.
Their descendants restored the homes, creating in 1965 the

Restaurante Rancho de Chimayo in Hermenegildo's home and in 1984 the Hacienda Rancho de Chimayo in Epifanio and Adelaida's home. I found the sense of history here intriguing.

The inn's rooms open off a walled courtyard with a sparkling fountain and bright flowers. The view is toward the mountains. French doors open onto a little balcony, and that's where I had my simple continental breakfast, although I was tempted to join other guests in the courtyard. The restaurant is justly famous: Lunch was a small *sopapilla* (puffed, slightly sweet Mexican roll) stuffed with chili and cheese and served with guacamole (avocado salad). For dinner I had *carné adovado*—pork marinated in chili, another specialty of the house.

My very large room had twin mahogany beds forming a king-sized bed. At the foot was a taupe velvet sofa, coffee table, and two wing chairs; every room has a similar area.

"We've traveled a lot in the States, and we always like to sit for awhile in our room, perhaps have some wine and cheese, and relax before we go out to dinner," says Florence. There's wine in the kitchen of the office/lobby for whoever wants it, and a bottle of wine is placed in your room if you notify ahead of a special occasion.

Other evidences of thoughtfulness were the small cans of fruit juice I found in my room. ☞ Each room is practically a suite, there's so much space, and the antique furniture is well selected. I particularly admired my room's mahogany dressing table and antique blanket stand holding a white woven afghan in case I got chilly. I asked Florence how they were lucky enough to have so many lovely pieces.

"We searched all of San Antonio, Austin, and Denver for our antiques!" Florence says. She and Arturo have done a wonderful job, recreating the distinctive charm of the Colonial New Mexico of their ancestors.

How to get there: From Highway 60 north of Santa Fe, take Highway 76 east ten miles to Chimayo. The highway runs right between the inn and the restaurant.

∽

E: In my room, details like the pink linens, rose lace shower curtain, and old prints on the walls made it seem just like home, or like home ought to be!

St. James Hotel
Cimarron, New Mexico
87714

Innkeepers: Pat and Ed Sitzberger
Address/Telephone: 17th & Collinson streets, Rt. 1, Box 2; (505)
    376–2664
Rooms: 3 with private bath in hotel, 12 with private bath in annex.
Rates: $35 to $85. Mature children only. Pets in annex only. MasterCard,
    Visa accepted.
Open: All year except Christmas Day.
Facilities and Activities: Coffee shop, dining room, lounge, gift shop,
    pool, game room, meeting rooms. Hunting, fishing, skiing.

Cimarron means "untamed" in old Spanish, Pat told me, and
that's what the St. James was in its heyday. Which is strange,
because Henry Lambert, who built the hotel in 1875, came from
a country considered the quintessence of civilization: France.
Chef Lambert cooked for Napoleon Bonaparte and later for both
Abraham Lincoln and Ulysses S. Grant. What was he doing in
wild Cimarron?

He was looking for gold in 1863, says Pat, and he must have
found it, because the St. James is an unexpectedly elegant find in
this mountain town of approximately 900 souls.

The handsome building is as full of antiques as it is of

history. ☛ Frederic Remington painted in the hotel. Lew Wallace was a guest; Zane Grey wrote one of his Western sagas here. Buffalo Bill Cody, Annie Oakley, and Blackjack Ketchum stayed here, too.

But some of the guests may not have been welcome. Jesse James and Wyatt Earp, well, perhaps, but certainly not Clay Allison, the desperado who danced on the bar, killed fifteen men, and left ☛ the famous bullet holes in the walls and ceiling of what is now the dining room.

"Everyone wants to see the bullet holes," says Pat, and I was no exception. But I also wanted to see the main floor ☛ rooms that are kept as a museum, full of beautiful antique furniture. (Upstairs and annex guest rooms are modernized and comfortable.) The lobby, too, is reminiscent of gracious and spacious living. A huge painting of one Don Diego de Vargas hangs alongside that of Junipero Serra, a Spanish priest and missionary. Ornate wire cages contain tropical birds; Japanese *koi* (carp) swim in a small pool. The furniture is the hotel's original.

But that's as far as the formality goes—the St. James is a people place. "I'm a people person," says Pat, "and I try to know every guest who stays here. This is our home—Ed was born and raised across from the hotel, and he grew up playing here."

The restaurant menu, surprisingly sophisticated, features everything from escargot for an appetizer to broiled swordfish steak. I had pasta with white clam sauce—a delicious medley of clams and pasta blended with fresh vegetables, herb butter, and white wine.

How to get there: From Highway 64 into town, follow the signs south across the railroad tracks to 17th and Collinson. The hotel is on the northeast corner.

The Lodge
Cloudcroft, New Mexico
88317

Innkeepers: Carole and Jerry Sanders
Address/Telephone: P.O. Box 497; (505) 682–2566
Rooms: 47, including 3 suites; all with private bath.
Rates: $55 to $70; suites, $95 to $120. No pets. Smoking discouraged.
   American Express, MasterCard, Visa accepted.
Open: All year.
Facilities and Activities: Restaurant and lounge, saloon on weekends,
   swimming pool, Jacuzzi. 9-hole golf course, skiing. Village with
   shops and restaurants, Sacramento Peak Observatory at Sunspot.

☛ Set like an eagle's aerie 9,000 feet high in the clouds
overlooking the San Andres Mountains, the Black Range, and
White Sands National Monument below, The Lodge looks like
the mansion of a prospector who finally struck gold.

   Glassed-in verandas, sprawling wings, gabled windows, and
a five-story copper-clad tower, all in a mixture of styles no one
can quite put a name to, make the inn's appearance as colorful as
its history.

   A fanciful façade, unchanged by numerous interior renovations, graces a hostelry that was built in 1899, burned and rebuilt
in 1911, and has never closed its doors since.

I was interested to learn that stars such as Judy Garland and Clark Gable had signed in, as well as presidents and astronauts. Even Pancho Villa was a guest, when he was an escapee from Mexico in 1911.

The two-story lobby is surprisingly cozy, like a larger-than-life but wonderfully comfortable living room. I was startled by the huge stuffed bear that guards the great high fireplace, which takes off the mountain chill present even in the summer.

Hallways and stairways branch off the lobby like a rabbit warren, but an elegant one. Rooms are furnished with antiques, are all sizes and shapes, and offer different views. Maybe you'll get a pine-studded mountain, maybe the golf course (highest and most scenic in the country), or even the glistening White Sands National Monument miles away.

A sight for Victorian eyes, the Honeymoon Suite is all red velvet and gold with a red-satin-covered four-poster topped by a gold and mirrored crown. Complimentary champagne and breakfast comes with all this!

Innkeepers Carole and Jerry have capitalized on the myth of the beautiful Rebecca, flame-haired ghost of a redheaded maid who disappeared when her lumberjack lover found her in the arms of another: They've named their haute cuisine restaurant after her.

"She's a friendly spirit," says Carole. "She roams the corridors in search of a new lover, particularly haunting Room 101, the Governor's Suite."

Chef David Lafferty serves such stellar attractions as flaming peppercorn tournados or brings chateaubriand, flaming, to your table; and I could die for the house dessert, called "DBC" for Death by Chocolate!

Another ghost might haunt The Lodge: The long polished wooden bar in the lounge belonged to notorious Prohibition gangster Al Capone.

How to get there: Cloudcroft is approximately 8 miles east of Alamagordo on Highway 82. Signs point to The Lodge.

*

E: *This is an exceptionally fine place to stay. The location (what a view!), the unique lodge, the hospitality—all make for a winner.*

The Spanish Stirrup
Guest House
Demming, New Mexico
88030

Innkeeper: Elizabeth May
Address/Telephone: Route 1, Box 206; (505) 546–3165
Rooms: 2 bedrooms with private bath; 2 suites with kitchen and private
   entrance.
Rates: $40 to $50, including ranch breakfast. Pets by prior arrangement.
   Lunch and dinner by reservation. MasterCard, Visa accepted.
Open: All year.
Facilities and Activities: Rock Hound State Park, Black Range Moun-
   tains; hiking, rock hunting. Mexican border 30 miles away.

Elizabeth May, an old hand at hospitality, owned and ran
The Spanish Stirrup as a guest ranch for twenty years. "We had
livestock, horses, and cattle, branding in the spring and fall."
Then she sold it but was persuaded to stay on and run it for the
new owner.

"Sure, I guess I enjoy it," she confesses. "I've been at it long
enough! Met lots of great people, still have 'em coming back who
used to come thirty years ago."

The Spanish Stirrup is that cozy. The large parlor has oval

rag rugs on the floor, deerheads and antlers over the mantel. The fireplace was built years ago by Elizabeth's husband, and it's made mostly from geodes, the hollow nodules of stone lined with crystals that rock buffs come to the area to hunt for. Geodes come in all sizes, and when they're split and polished they reveal wonderful depths of color and glitter.

The centerpiece of the inn is the Spanish stirrup it's named for. It hangs on a wall facing the front door, and it's a treasure, a real one. Edgar May found it on the ranch in 1912 in a crevice in the rock, and conjecture is that the conquistadores might have lost it.

"None have been made since the sixteenth century," says Elizabeth. "The *padres* in Mexico forbade it, because it resembles a cross."

The inn's rooms are simple and rustic, with Wedgewood Oak from 1949 that Elizabeth says is not made any more. Everything is clean and light and bright. The game room at the end of the long center hall has books, a piano, and a modern note—an exercise bicycle! More books and magazines line the hall, as do family photographs: Elizabeth's grown sons, Harley, Ross, and Clyde, were rodeo cowboys in their youth.

Breakfast is a collection of—are you ready for this?—biscuits, muffins, rolls, cereal, scrambled eggs, bacon or ham, sausage, *jalapeño*, strawberry and prickly-pear jellies, fresh fruit in season, juice, coffee, and tea. Getting fed like a ranch hand was no hardship for me!

How to get there: Take Rock Hound State Park Road 12 miles southeast of Demming, turn right, and follow the curved road for 7 miles. Spanish Stirrup will be on your left, up a small hill.

❧

E: *I stopped in town to make sure my directions were right and was cautioned to "be sure to have some of Elizabeth May's cooking, she's been famous for it out here for years!"*

Elephant Butte Inn
Elephant Butte, New Mexico
87935

Innkeepers: Carrie and Bill Saegart
Address/Telephone: P.O. Box E; (505) 744–5431
Rooms: 48, one a suite; all with private bath
Rates: $38 to $82. American Express, MasterCard, Visa accepted.
Open: All year.
Facilities and Activities: Restaurant, lounge with live entertainment
   open Wednesday through Sunday winter, seven nights summer.
   Fishing and boating on Elephant Butte Lake, tennis, golf; Las
   Palomas hot mineral springs in nearby Truth or Consequences.

Elephant Butte Inn is more a resort than an inn. 🖙 It overlooks large Elephant Butte Reservoir, one of the Rio Grande lakes
that string down the state. And there are all the activities that go
with a resort area: two tennis courts, a 9-or-18-hole golf course,
and a marina that provides boat rentals for water skiing, pad-
dling, or fishing.

You can fish either in the lake or the Rio Grande, catching
bass, blue gill, and trout. Or you can indulge in nature
watching. 🖙 "The inn's pets," Carrie says, "are the road runners
nesting in the yucca plants. We have people out every night
trying to take pictures of them!" Rabbits and quail are here, too.

Bill Saegart is a geologist, and during my visit a big geologists' convention was going on. The Saegarts settled down into innkeeping after being world travelers.

"We're here to mingle with people who travel and to share our experiences with them," says Carrie. Both hail from Florida, where they also had an inn. "Although we didn't have food service there, we always had cookouts with our guests."

Summer nights, there's often a chuckwagon out on the patio, serving barbecue to the tunes of a live band. Indoors, restaurant breakfasts specialize in fried oysters and chili *releños*. Lunch might be a Chelsea sandwich, and dinner specialties include lobster bisque, Cornish hen stuffed with grapes and pecans, and pecan, apple, or chocolate pie to top it off.

Rooms are spacious and clean, with new furniture, color television, double long-boy beds, and a great view of the lake.

How to get there: Elephant Butte is on Highway 52, 5½ miles north of Truth or Consequences.

The Galisteo Inn
Galisteo, New Mexico
87540

Innkeeper: Annie Campbell
Address/Telephone: Box 4; (505) 982–1506
Rooms: 9; 2 with private bath, 7 share 3 baths.
Rates: $45 to $90 (seasonal rates). Includes continental breakfast. No
    children (except babes in arms) or pets. Smoking in designated
    areas only. MasterCard, Visa accepted.
Open: All year.
Facilities and Activities: Heated pool, Jacuzzi, sauna, exercise center;
    horseback riding. Dinner by reservation only; special diet requests
    honored. Old pueblo, old church, old Spanish graveyard nearby.

This classic Spanish-adobe inn is more than 250 years old,
but don't worry, it's been remodeled. But not so that it no longer
fits in with its surroundings, which include ☞ some of the oldest buildings in America. "People seem to associate that with the
northeast, but the Spanish were here before the Pilgrims," chef
Amy Toms reminds me.

The inn is situated on eight acres of land under huge old
cottonwood trees. It's a long, low building hidden behind a long,
low adobe wall, and I almost missed it. Galisteo is just a mark on
the map, and I don't advise looking for it in the dark.

But what a wonderful place to discover, even though I had a little difficulty finding it! Staying here is like going on a retreat. The simple rooms have whitewashed walls with wood *vigas* above. Handmade furniture and hand-woven rugs are the décor; some rooms are angled, and some have adobe fireplaces. All are clean, simple, and uncluttered.

☛ The food is healthy and natural. Breakfast was both fresh and dried fruits—apricots, peaches, apples, and raisins—as well as fresh-squeezed orange juice, coffee and tea, and blue corn—*piñon*-nut muffins. The muffins were so good I begged the recipe from Amy.

Blue corn (native grown and sporting a bluish tint) is used a lot because the inn believes in suiting the cuisine to the countryside. Dinner began with a tomato salad with avocado dressing, accompanied by a fresh-baked loaf of blue corn–pepper bread made with mild chilies. Main course was chicken enchiladas, also made with blue corn, smothered with a mild green chili sauce and served with deliciously flavored black beans, seasoned with garlic, chicken stock, and *nopalitos* (cactus; you buy it in cans or jars).

Dessert was homemade cinnamon–*piñon*-nut ice cream and *sopapillas* (puffy, slightly sweet Mexican rolls) with honey. This was truly a feast.

"But we don't serve only Mexican food," says the chef. "Everything from quail to vegetarian—we have a lot of health-conscious people who come here."

Annie Campbell is from New Zealand, and in her lovely accent she describes innkeeping: "Getting to know a small part of people's lives—it's really lovely."

How to get there: From Albuquerque, take I–10 east to Moriarty, then 41 north toward Santa Fe through Galisteo. Or take I–25 north, then 285 south toward Lamy, then 41 south to Galisteo. From Santa Fe, also take I–25 north, then 285 south toward Lamy, then 41 south to Galisteo.

Llewellyn House
Bed & Breakfast Inn
Las Cruces, New Mexico
88005

Innkeepers: Linda and Gerald Lundeen
Address/Telephone: 618 South Alameda Boulevard; (505) 526–3327 or
526–6978
Rooms: 6; all with private bath (one is a suite with kitchenette).
Rates: $28 to $65, including breakfast and afternoon social. (Summer
season, second night ½ price.) Pets OK if kept in room. Smoking in
3 of the bedrooms and in the common rooms. American Express,
MasterCard, Visa accepted.
Open: All year.
Facilities and Activities: Library, TV room; bicycles. Inn kitchen open
for guest use. Theater weekends with the American Southwest
Theater, directed by Mark Medoff. The innkeepers, actively involved
with the arts in Las Cruces, publish a newsletter keeping guests
informed.

Linda and Gerald call Llewellyn House an "Inn of the Arts."
Walking in, I found myself in the Linda Lundeen Gallery. I wan-
dered through 🖝 a maze of wonderful prints and paintings on

my way to the inn rooms at the back of the gallery. (I later found out that there's a side entrance directly into the inn.)

Gerald is an architect; Linda has the gallery. Both are wide-awake, vital, energetic people who make guests feel a part of the electricity in the air.

"Our guests are part of the family immediately—we treat them like that," says Linda. "We have a man from Bogotá, Colombia, a regular guest, who needs a phone, so we put a jack in his room."

The inn has 📌 all sorts of international guests, and you're bound to meet very interesting people, perhaps even in the kitchen! I liked having the freedom of this modern, attractively tiled room, where a guest from Portugal was poaching his own eggs and an actor was fixing his health breakfast. Linda told me about another guest who baked a wonderful cheesecake and went ahead and served it to everybody. I wish I had been there then!

Each artistic room is named for an artist, mainly those of the Southwest, names like Georgia O'Keeffe, Fritz Scholder, and Olaf Weighorst. The Weighorst Room has headboards cunningly made from antique gas-grate hoods and padded with decorator fabric matching the bedspreads. I loved the bathroom's footed tub, painted bright red.

Breakfast weekdays is continental, but on weekends Linda cooks waffles, popovers, scrambled eggs, but "no fried meats." The daily afternoon *menienda,* an afternoon social hour from 5:00 P.M. to 7:00 P.M., is complete with wine and southwestern hors d'oeuvres—chili con queso and guacamole—and perhaps a shrimp soufflé.

"We all interact," says Linda. It's easy to see how, too, at the Llewellyn House.

How to get there: The inn is on Alameda Boulevard next to the First National Bank Tower, the only high-rise on the street.

❋

E: *Very special are the inn's theater weekends, with a Saturday luncheon and critique attended by either playwright or performers, play attendance in a group, and late champagne supper at the Desert Rose, where guests ask questions and get feedback from innkeepers and artists.*

Carriage House Inn
Las Vegas, New Mexico
87701

Innkeeper: Kera Anderson
Address/Telephone: 925 6th Street; (505) 454–1784
Rooms: 7; 3½ baths.
Rates: $27 to $39, full breakfast included. No pets. MasterCard, Visa
accepted.
Open: All year.
Facilities and Activities: Kitchen available to guests. Walking tour of
historical district, water-skiing at Storrie Lake 5 miles north of town,
cross-country skiing at Sipipu Ski Area. Fishing in Santa Fe and Kit
Carson national parks.

It's always fun to find something different at an inn, and
Kera Anderson's is 🖝 also an antique shop. As I entered and
walked down the wide hall, I could see treasures in the large
rooms on each side. There are treasures in all the other rooms,
too, and if you take a fancy to any of them, Kera will be happy to
sell them to you. I was taken by the 1880s pump organ in the
dining room, though not enough to take it with me. But it certainly is handsome.

Kera's breakfasts are gourmet, with such tasty treats as
shrimp-and-bacon quiche, eggs Benedict, or ham-and-Swiss om-

elets accompanied by country-fried potatoes. Homemade dough-nuts and chocolate-chip or honey-and-bran muffins, too, are served on the antique tables in the dining room. Kera also always serves a fruit-and-yogurt dish, as well as orange juice, coffee, and tea.

The bay window in the dining room lets lots of light shine on the buffet, which turns out to be a bar from an old Texas saloon. Carriage House Inn is full of such surprises.

The common room has television and games. There's a night manager on duty; Kera and her children live in the carriage house in the rear that gives the inn its name.

The wide upstairs hall leads to rooms that are color-coded. My favorite is Number 3, the Peach Room, with its antique four-poster covered with a crocheted spread.

Bathrooms are large with claw-foot tubs. Kera rebuilt the entire inside of the house, and each room's fresh-sprigged flower curtains and bedspreads reflect newly painted walls.

The third-floor suite, with its own kitchen, can be used as three singles or as a three-bedroom suite. Summertimes, guests can sit on the upstairs porch amid its lovely plants.

For dinner, Kera will recommend several restaurants serving good food not far from the inn.

How to get there: Take University exit off I–25 to 6th Street and turn right to number 925.

E: Although this inn is fine just as it is, Kera plans to remodel still more rooms in this huge old house!

Plaza Hotel
Las Vegas, New Mexico
87701

Innkeeper: David Fenzi
Address/Telephone: 230 On the Plaza; (505) 425–3591
Rooms: 37, including 4 suites; all with private bath.
Rates: $45 to $75; each additional person $5; children under 12 free.
$25 pet deposit. All major credit cards accepted.
Open: All year.
Facilities and Activities: Restaurant, lounge. Use of New Mexico High-
lands University pool and racquetball courts. Near 18-hole golf
course, Armand Hammer's United World College.

This one-hundred-year-old hotel was remodeled in 1982, but,
says front-desk manager Barbara Garcia, the renovation didn't
vanquish the resident ghost, an old man in a top hat and old-
fashioned clothes. "He does little pranks," she says. "Guests see
him, and then he vanishes."

I wouldn't blame him for wanting to hang around this
charming hotel, ☞ situated right on Las Vegas's tree-shaded old
plaza. The large lobby has new wicker furniture and ☞ an old
upright piano that guests actually play. Grand double stairways
lead to the wide halls of the three-story structure.

The large rooms are furnished in antique style, and I particularly liked my large dressing room. I was pleased to learn that every room offered such roomy luxury. They really knew how to build spaciously in the good old days, which is why it's always a pleasure to stay at one of the past's remodeled "grande dames." I liked the ambience, too, of this small hotel.

"A lot of our guests tell us they feel at home, not at a hotel," says Barbara. "But then, we treat them like family. We try to make people feel extra special."

You'll feel like a lumberjack after you fill up on the hotel's lumberjack breakfast of eggs, bacon, and hotcakes. The "Tom Mix" at lunch is a great mix, too, a giant sandwich of turkey, ham, bacon, lettuce, tomato, cheese, and avocado.

For dinner, the hotel is known for its Mexican food. Especially tasty are the chicken *fajitas*. If it's possible that you could still be hungry, there's ☞ popcorn on tap all the time in Byron T's, the hotel lounge. While you're in there, you might catch a glimpse of that funny old man in the top hat and the old-fashioned clothes.

How to get there: From I–25 go north on Grand Avenue. Follow the signs to Old Town Plaza and the hotel.

Wortley Hotel
Lincoln, New Mexico
88338

Innkeeper: Kay Dennis
Address/Telephone: P.O. Box 96; (505) 653–4500
Rooms: 8; all with private bath.
Rates: $35 to $46. Pets OK with prior arrangement. MasterCard, Visa
   accepted.
Open: All year.
Facilities and Activities: Restaurant closed on Tuesdays and Wednes-
   days, may be closed Christmas week. Lincoln Days and Billy-the-
   Kid Pageant first full weekend in August; historic courthouse where
   "the Kid" made his famous escape; Tungstell Store Museum and
   Visitors Center.

Lincoln has a mighty reputation for a small town of only
sixty-two residents! This was the place where Billy the Kid passed
into history by making his famous jail break from the Lincoln
County Courthouse across the road from the Wortley
Hotel. ☛ The hotel sure could tell a tale or two, and I found it
great fun to stay where "the Kid" had been!

The hotel was built in 1872 to provide meals and lodging for
men working for L. G. Murphy, who owned the big saloon and
store in town. It's simple, unpretentious, and relaxing,

88

with 🖝 rockers and other old-fashioned chairs on the long front porch. I found two of the town's older citizens rocking away, ready to pass the time of day with me.

"Most of the people who come here want to just relax, visit the museums, sit on the porch, and rock—there are no TVs and telephones," says innkeeper Kay. She's a volunteer innkeeper; the hotel is kept open by the Lincoln Pageant and Festivals Corporation, a nonprofit, civic-minded organization.

"We felt that the hotel should be kept open. It's important to Lincoln and to our history," Kay says rightly. An added bonus is that she enjoys her job. "You meet the nicest people here; it's great fun and terribly interesting."

Rooms are whitewashed, with nineteenth-century antique furniture and lace curtains in the windows. The restaurant serves breakfasts of blueberry pancakes, *huevos rancheros*, and super omelets. Dinners are the western favorites of chicken-fried steak and roast beef. Desserts are delicious homemade cobblers of peach, apple, cherry, and blueberry.

Kay sums up the attraction of the Wortley: "It's 🖝 strictly a get-away place, strictly a country inn." Exactly what I was looking for!

How to get there: Lincoln is three blocks long, a little village on Highway 380. If you go too fast, you'll miss it altogether! If you're going west, the inn will be on your right.

Inn of the Mountain Gods
Mescalero, New Mexico
88340

Innkeeper: John Livingston
Address/Telephone: P.O. Box 269; (505) 257–5141
Rooms: 250; all with private bath.
Rates: $65 to $75, January 1 to May 31; $85 to $95, June 1 to December 31. Pets permitted if kept on leash in public areas. American Express, MasterCard, Visa accepted.
Open: All year.
Facilities and Activities: Dining room, lounge; food served at golf shop, pool, and Top of the Inn summers only. Swimming pool, tennis courts, 18-hole golf course, trap shooting, bicycling, volleyball, badminton, horseback riding, fishing, and hunting all seasonal. Horseracing season in nearby Ruidoso; skiing Ski Apache; boating and fishing on Lake Mescalero.

The Inn of the Mountain Gods has a romantic slogan: "Come walk where the gods have tread." The inn was built in 1973 in the heart of the Mescalero Apache Indian Reservation in southern New Mexico, a ◖ land of pure air and pine-studded mountains topped with snow and laced with cool green-blue lakes and streams rich for hunting and fishing. You can really feel renewed here, even if you don't go in for the hunting and fishing.

I found the legend behind the inn's name very appealing. The gods, say the Apache, came down from the sacred mountain of Sierra Blanca to give them this beautiful land, driving away evil and bringing them good fortune.

Good fortune for anyone, Apache or otherwise, is a holiday at this super resort. It's on sparkling Lake Mescalero, ☞ within a 460,000-acre reservation. (Which is where the hunting comes in. If you make prior arrangements, you get an Indian guide who really knows what he is doing.)

This is an inn conceived and executed on a grand scale. The covered entryway, bridging a rock-tumbled stream, leads to an awesome lobby. In the center, the octagonal copper fireplace reaches up three stories. Beyond, the three-story window-wall gives one ☞ a magnificent view of Sierra Blanca, towering on the horizon behind Lake Mescalero.

Rooms are large and pleasant, with ☞ each one opening off a balcony, taking advantage of the gorgeous scenery. There's luxury here, but no ostentation, no stuffiness. Friendly and folksy is the atmosphere, with everyone, from desk clerk to pianist in the piano bar alongside the window-wall, ready to pass the time of day.

The Dan Li Ka Restaurant serves fine continental dishes with daily specials. I had veal Michelle: medallions of veal topped with crab, mushrooms, avocado, and shallots in a brandy sauce and served with saffron rice and a julienne of carrots, turnip, and zucchini. For dessert I enjoyed the chocolate butter-cream torte. Portions are huge—but not too huge for appetites charged up by all the activities that interest even the laziest inn guest.

How to get there: The inn is 3½ miles west of Ruidoso on Highway 70.

Mesón de Mesilla
Mesilla, New Mexico
88046

Innkeepers: Merci and Chuck Walker
Address/Telephone: 1803 Avenida de Mesilla; (505) 525–9212
Rooms: 13; all with private bath.
Rates: $45 to $75, seasonal, gourmet breakfast included. Children 12
    and older, pets by prior arrangement. American Express,
    MasterCard, Visa accepted.
Open: All year.
Facilities and Activities: Restaurant open for lunch Wednesday, Thurs-
    day, and Friday; for dinner Tuesday through Saturday; Sunday
    brunch. Swimming pool, bicycles. Old Mesilla Plaza, with shops
    and restaurants and where Gadsden Purchase Treaty was signed, is
    within walking distance. Billy the Kid was imprisoned on the plaza.

Mesón de Mesilla is innovative in that it's solar heated. Innkeeper Chuck Walker did research at nearby New Mexico Solar
Institute before building the inn.

Everything is new and fresh and bright. ☛ All rooms open
off the wide balcony, which encircles the building. The painted
tile work in the entryway is especially attractive.

The parlor has a fireplace, great for chilly New Mexican
evenings, a television, a VCR, a game table, and board games. A

pile of towels waits by the door for guests heading for the pool just outside.

Merci left the public relations business and Chuck the insurance business to become innkeepers. Chuck takes his hosting seriously enough to be very disappointed when a guest declines the gourmet breakfast he takes pride in.

He didn't have that trouble with me. My problem was deciding whether I would have the eggs Benedict or the lemon soufflé French toast! I chose the latter, and the plate was garnished with fresh fruit in a positively French manner.

"You have to love people to be in this business," says Chuck, "and I meet the most marvelous people in the world." He joked that when he was in the insurance business, people avoided him at parties, and now they don't run anymore. "I've turned eighteen years of total rejection into three years of total acceptance," he said happily.

He and Merci patterned their inn after California ones that they admired, those with "a fine restaurant, good food, small size, and an intimate atmosphere. That's what appeals to us," says Merci.

Chef Bobby Herrera, who has been with the inn since its opening, offers three specials for lunch each day. The dinner menu features such specialties as filet de salmon champagne, scampi alla pescatora, and beef Wellington.

The Walkers delight in sending guests to "the best theater in the Southwest," directed by playwright Mark Medoff. They'll also pack lunches for hikers to Aguirre Springs, reached by a hiking trail overlooking a New Mexican missile range.

How to get there: Take exit 140 off Highway 10 or I–25 to University Avenue, then to Avenida de Mesilla.

❋

E: *Muppet the Maltese (dog) trots out to say "Hello" to everyone, and then resumes minding his own business.*

Montjeau Shadows Inn
Nogal, New Mexico
88341

Innkeepers: Pauline and Howard Skeean
Address/Telephone: Bonito Route; (505) 336–4191
Rooms: 7; 2 with private bath, 5 share 3 baths.
Rates: $35 to $45 in summer, $40 to $50 in winter, breakfast included;
  wine served afternoons at "4:30-ish." Children over 12 OK. No pets.
  MasterCard, Visa accepted.
Open: All year.
Facilities and Activities: Lunch by request if convenient, dinner by
  reservation; without reservation, guests take potluck. Hiking paths
  on 10 acres. Fishing on nearby Bonito Lake; skiing at Ski Apache;
  horseracing in Ruidoso.

Howard is both gourmet cook and wit. When asked by a
guest just what makes a country inn different from a motel, he
answered, quick as a flash. "A lot more ambience and no swimming pool!"

Pauline was just as quick when she said that Howard thinks
he's a wit, but he's about half right. The Skeeans complement
each other, and both are a lot of fun. With them, I certainly didn't
miss a swimming pool. Their idea of country fun, aside from
joking, is to sit on the porch and watch the hummingbirds or hike

down one of the nature trails to the tree house. They're famous for their hummingbird-watch in summertime: Howard sets up feeders, which also attract many other species and make for great bird watching.

The inn's sundeck and the porch beneath it offer a gorgeous view of the mountains all around. The house, perched high on a hill, is surrounded by 200-year-old junipers, as well as *piñon* and ponderosa pine.

Montjeau Shadows was built in 1980 as a private home, in the style of a Victorian-era farmhouse. The two-story living room has ☛ a stained-glass skylight that is illuminated at night. The balcony overlooking the room has bookshelves and a French door leading to the sun deck.

There's a lounge with yet more books and a television set. Down in the inn's lower level, there's a large game room with bar, pool table, and a separate lounge with a sofa bed for yet more guests.

I enjoyed the small basket of fruit I found in my room and the candy on my pillow, both welcoming touches. Newlyweds get complimentary champagne.

Many of the nature trails have picnic tables, and I took my breakfast outside to eat. If I'd wanted a picnic lunch, Pauline or Howard would have been happy to fix it for me.

"We make our own everything," Pauline says with a laugh. ☛ She keeps track of the menus of meals served and never serves the same dish twice. Although they prefer to plan for groups, they never turn down hungry guests who may not have reserved ahead. "We've got to cook for ourselves, so we usually plan expandable meals, just in case," Howard says. Favorites are chicken cacciatore and bananas Foster.

Pauline likes to take snapshots of all the guests and mails an extra print to them as a reminder of the great time they had at Montjeau Shadows!

How to get there: Take Highway 37 north of Ruidoso, between mile markers 15 and 16. Turn west at the inn sign.

Shadow Mountain Lodge
Ruidoso, New Mexico
88345

Innkeepers: Frances and Curley Williams
Address/Telephone: 107 Main Road; (505) 257–4886
Rooms: 19; all with private bath, 9 with wet bar, 10 with full kitchens.
Rates: $55 winter, $69 summer. No children or pets. American Express,
　　MasterCard, Visa accepted.
Open: All year.
Facilities and Activities: Skiing in winter at Ski Apache, horseracing in
　　summer at Ruidoso Downs, 35 miles from El Malpais, world's larg-
　　est lava flow.

Shadow Mountain Lodge is on green and well-tended grounds under tall, tall trees. It has one story, and rooms are strung along a long veranda. They're large, 400 square feet, with wood-paneled walls and brown-and-tan color scheme; all have fireplaces.

Guests who return to the lodge often bear gifts for Frances—hand-crocheted potholders, fancy candles, a big bag of shelled pecans. Why? Perhaps because ☛ Frances says she tries to treat her guests the way she likes to be treated.

"I spend a lot of time on the porch, visiting with my guests," she told me. "If they get sick, well, I fixed chicken soup for one girl who was ill. I took a man to the hospital at 1:00 A.M. once; his wife was too distraught." Frances sums up her innkeeping philosophy in one sentence: "I want 'em to feel at home."

I had no trouble feeling at home in Number 15—it was almost like a suite. I entered into a kitchen-and-dining area, which adjoined a sitting area with lounge chairs facing the fireplace. Beyond, a king-sized bed faced a large stone fireplace just waiting for a roaring fire.

The fire didn't roar, however, until Frances gave me a helping hand! But it sure was a pleasure when it finally caught, because the air can be chill in the mountains in the evening. ☛ There's a big pile of firewood behind the lodge office, and guests help themselves.

The kitchen is complete down to dishes, silver, coffee-pot, and paper towels. If you don't want to cook, Frances will recommend some great eating places in town.

Frances gets her guests tickets to the Jockey Club at Ruidoso Downs, as well as counter and box seats; she calls the track to make reservations. "Whatever they want, I do." She says she loves her job. "Everybody thinks I'm crazy, but it suits my personality!"

It suited my personality to sit in the sun on the porch and breathe in that clean mountain air and listen to the quiet.

How to get there: Turn off Highway 70 and come through town on Sudderth Drive (the main street) as far west as you can go. At the dead-end traffic circle, take the road to the right; the inn is immediately on the left.

Chinguague Compound
San Juan Pueblo, New Mexico
87566

Innkeepers: JB (Joan) and Philip Blood
Address/Telephone: Box 1118; (505) 852–2194
Rooms: 2 1-bedroom guesthouses, each with private bath; 1 2-bedroom guesthouse with 2 baths.
Rates: $65 to $125, May 1 to September 30; $65 to $150, October 1 to April 30; includes breakfast. Children welcome. Pets by prior arrangement. MasterCard, Visa accepted.
Open: All year.
Facilities and Activities: All units have fully equipped kitchens, living areas with kiva (Indian "beehive") fireplace, and screened porches. Library, games, and television. Indian events in the Eight Northern Pueblos; Santa Fe Opera House 17 miles south, July–August season.

You pronounce *Chinguague* "ching-wa-yea," which isn't hard at all—my difficulty was in remembering it! Named for the *arroyo* you have to cross to get to this fascinating inn, it means "wide place" in the language of the San Juan Indians.

Before I could cross the *arroyo*, I had to drive through the town of San Juan Pueblo and ask for help in finding it. The obliging switchboard operator at the police station said they often send inn guests on their way with a police escort, but this time she called Philip Blood, who came and got me. (He was coming into town to get the mail, anyway.)

By now I imagine you've tumbled to the fact that this is an unusual place. ☛ Situated on the banks of the Rio Grande in the midst of the San Juan Indian reservation, Chinguague Compound is an idyllic retreat of individual adobe *casitas*. Contented guests take long walks along the river, go fishing or bird watching, read from hundreds of available books, play the classical-music records, loaf, and watch the sunrise and sunset over the Sangre de Cristo Mountains.

"When people come here the first time, they don't believe it," says JB, who claims to be on perpetual vacation. Both she and Philip are fugitives from back East, delighted to be in the inn business.

"It's fantastic—we've met people from all over the world. We find bed and breakfast people just wonderful. We invite all our guests to breakfast, though they can cook their own, but we've even had a guest with dietary restrictions who would come— she'd just bring her own breakfast!"

It's hard to stay away. Aside from the good company, guests dine on cornmeal pancakes with New Hampshire maple syrup, sausage, homemade granola and coffeecake, and fruit-and-yogurt parfait. ☛ JB and Philip grow their own corn and grind it; they also make apricot preserves and plum or peach honey from their own trees. They even grind whole-wheat flour from wheat sent by a friend in Thomas, Oklahoma!

How to get there: Take Highway 285 north to 68 north to white water tank. Turn left into San Juan Pueblo and ask for help at the police station on the right by the post office. (Or call, and help will be forthcoming.)

෴

E: *Even the Dobermans are friendly here: Hildi, short for Bruinhilda, and Cleo are sisters, though from different litters.*

Pine Cone Inn
Sandia Peak, New Mexico
87047

Innkeeper: Lois Johnston

Address/Telephone: P.O. Box 94, 13 Tejano Canyon Road; (505) 281–1384

Rooms: 3; 1 for ladies only, share bath with innkeeper; 2 share bath and kitchen, can be suite.

Rates: $25 to $100, with special 3-day and weekly rates. Includes continental breakfast. Children welcome in suite. No pets. MasterCard, Visa accepted.

Open: All year.

Facilities and Activities: Sun room, games, fenced play area for children. Picnic and barbecue area. Pine Cone Trail, Skiing at Sandia Peak 5 miles up trail, ½ block from Cibola National Forest, Turquoise Trail scenic and historic area. Tinker Town Museum.

Lois Johnston is an interior designer, and her inn is a warm reflection of her talents. It's beautifully decorated with warm woods, designer furniture, and fabrics. It's also a reflection of her warm personality. Guests play the piano, drink wine in front of the fire, play games in the sun room, and take 🖙 breakfast out under the Ponderosa pines, the cedar, and the piñon trees that surround the inn.

"I open my whole house," she said as she fed me her delicious orange-walnut bread in the windowed dining room. "First of all, I love to share the beauty of what is here. New Mexico is truly a place of enchantment."

Nature is here in abundance: the inn is set in the woods leading up the mountain. I sat in the dining room and looked out at the tassel-eared squirrels and the stellar bluejays, the latter a vivid blue especially keen against the winter snow.

"They come all winter," Lois said, picking fall apples and pears from her trees for me to munch on as we toured the inn grounds. Her flowers are a delight, too. "I just sprinkle seeds, and flowers come up." The cosmos, pansies, petunias, and geraniums end up gracing guests' bedrooms.

Lois has many lovely pieces of furniture. I particularly admired the unusual English stained-glass and cherry-wood hutch in the living room. Lois said that her grandmother brought it from Oxford; Lois' grandfather had been a Rhodes scholar.

Lois serves breakfast on china and silver and puts cookies in her guests' rooms. Breakfast is usually fresh fruit, juice, bran and blueberry muffins, and sometimes Danish pastry. Honeymooners will find champagne cooled and waiting, along with fresh fruit. For dinner Lois heartily recommends Pete's Mexican Cantina nearby or Bella Vista, which she says is the largest restaurant in the Southwest.

I can see why many of Lois' guests are people who "just follow the highway up here, with no hassling of traffic. I get judges, retired Dallas Cowboys, artists, and a lot of businessmen who want to relax their brains before going back to work!"

How to get there: From Albuquerque take I–40 east to exit 175 (Highway 14). Go six miles to Highway 44, then left one mile to red-and-white-striped sign. Turn left, then right immediately, and you will be on Tejano Canyon Road. The inn is on the left.

✳

E: *Chayne and Tillie, inn cats, won't bother you unless you invite them. But they like people and aren't at all averse to jumping into your lap.*

El Paradero en Santa Fe
Santa Fe, New Mexico
87501

Innkeepers: Ouida MacGregor and Thom Allen
Address/Telephone: 220 West Manhattan Avenue; (505) 988–1177
Rooms: 12; 6 with private bath.
Rates: $46 to $90 (weekly rates off-season), including full gourmet breakfast. No infants. Pets by prior arrangement. Smoking in designated areas only. MasterCard, Visa accepted.
Open: All year.
Facilities and Activities: Historic Santa Fe Plaza, with art galleries, restaurants, and historic buildings, is a five-minute walk away.

El Paradero is Spanish for "the stopping place," a lovely name for this warm and cordial inn. Ouida and Tom are professionals in the best sense of the word, dedicated to and loving the work they have chosen for themselves.

In extensively remodeling this Spanish farm house, they have nevertheless kept the ☛ rambling, rabbit-warren character of the old adobe house. Santa Fe's Historic Styles Commission approved the plans to leave the old farm house a hodgepodge, and the effect is delightful.

The front part of the building is more than 200 years old. Space was doubled circa 1840–1860 with a territorial-style addition. To complete the charming, diverse appearance, the 🖙 front door is 1912 Victorian, with oval, beveled glass. The painted walls are textured buttermilk and sand, and all is concealed behind a high adobe wall.

Inside, all is light and airy, with high *viga* ceilings, big windows, and Mexican tile floors. Green plants hang from the skylight in the breakfast room, the picture window opens onto the patio, and through the serving window I could see the hand-painted tile decorating the bright, clean kitchen.

There's a lot of common space in this inn. A main *sala,* a cozy television lounge, two dining rooms, patios, and the courtyard are available to guests all day and evening. Wine and tea are served afternoons amidst convivial company.

"A lot of our guests are artists and writers, and it's fun for them and fun for us," says Ouida. 🖙 She grows parsley and other herbs, and each breakfast is a gastronomical adventure. *Huevos* avocado, two poached eggs on an avocado half with salsa and cheese, take my vote. And always, there are freshly squeezed orange juice, fresh fruit, freshly ground coffee, and for tea sippers like me, forty-five varieties!

Santa Fe, a tourist town, has many fine restaurants. Ouida and Tom will gladly recommend their favorites; most are around the Plaza, within walking distance of the inn.

How to get there: From I–25 south take the Old Pecos Trail exit into town. Take a left on Paseo de Peralta and turn right on Galisteo. The inn is on the southeast corner of Galisteo and Manhattan. From I–25 north take the St. Francis exit, follow it to Hickox, turn left before it becomes Paseo de Peralta, cross Cerrillos Road, and turn left on Galisteo.

Grant Corner Inn
Santa Fe, New Mexico
87501

Innkeepers: Louise Stewart Walker and Pat Walker
Address/Telephone: 122 Grant Avenue; (505) 983–6678
Rooms: 11; 5 with private bath, 6 share 3 baths.
Rates: $45 to $100, May through November; $50 to $110, December
  through April; includes gourmet breakfast and evening wine and
  hors d'oeuvres. Children over five OK. No pets. MasterCard, Visa
  accepted.
Open: All year except last three weeks in January.
Facilities and Activities: Thanksgiving, Christmas, and New Year's Day
  dinner for guests. Afternoon tea open to public. Yearly bazaar between Thanksgiving and Christmas. One block from historic Old
  Santa Fe Plaza.

On each guest-room door of this handsome Santa
Fe–Colonial home hangs a red-velvet-and-lace heart that says
"welcome." This should give you a good idea of what's in store for
you at this cordial inn.

"We can't really pamper our guests," Pat claims, "but we can
come pretty close."

"Close" like fruit, fresh flowers, and ice water in your room
and a terry robe if you're sharing a bath. "Close" like a personal

welcome card from Louise, Pat, and Bumpy (Elena, age 6). "Close" like warm, personal care not only from the Walkers but from all the inn staff.

Begin with this truly outstanding tall blue-and-white house on the corner of Grant Avenue. It's surrounded by a spanking white picket fence and ☛ absolutely draped in weeping willows. Inside, blue and white walls, white drapes, and the warm woods of antique furniture meld with the large antique oriental rugs covering polished wood floors.

Louise is an interior designer with a background in the hotel business, and Pat is a teacher of space planning and design, so you can see why Grant Corner Inn is pretty much of a masterpiece.

Pat also doubles as chef, creating eggs Florentine, banana waffles, and his special New Mexican soufflé. Louise has just completed *The Grant Corner Inn Breakfast and Brunch Cookbook*. Need I say more?

Breakfast is served in front of the blazing dining-room fire wintertime. Summers, you can have it on the front veranda under the willows. Teatime brings out all sorts of pastries and muffins, as well as zucchini bread and carrot cake, all made fresh in the kitchen daily. Herbal teas are featured, and you can even have an ice-cream sundae.

The Walkers are eager to provide guests with information on local events, such as the Indian pueblos and their dances and music and art festivals, and on restaurants, shops, and museums.

How to get there: The inn is on the corner of Grant and Johnson just south of Santa Fe Plaza. Grant is the street that borders the plaza on the west.

∽❧

E: *There's a sense of humor at work here, too. The reverse side of the stuffed velvet heart on your door will say "Beware of occupant."*

Inn on the Alameda
Santa Fe, New Mexico
87501

Innkeeper: Patty Jennison
Address/Telephone: 303 East Alameda Avenue; (505) 984–2121
Rooms: 36; all with private bath.
Rates: $80 to $200, summer; $60 to $150, November 1 to May 31;
    continental breakfast and cocktail hour included. Pets by prior ar-
    rangement. American Express, MasterCard, Visa accepted.
Open: All year.
Facilities and Activities: Spa, access to swimming pool and weight room
    a mile away. Newsstand–snack shop. Palace of the Governors; mu-
    seum of fine arts; Santa Fe Plaza with shops, galleries, and restau-
    rants.

"Just imagine an absolutely enchanting small hotel in old
Santa Fe," invites the Inn on the Alameda's brochure.

I have to say it's not hype—it's true. This spanking-new
pink-adobe inn is New Mexico on the outside but small European hotel indoors: You can tell from things like the concierge
calling you by name, fresh flowers, and the smell of coffee and
fresh bread in the morning.

"Hospitality is my thing," says Patty Jennison, her voice bubbling over with enthusiasm. "Every one of our employees is a concierge!"

They mingle with guests at breakfast and the cocktail hour, so you never need to feel like you don't know anyone in town. Breakfast is served in what the inn calls its 🖝 "country kitchen," a bright, painted-tile-decorated room just beyond the sitting room–library. Or you can have your selection of freshly baked croissants, bagels, English muffins, and Danish, along with your fresh-squeezed orange juice and coffee, either in your room or on the patio—whatever makes your day start right.

Cocktails, offered in front of the fireplace from 4:00 P.M. to 8:00 P.M. for guests only, consist of premium liquors and a full wine selection. After an afternoon of "doing" Santa Fe, what a nice way to relax and meet fellow guests.

The inn's 🖝 location is fabulous: one block from Canyon Road, Santa Fe's original artist colony, and three blocks from the famed Plaza, which is just far enough away to ensure the inn's tranquillity, yet near enough to walk to the many fine restaurants that inn personnel will recommend to you for lunch and dinner.

Each of the thirty-six rooms has its own individual character, and some have private balconies. The furnishings are a fine mix of native American and Hispanic styles, reflecting the unique blend of Anglo, Hispanic, and Navajo cultures that is Santa Fe.

Perhaps this mixture is what makes Santa Fe open, receptive, and friendly to visitors regardless of where they're from. The Inn on the Alameda reflects this openness. Patty reports that many guests have commented that the inn is more professional than a bed and breakfast, more personal than a hotel.

How to get there: Drive north on Old Santa Fe Trail (past the State Capitol) across the river to Alameda. Turn right on Alameda and drive three blocks. The inn is on the northeast corner of Alameda and Paseo de Peralta.

❋

E: *I like what official concierge Paul Cimino has to say: "We're kind of a hybrid. We like to be elegant, yet we want to know all our guests."*

Preston House
Santa Fe, New Mexico
87501

Innkeeper: Signe Bergman
Address/Telephone: 106 Faithway Street; (505) 982–3465
Rooms: 8; 4 with private bath, 2 share bath, 2 in separate bungalows
    with private bath.
Rates: $45 to $98; extra persons, $7. Generous continental breakfast
    included. Infants or children over 6 only. Pets by prior arrangement.
Open: All year.
Facilities and Activities: Afternoon snack 3:00 P.M. to 4:00 P.M. Historic
    Santa Fe Plaza, with shops, art galleries, and the Palace of the
    Governors.

    This charming house is the only Queen Anne in New Mexico, Signe told me. She added, "This house has been a real pleasure. It's different from anything in Santa Fe or in all of New Mexico, and the minute I saw it, I wanted to own it!"

    It was built in 1886 and has some wonderful features. The large arched window halfway up the stairs faces west, and ☛ the window seat on the large landing is a favored spot for afternoon refreshment.

    The staircase itself, all gold and black lacquer, is very unusual. Sarah Harwell, member of the staff, told me, "it was built

108

by Orientals who came to build the railroad." It's a marvelous architectural detail.

Signe, an artist, remodeled the house and turned it into an inn because it seemed the perfect thing to do with it after it became hers. Many of Signe's paintings grace the walls of her inn and are for sale.

Because of her artist's vision, Signe wanted guests to see her inn as an exciting experience, not just as a place to spend the night. My favorite room is No. 1, whose fireplace is of tile with a built-in wood cupboard. The flowered wallpaper, high ceilings, and oval lacquered oriental nightstands flanking the king-sized bed made a hit with me.

The parlor has a television as well as an antique armoire, its furniture is upholstered in a cool white, and its fireplace is of tile, too. Breakfast is served in the large dining room, and it's generous. Pear streusel, bread pudding, sour-cream coffee cake, four cold cereals, yogurt, and fruit salad are accompanied by homemade jams and jellies.

After baking in the evening, it's Sarah who often serves breakfast. "But mostly, everybody here does everything," she says. After a waitressing stint elsewhere, she finds innkeeping infinitely superior. "This is such a different atmosphere—you get to know people instead of merely serving them." That pretty much sums up the spirit of innkeeping, I think.

From the third-floor room, another favorite, there's a wonderful view and ☛ an outside spiral staircase to the garden below.

How to get there: Take Palace Avenue four blocks east of downtown. Turn left on Faithway, just one block long, and the inn will be on your right. (There's the Holy Faith Episcopal Church on the corner for a landmark.)

Pueblo Bonito
Santa Fe, New Mexico
87501

Innkeepers: Jan Rogers and Nita Downey
Address/Telephone: 138 West Manhattan Avenue; (505) 984–8001
Rooms: 12; all with private bath.
Rates: $75 to $100, including continental breakfast and evening wine
  and hors d'oeuvres. Pets by prior arrangement. MasterCard, Visa
  accepted.
Open: All year.
Facilities and Activities: Laundry facilities, kitchenettes. Five-minute
  walk from Santa Fe Plaza with shops, art galleries, restaurants, and
  historic buildings.

Pueblo Bonito is well named—though it's on a city street
corner, it's 🖝 so privately enclosed behind its thick adobe walls
that it looks like a real Indian pueblo, somehow left over when the
city grew around it.

Actually, it was a small apartment house, and Jan and Nita
are being quite descriptive when they call the rooms *casitas*,
little houses. Each one, named for an Indian tribe, has been
beautifully renovated, and each is almost a small suite.

The rooms are furnished with attractive artifacts of the
Southwest. Navajo rugs, baskets, and, on the walls, sand paint-

ings blend with Pueblo and Mexican pottery, antiques, and works of local artists. Each *casita* seems brighter and fresher than the next, and each has a corner adobe fireplace.

Pueblo Bonito was once a private estate, which accounts for the privacy of the compound. Within you'll find flagstone paths, private courtyards, and so many huge old trees that the building is almost completely hidden from the street.

But there are ☛ sun decks that give a fine view of the winding streets of Old Santa Fe, framed by the Sangre de Cristo Mountains in the distance.

There is no central meeting room, so ☛ this inn is perfect if you want privacy. Both breakfasts and evening wine with nibbles are brought to the room and served in front of the fire.

Breakfast, served when I "ordered" it, included freshly squeezed orange juice, fresh ground coffee, croissants, and homemade muffins with jellies; and there's always fresh fruit (I had cantaloupe).

Neither Rosie the Lhasa apso nor Pud the springer spaniel mingles with guests; they stay quietly in their quarters. At Pueblo Bonito, therefore, you can be sure of peace and quiet right in the heart of Santa Fe. Yet for shopping and dining, the famous Plaza, with all its bustle and excitement, is just a few blocks away.

How to get there: Manhattan is one block south of Alameda, and the inn is on the corner of Manhattan and Galisteo.

Rancho Encantado
Santa Fe, New Mexico
87501

Innkeeper: Betty Egan
Address/Telephone: Rt. 4, Box 57C; (505) 982–3537
Rooms: 22, including suites and cottages; all with private bath.
Rates: $95 to $165. Children welcome. No pets. All major credit cards
  accepted.
Open: March 21 to January 5.
Facilities and Activities: Restaurant, cantina; library, games; pool, ten-
  nis, horseback riding.

The main lodge of today's Rancho Encantado was built in
the late 1920s. It was a small country inn with twelve rooms and
two separate cottages, all enjoying a view of the Sangre de Cristo
Mountains and 168 acres of desert. The Egan family bought the
spread in 1968, and old-timers wouldn't know the place now.

The former modest guest ranch is now a luxurious resort,
but the inn ambience has remained unchanged. Betty Egan re-
gards her guests as friends, inspiring her staff to maintain the
warm and intimate atmosphere of the original inn. ☛ Every
guest is treated like a celebrity, and those who look familiar probably are—the resort has hosted many famous personalities, from
Henry Fonda to Nelson Rockefeller.

112

New rooms of adobe, brick, and hand-painted tile are decorated with Indian rugs, wall hangings, and other arts and crafts of the region, and all are true to the traditional ranch style of the original.

I walked over a picturesque little bridge to reach the newest *casitas*. More luxurious, they have front porches, fireplaces, sitting areas, large dressing rooms, and such details as ☞ skylights in the bathroom, as well as the gorgeous view afforded the whole ranch.

In the main lodge the dining room and cantina, with adobe walls, tiles, and wood-beamed high ceilings, offer several tiers of dining. Thick, juicy steaks vie with sole Meunière or roast duck Montmorency amid whitewashed walls and warm woods. Try guacamole with blue-corn *tostados* for an appetizer.

Have your morning meal in the Southwest motif, with a breakfast burrito—scrambled eggs and mushrooms rolled in a flour tortilla. Then it's off for the summer sports and the horseback riding or just sightseeing along the trails first trod by those conquistadores looking for gold. The ranch is located between Santa Fe and Taos.

How to get there: Take I–84 north from Santa Fe to the Tesuque exit. Take Highway 22 past Tesuque about 2 miles; the inn is on the right.

Bear Mountain
Guest Ranch
Silver City, New Mexico
88062

Innkeeper: Myra McCormick
Address/Telephone: P.O. Box 1163; (505) 538–2538
Rooms: 15 (some suites); all with private bath.
Rates: $46 to $69, AP. Children and pets accepted. No smoking in the
   dining room. No credit cards accepted.
Open: All year.
Facilities and Activities: Bird-watching room, birding being a specialty
   of the inn, with a full schedule of classes and nature clinic. Gila Cliff
   Dwellings; prehistoric Indian sites; ghost towns; fishing, rock-
   hunting, horseback riding.

Love of nature and care for her fellow humans mark Myra
McCormick and her unique guest ranch. "Tell me your interests," she says, "and I'll plan a tour for you, guided or otherwise."
Her list of suggestions is wide, encompassing geology, archeol-
ogy, caving, white-water rafting, wild-plant seeking, fossilizing,
fishing, hiking, birding (a favorite), or just plain "soaking up sun
on the front porch."

Peace, solitude, friendliness—and health—are the watchwords of Bear Mountain. Myra has a care for the health of her guests, and food is all home cooked, down to the jar of granola I helped myself to at breakfast.

A dinner of oven-baked chicken and scalloped potatoes is bound to have at least two vegetables, in addition to the delicious mixed-fruit salad. "I try to have a green and a yellow vegetable— it's good for people," says Myra.

"So many who come here are intelligent people. They're really thinking, and they tell me that, as they travel across the country, they get fed up with baked potato and tossed salad, and they're hungry for vegetables."

My room reminded me of the 1920s and '30s—clean, comfortable, and not too fancy or fussy. Rag rugs are on the varnished floors, plants are everywhere, and the rooms are bright and sunny with the light from large, old-fashioned windows. Corner suites have sun porches, with marvelous views of the surrounding mountains.

 Meals, cooked from scratch from all-natural foods, are served family style, all you can eat. After spending all day in the great outdoors, I worked up quite an appetite and really dug in.

Myra also provides sack lunches of home-baked bread to take walking, so you won't have to interrupt your nature-seeking. "Very seldom do people stay in," she says. "The big thing for people who come here is to be *out all day long.*"

Tess and Sport are "Heinz 57" dogs. "What amazes everyone," says Myra, "are Sport's blue eyes."

How to get there: From Highways 90 or 180, when you get to Silver City, take 180 to the 4th traffic light. Take the right fork; that's Alabama. Turn north and go 2.8 miles, cross the first cattle guard, and go left on the dirt road .6 of a mile. Don't worry, there are signs to guide you.

E: *I knew that the ranch was famous for its home-baked breads, and I couldn't wait to try them. My favorite was the orange-swirl bread. Delicious!*

115

American Artists Gallery House
Taos, New Mexico
87571

Innkeepers: Myra and Ben Carp
Address/Telephone: Frontier Road (mailing address: Box 584); (505) 758–4446
Rooms: 3 share two baths. (One can have private bath.)
Rates: $45 to $65, $5 more on holidays; includes full breakfast and evening desserts. Children welcome; no pets. No smoking. Cash and personal checks only.
Open: All year.
Facilities and Activities: Interaction with the art community, history and culture of area, geology, tours, hot springs.

Here's ☞ an inn where you truly become part of the family—an artistic, educated, and cultured family at that. Myra taught in a private school in New York City, where Ben was a high-school administrator. Their low adobe Taos house is an art gallery, hung with the works of the well-known Southwestern artists whom Ben represents. "Here you can live with a work in anticipation of buying it, or just enjoy it," says Ben. Both innkeepers, true to their past profession, are enthusiastic teachers as well as gallery and innkeepers.

"I lay out tours on maps of the area," Ben says. "We want our guests to get the maximum benefit from their experience in Taos."

The bright, colorful, and comfortable rooms, hung with art, are overflowing with books on any subject. Stereos with classical albums are close at hand. I spied a typewriter. Ben smiled as he told me that guests could use it "with permission."

 The inn often has happy "happenings." Gourmet-chef visitors insist on making dinner for the Carps and include inn guests. "When we're having guests for barbecue, you're in, you're part of our group," Ben says. "That sort of thing happens here quite often."

At night there's dessert and company. "Ben serves up the desserts," says Myra. "That's his department. You'll get ice cream and pie, or perhaps gourmet goodies from Epicurean Palate, Taos's annual fund-raising event, where artists bake goodies for sale."

Myra's specialty is breakfast. Would you prefer the gourmet or the New York experience? Never mind, says Ben; it all depends upon the whim of Myra whether you have soufflé with baked tomato and cheese, croissants, muffins, and toast or bagels with cream cheese and lox (smoked salmon), smoked trout, kiwi fruit, and cheeses.

You come to Taos for a reason, Ben says. He and Myra are really dedicated to helping you realize it in the short time you're here. In addition, "We make such good friends, they come down when we have our artist's Masked Ball!"

How to get there: Coming into Taos from the south on Old Santa Fe Road (the main highway through Taos), turn right on Frontier, located between the Allstate Insurance building and the Ramada Inn. The inn will be the last house on the right, at the end of the road.

❋

E: *Tovah, the "Taos Mix" pooch, is very friendly, but she gets locked up by 6:00 P.M..*

Casa Europa
Taos, New Mexico
87571

Innkeepers: Lyle Fluitt and Jim Hutchinson
Address/Telephone: Upper Ranchitos Road (mailing address: Box 157);
(505) 758–1356
Rooms: 3 suites; all with private bath.
Rates: $60 to $150, May through September; $50 to $100, October and
November; check rates for rest of year. Special weekly rates. Includes breakfast and afternoon tea; box lunches and dinners by
reservation. Responsible children only. Pets by prior arrangement.
Cash and personal checks only.
Open: All year.
Facilities and Activities: Three wet bars in public areas. Center for art
collectors, not far from Taos Plaza.

Staying at Casa Europa is ☛ like moving into a bright, glittering jewel of a museum, a clean whitewashed adobe house
made just to show off a lifetime collection of art, sculpture, oriental rugs, and fine furniture. The mixture is incredibly eclectic,
from Remington bronzes to full-size suits of Spanish armor to the
life-size Katchina doll high on the balcony library. The house
itself is a treasure, with its ☛ fourteen skylights and circular
staircase to the gallery above the main salon. Appearing decep-

tively small from the outside, the many common rooms (very uncommon!) lead to three exceptionally spacious and elegant suites, one downstairs, two up. ☞ Breakfast is served on Waterford crystal and silver and a different set of fine china each day. (The many sets make a lovely display in built-in glass china cabinets.)

Casa Europa represents a forty- to fifty-year collection of art and artifacts of the Southwest by the innkeepers. Lyle describes himself as a "burned-out Wall Street broker and ex-rancher who retired from the fray and came home to New Mexico." Jim is also an ex-rancher who retired early. They both agree on why they've furnished their inn with so many outstanding things.

"We spent a great deal of time collecting furniture, art work, crystal, and china, and we decided to use it. Why save it?"

Lyle and Jim have thought of everything possible to make their inn an outstanding one. Mints are placed nightly on the down pillows, stamped envelopes are at hand, and three wet bars are stocked with ice, mixers, and Perrier water. Also provided are fruit and flowers and afternoon tea, a safe for your valuables, electric gates and secured parking, and an upstairs entrance and foyer. All this, and three of the most exquisite suites you could imagine. You'll just have to go and see for yourself.

The blue-and-white sparkling kitchen is a perfect place for two gourmet cooks. Here Lyle and Jim turn out their traditional American breakfast and make a lovely occasion of afternoon teas—finger sandwiches of watercress, cucumber, and cheese; zucchini bread; pastries; and fresh fruit.

How to get there: Take Ranchitos Road (on the southwest corner of Taos Plaza) 1½ miles southwest to the intersection of Highway 3 and Ranchitos. The inn is just north of the intersection. It's best to call first so the inn gates will be open for you.

༄

E: *On the pleasures of innkeeping, both men spoke at once: "Every guest so far has invited us to visit them! They borrow books and send them back, with more, to add to our over-1,000-volume library."*

El Monte Lodge
Taos, New Mexico
87571

Innkeepers: Pat and George Schumacher
Address/Telephone: Kit Carson Road (mailing address: P.O. Box 22), (505) 758–3171
Rooms: 13, including one suite; all with private bath, some with kitchenette and fireplace.
Rates: $49 to $55. Children, pets, smoking permitted. All major credit cards accepted.
Open: All year.
Facilities and Activities: Large picnic, barbecue, and play area. Within walking distance of Old Taos Plaza, art galleries, shops, and restaurants. Laundry.

El Monte Lodge at first glance may look more like a motel than an inn, but don't let that fool you—the atmosphere is right. ☛ Mints will be placed on your pillow at night, and Pat and George are always ready for a chat in the small sitting area of the lobby. Fireplace, books, and green plants make it cozy; maps and brochures make it informative; and restaurant menus guide you to delicious New Mexican dining.

"We should have started this when we were young," Pat

says. "We both love people and we love it!" The coffee pot is always on, as well as a handy ice-making machine.

The lodge is fifty-five years old, George told me, according to a retired math teacher from Taos High School. "Last year I had a man call who said, 'I'm 93 years old, and in 1933 I stayed at the Monte.'"

Pat's pride is sharing letters and comments from guests, and I enjoyed reading them. Words like "It's *beautiful,* so clean and modern" or "A very special place, very homey with unusually thoughtful appointments" reaffirmed what I could see for myself.

Behind the main building, huge old cottonwoods shelter a well-kept barbecue and picnic area, and there's a fenced playground for the kids. Everything is spotless in the cabins, grouped in a half-circle facing the main building.

From the large apartment with fireplace to the smallest room with one double bed, desk, chair, and dressing room, all appointments are warm and comfortable. Kitchen units have drop-leaf tables, and the suite has a connecting bath and fireplace.

As one guest wrote, "Our room at El Monte has character and style, everything was spotlessly clean, innkeepers friendly and helpful."

But I thought this was the best accolade of all: "It seems . . . a perfect visit."

How to get there: From the traffic light at Taos Plaza, go east on Kit Carson Road for approximately ½ mile. The lodge will be on your left.

Hacienda del Sol
Taos, New Mexico
87571

Innkeepers: Jim and Mari Ulmer
Address/Telephone: Highway 3 North (mailing address: P.O. Box 177); (505) 758–0287
Rooms: 3; one with private bath and Jacuzzi, 2 share bath.
Rates: $24 to $39, including breakfast. Children over 3 OK. Pets by prior arrangement. Smoking in designated areas only. MasterCard, Visa accepted.
Open: All year.
Facilities and Activities: On the edge of the Taos Indian Pueblo. One mile north of Taos Plaza with its art galleries, shops, and restaurants.

Mi casa es su casa (my house is your house) is the motto of Hacienda del Sol, and innkeepers Mari and Jim live that sentiment to the hilt. Guests, welcome to do homey things like helping themselves to sodas out of the fridge, often are reluctant to leave.

"Wouldn't you like to adopt us?" one young couple plaintively asked. "We'd hardly bother you at all, we'd just stay here and chop wood for you."

Mari laughs as she recounts that tale. "We're a regular family house party," she says, explaining that the no-smoking rule is largely so "you can smell the bread baking." Her breakfast, of bread baked in a clay pot, pecan coffee cake, hot stuffed oranges, and pecan butter on the homemade bread, with a cold-fruit plate for contrast, ☛ was featured in *Women's Day* magazine (May 22, 1985).

The inn's story is part of Taos history. Mabel Dodge Luhan, the wealthy arts patron who brought Georgia O'Keeffe and D. H. Lawrence to Taos, bought this home as a hideaway for her Taos Indian husband, Tony, "so he wouldn't feel like a fenced-in bear," says Mari. Georgia O'Keeffe painted her *Sunflowers* here.

The inn, like so many New Mexico homes, is an old adobe building hidden behind a wall. But it backs up to 95,000 acres of Indian land, with a beautiful view of Taos Mountain, the Magic Mountain of the Taos Indians. ☛ On moonlit nights when the coyotes howl, the Indians answer with their drums. A near neighbor is Tony Luhan's grandson, Standing Deer.

The Sala de Don was Tony's room, with antique Spanish bed and armoire, an adobe fireplace, and books in a wall recess. Escondido has two skylights, a blue four-poster bed, and books and games. Simple pleasures are the rule here.

"We don't charge extra for no TV," Mari says with a twinkle. "We play music, games, read books." She and Jim greet guests with sangria on the patio in summer and hot spiced rum in front of the fire in winter.

This location is relatively new for the Hacienda del Sol. In the past the inn was located at the opposite end of town, tucked away in a spot difficult to reach and without a view. "We're getting younger," Mari says. "Our other inn was 300 years old, the new just 200."

The Ulmers are experts on where to eat in Taos and steer their guests to all the good food to be had in local restaurants.

How to get there: The inn is one mile north of Taos Plaza, off Highway 3 North. Turn right immediately before the Lottaburger (half a mile past the post office). The inn is beside the restaurant but well hidden behind a fence of palings on your left.

La Posada de Taos
Taos, New Mexico
87571

Innkeeper: Sue Smoot
Address/Telephone: 309 Juanita Lane (mailing address: Box 1118); (505) 758–8164
Rooms: 5, including cottage with kitchen; all with private bath.
Rates: $55 to $75, including hearty breakfast. Pets permitted by prior arrangement. Cash and personal checks only.
Open: All year.
Facilities and Activities: Within walking distance of Old Taos Plaza, art galleries, museums, restaurants. Downhill and cross-country skiing, hiking, rafting, fishing, horseback riding.

Sue Smoot has the reputation of knowing what she wants and wasting no time getting it. A few years ago she breezed into town from New York City with an architecture degree under her arm, bought an old adobe hacienda, and practically restored it herself.

The result is a cozy mix of Southwest style and items Sue brought with her from New York. ☛ Mexican carved headboards set off batik tapestry; oriental carpets cover both polished wood floors and blue linoleum.

But best of all is Sue's enthusiasm, which is very catching.

124

Two young guests from New York came in beaming during my visit. She had helped them plan their day.

"Lovely day! We went out to the Taos Pueblo, and I rode a horse for the very first time!"

Sue flashed her wide smile. "I can keep them busy! I send them to horseback riding, I plan day trips which may culminate in long or short hikes . . . art galleries, paintings, pottery, jewelry."

Energy and enthusiasm begin at breakfast, at which Sue serves egg burritos (eggs, beans, and cheese wrapped in a soft tortilla); hot red salsa (on the side); cantaloupe boats filled with grapes; apples; and oranges.

"We all eat together; that's where the fun is," Sue says. "My guests really enjoy it." The long dining room faces French doors opening onto the east garden and sunshine. Behind, in the lounge, bookshelves are stocked for good reading before the tile fireplace. Several of the rooms have a wood-burning stove or fireplace. The kitchen is redolent of thyme or marjoram. ☛ Little notes in guest rooms asked me if I preferred other than black coffee, and was I a vegetarian?

Sue tackled her architecture degree after a career in modern design and advertising. She wanted a New England inn, but that proved to be beyond her means, so she went West like many a pioneer before her. "I take what I'm doing seriously, but it's what I want, so I'm also having a great time!"

How to get there: From the traffic light at the Plaza and Kit Carson, go west on Don Fernando, then left on Manzanares one block to Juanita. Turn right on Juanita, a one-block unpaved street. The inn will be on your right at the end.

✳

E: *Pearl, the Australian sheepdog, reflects her owner's philosophy. "She's a sweetheart," says Sue. "She loves people, she's in the right business!"*

Mabel Dodge Luhan House
Taos, New Mexico
87571

Innkeepers: Kitty and George Otero
Address/Telephone: Morada Lane (mailing address: Box 3400); (505)
754–9456
Rooms: 14; 6 with private bath, 8 share 4 baths.
Rates: $45 to $75, full breakfast included. No pets. Smoking in desig-
nated areas only. MasterCard, Visa accepted.
Open: all year.
Facilities and Activities: Lunch and dinner served to groups; on holi-
days, to individuals also. Inn is State and National Historic Site;
offers films and videos of area culture and history. Borders Taos
Indian Reservation, near Kit Carson National Park. Winter skiing,
summer rafting.

This inn has quite an artistic and literary history. Mabel
Dodge Luhan was a wealthy patroness of the arts, and to her
home in Taos came Georgia O'Keeffe, Thomas Wolfe, Aldous
Huxley, Willa Cather, D. H. Lawrence, and others. You can
see ☛ the artistic endeavors of writer Lawrence in the upstairs
tower bathroom: He hand-painted designs on the windows, which
go down to the floor on all four sides of the room!
The building was 150 years old when, in the 1920s, Mabel

and her husband, Tony, enlarged it to its present twenty-two-room size. The gates of the adobe wall that hide the inn are ancient altar pieces, and all main rooms have ceilings of *viga* and *latia* construction. ☛ Hand-carved doors cover arched doorways.

There were no stairs in the original house—evidently the original inhabitants climbed ladders from one level to another, just like real pueblo dwellers! Kitty Otero cautioned me to watch my head as we climbed the narrow, steep stairs that were added indoors to reach the solarium at the top.

The guest rooms give me a feeling of a summer home in the mountains—the mountains of the Southwest, of course. Walls are whitewashed, simple curtains hang at the windows, and the furniture is a collection of interesting old wooden pieces. Many of the rooms have a fireplace.

Outside on the spacious grounds, there are what amounts to bird-house apartment houses, so large they stand on dual posts. "In summer, twenty-one bird species nest here," says Kitty. In the large courtyard two sculptured deer looked, for a moment, almost real—beautifully poised, ready for flight.

Guests can relax in any of the inn's main rooms. There's a piano in the lounge, and all evening you can help yourself to interesting conversation, coffee, herbal teas, and cocoa in the dining room. ☛ Breakfast is as interesting as the inn: *chiliquiles* (a casserole of egg, chicken, chili, corn chips, and cheese) served with flour tortillas, coffee, tea, milk, and orange juice.

For dinner Kitty recommends New Mexican food at Ogelvie's or Michael's Kitchen, where a specialty is *sopapillas* stuffed with ground beef, beans, and green chilis and then covered with cheese, lettuce, and tomato.

How to get there: From the stop light at Taos Plaza, go east on Kit Carson for about ½ mile to Carl's Trading Post on your left. Behind is Morada Lane, which you take all the way to the end. Signs and arrows point the way to Las Palomas, another name for the Luhan House.

༄

E: *"What we're offering here is the opportunity for people to know Taos in a different way," says Kitty enthusiastically of the special lectures and enrichment programs available at the inn.*

Sagebrush Inn
Taos, New Mexico
87571

Innkeeper: Ken Blair
Address/Telephone: P.O. Box 557; (505) 758–2254
Rooms: 63; all with private bath.
Rates: $38 to $95. Pets by prior arrangement. All major credit cards accepted.
Open: All year.
Facilities and Activities: Steak house, restaurant, bar with live entertainment; swimming pool, two hot tubs; tennis courts, fishing, hunting, horseback riding, skiing, hiking. Taos Indian Pueblo; Taos Plaza.

"It's a family affair," Ken Blair says with a laugh, speaking of his inn. "With five kids, and wife, and daughters-in-law—and seven grandchildren who I hope at some point in time will be involved . . ."

Ken can use all the help he can get. This large and interesting historical inn was built in the old pueblo-mission style, spread out long and low. And the inn's traditions of service, fiercely guarded by Ken and staff, go back awhile.

The inn, a two-story structure with one third-floor room, was built in 1929. That top room is famous because, for about six months, Georgia O'Keeffe painted in it. It was my luck to spend the night there, and I'm wondering if it will bring out some latent artistic talent.

It was inspiring, with 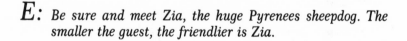 high windows on all four sides, looking out at the Sangre de Cristo Mountains. The rustic ranch furniture, the clothes cupboard, and the many bathroom windows were all hand-painted with bright decorations in primary colors. I loved it.

Dinner was a treat, too, and unexpected in the land of tacos and tortillas. I had a boneless breast of chicken sautéed in a wine sauce, wild rice, and Italian green beans with a wonderful seasoning I couldn't identify; and the portions were a challange. The salad bar was delightfully fresh.

The inn won *Lodging Hospitality* magazine's lobby award in 1983. The large white-adobe fireplace lights up Ken's colorful collection of native art.

"I think I have one of the largest art collections in town," he says of the rugs and paintings that decorate all areas of the inn. New Mexican artists like R. C. Gorman and Robert Daughters abound, so there's no loss if you don't make it to any of Taos's many art galleries—this inn is as good as a museum.

How to get there: Sagebrush is located two miles south of Taos on the Santa Fe Road. It will be on your left heading into Taos. You can't miss the big sign.

❁

E: *Be sure and meet Zia, the huge Pyrenees sheepdog. The smaller the guest, the friendlier is Zia.*

Taos Inn
Taos, New Mexico
87571

Innkeeper: Bruce Ross
Address/Telephone: North Pueblo Road (mailing address: P.O. Drawer N); (505) 758–2233
Rooms: 40; all with private bath.
Rates: $45 to $85. No pets. American Express, MasterCard, Visa accepted.
Open: All year.
Facilities and Activities: Restaurant and bar; outdoor heated swimming pool open Memorial Day to Labor Day; Jacuzzi. Taos Pueblo, Taos Art Festival, Mountain Balloon Rally. Near art center, horseback riding, skiing.

☛ The lobby of this inn was originally the town square—really and truly. The town's well still occupies the room's center, but now, encircled by a seat, it's a happy meeting place.

Surrounding rooms, like Doc Martin's Restaurant and the Adobe Bar, were once small buildings on the square. The whole square has been roofed over, two stories high, but with native wood *vigas* and *tillas;* so the sun still shines through, dappling the green plants with bright light.

"We believe that today's traveler is looking for something

different and unique," says the inn's Stacy Rychener. This traveler certainly found it at the Taos Inn. I was particularly impressed by the adobe fireplace in my room, even when I found out that all the rooms were so adorned. Each fireplace is different, having been designed and painted by local artist Nona Wesley.

Since the Taos Inn grew from a collection of small adobe buildings, rooms outside the main building are grouped on their own patios or small courtyards, and each one has a story. Rooms are furnished in warm Southwestern style: tans and blues and browns. Bedspreads are hand-loomed Indian weaving, armoires are rustic antique, and other furniture is crafted "Taos style."

The two-story lobby has balconies overlooking the well that are popular spots for cocktails. "On New Year's Eve and Halloween, we have parties for our guests," Stacy says. "On the balcony at Halloween, we have 'Psychic Row'—three or four local psychics give readings. It's really popular."

There's parking in the rear for hotel guests, no mean offering in this popular tourist town. Just around the corner is Taos Plaza, filled with art galleries, boutiques, and shops featuring Indian jewelry, pottery, and woven goods. Every parking spot is always taken.

How to get there: The inn is located on North Pueblo Road, one block north of the Plaza traffic light.

E: *The food's no slouch here, either. My turkey-rice salad plate at lunch on Doc Martin's patio was a picture in pretty edibles; the* fajitas *and margaritas in the Adobe Bar were super, too.*

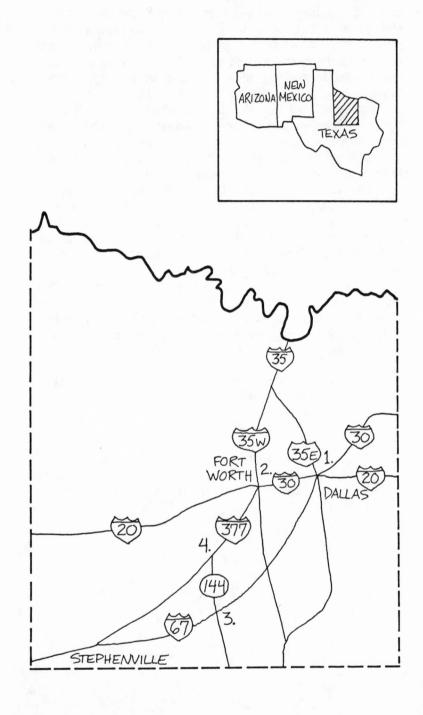

North Texas

Numbers on map refer to towns numbered below.

The Adolphus Hotel
Dallas, Texas
75202

Innkeeper: Jeff Trigger

Address/Telephone: 1321 Commerce Street; (214) 742–8200, in Texas 800–441–0574, elsewhere 800–221–9083

Rooms: 435 (including 20 suites); all with private bath, many with refrigerator, large walk-in closets, and separate sitting areas.

Rates: $136 to $189; suites from $425 to $1,000. Complimentary champagne and hors d'oeuvre hour Monday through Friday. Children under 12 free in parents' room. No pets. All major credit cards accepted.

Open: All year.

Facilities and Activities: Two restaurants, two lounges, afternoon tea in lobby; fitness center; 24-hour concierge desk, parking, house physician. Right in the heart of downtown Dallas, within walking distance of Dallas Fine Arts Museum and city hall with avant-garde architecture and famous Henry Moore sculptures.

The Adolphus is more a work of art than a hotel. I walked into the main lobby and was dazzled by what the hotel calls ☛ "Dallas's most elegant living room." I danced over the thick, flower-patterned carpet to inspect a portrait of Napoleon hanging over an elegant love seat, while a pianist at a gleaming grand piano filled the air with lively music.

134

This was at the five-o'clock cocktail hour, an Adolphus tradition, during which guests and *their* guests are invited to enjoy champagne, hors d'oeuvres, and jazz from Monday through Friday. Weekends you're on your own, but this is no problem, considering the hotel's famous award-winning French Room, or Le Bistroquet, for informal meals and either the Lobby Bar or Palm Bar for other refreshments.

The Adolphus was described as "the most beautiful building west of Venice, Italy" when built in 1912. To think that it all began with bottles of beer! Adolphus Busch of the Anheuser-Busch brewery chose Dallas as his first out–of–St. Louis brewery. After a while he felt like Dallas was his second home; and when a city delegation called on him to propose that he build a nice hotel for the city, his response was exceedingly handsome.

The twenty-one stories, built of red brick and gray granite, are adorned with figures of cherubs and gargoyles, and the interior is splendid with antiques and art. But Busch was not without a sense of humor; the corner turret looks like a beer stein. Inside, I was a little disappointed to discover that the turret is actually the huge walk-in closet of Suite 1912. Too bad. But the view from the suite, out over the gargoyles, is great for feeling like you're lording it over Dallas!

How to get there: The hotel is 8 blocks from the intersection of I–35 and I–75 South; 6 blocks from I–75 and I–45 North.

✸

E: *This is truly living in the lap of luxury, whether you're in a "standard" room or a suite. Adolphus standards are high.*

Ambassador Plaza Hotel
Dallas, Texas
75215

Innkeeper: Ghulam Khan
Address/Telephone: 1312 South Ervay Street; (214) 565–9003, in Texas
    800–442–4839, elsewhere 800–527–3018
Rooms: 114; all with private bath and sitting areas.
Rates: $55 to $85. Children and pets accepted. All major credit cards
    accepted.
Open: All year.
Facilities and Activities: Restaurant and lounge; room service from 6:30
    A.M. to 10:30 P.M. Located across from Old City Park, within walk-
    ing distance of Convention Center, Reunion Area, historical land-
    marks.

The Ambassador Plaza opened in 1905 as the Majestic Hotel, and it's still quite majestic. It was completely renovated in
1983; and with its gold and mauve lobby and gleaming fountain
reflected in gilt and mirrored pillars, I thought I might be in a
beautiful but coldly formal place. But to give you an idea of how
appearances can deceive, one of the hotel's guests, an elderly
gentleman now in a wheelchair, has lived in the hotel for more
than thirty years!

"He was here all through the remodeling," says bellman

Moses James, "and as for who takes care of him, well, we all do. Like, we run errands, bring him his meals." I think it's quite remarkable.

But that's a reflection of the philosophy of innkeeper Ghulam Khan. "We are different than other hotels, we are small, we are like a family. We all work together and when needed, we help each other. Guests often travel alone, and we try to be friendly with them, say hello, talk to them. If there is anything they want, we say, 'Please, let us know, we will take care of it.' "

The hotel is ☛ the oldest in Dallas and can boast of having the first elevator, although its two upper floors are easily reached by broad staircases. The rooms are large, and I loved the ☛ tall brass hatracks in each room—wonderful to hang up everything from clothes to purse and tote bag.

The food in the Embassy Restaurant is delicious, everything from the shrimp scampi, served with carrots in a special sauce, to the mile high pie, a marvelous confection of chocolate crust and mocha ice cream topped with hot fudge and nuts.

But sweetest of all is the attitude of the Ambassador's crew, who make you feel that you can ask anything of them and it will be done with a smile.

How to get there: Take Central Expressway South to Highway 30W, exit at Ervay, and turn left at St. Paul. The hotel is at the V formed by the two streets converging.

Bradford Plaza Hotel
Dallas, Texas
75202

Innkeeper: Louis Frega
Address/Telephone: 302 South Houston Street; (214) 761–9090 or 800–822–2500
Rooms: 118; all with private bath. Children welcome; pets permitted.
Rates: $60 to $90, $200 for presidential suite. All major credit cards accepted.
Open: All year.
Facilities and Activities: Bar and grill serves breakfast, lunch, and dinner daily; special late-night menu; 24-hour room service. Within short walking distance of the West End Historical District, JFK Memorial, and Union Station.

If you're looking for the perfect small European-type hostelry in the middle of downtown Dallas, the Bradford Plaza just fits the bill. Small, intimate, and cozy yet luxurious, the hotel is a small jewel set just down the block from Dallas's restored Union Station.

☛ Being here is like turning back the clock to 1910, when the Bradford (called the Scott back then) first offered the kind of personalized service found in European inns. There's complimentary limousine service to take you farther downtown (if you want to shop at Neiman-Marcus, for instance, five long city blocks away, and you want to be pampered) as well as evening turn-down and a complimentary daily newspaper.

Everything seems golden at the Bradford. The small marble lobby is bathed in a golden light; so is the bar and Sam's Bar and Grill. That name sounds homey and the food is definitely Amer-ican, but the setting is, like the rest of the hotel, elegant. Sam's is patterned after a stylish New York café, with marble floors, oak-paneled walls, and good food, like New Orleans creole gumbo and all sorts of meats cooked over a Texas mesquite grill.

There's coffee in the lobby to which guests may help them-selves; there's also a most surprising thing in such an elegant inn— ☞ the friendliness toward pets. "Sure," says Brian Holle-man at the desk, almost surprised at the question. "You can bring your pet. Just keep it in your room, is all."

I didn't have to worry about my security, either, although I was in the heart of downtown Dallas overnight. There's covered parking with a 24-hour guard and mounted policemen on duty until 1:00 A.M. The fountains at Ferris Plaza Park lit up at night, and I felt like I had traveled abroad.

How to get there: Take the Commerce Street East exit off Stemmons Freeway (I–35) and turn right at the first light, which is Houston Street. The hotel is one block up, on your left.

᙭

E: *I was impressed with the third-floor exercise room for today's guest who wants to be fit as well as elegant.*

Dallas Plaza Hotel
Dallas, Texas
75201

Innkeeper: Bill Cunningham
Address/Telephone: 1933 Main Street; (214) 741–7700
Rooms: 173 suites; all with private bath.
Rates: $65 to $125, including continental breakfast. Nonsmoking floors.
No pets. All major credit cards accepted.
Open: All year.
Facilities and Activities: Bar and grill, exercise room, library. Two blocks
from original Neiman-Marcus store and other fine shopping; West
End historic District.

"We don't do a whole lot of group business," Bill Cunningham
says; "we're basically for the individual and family, people who
come looking for 🖝 both elegance and the personal touch."

I found both at this faithfully restored historic hotel, originally the first Conrad Hilton Hotel to bear his name. Rich wood
paneling, crown molding, etched glass—this is elegance at its
height. Add fine period furniture, potted palms, and a caring
staff, and you have the intimate feeling of Europe's small hotels.

Bill came to the Plaza from a more commercial hotel; and he
says with genuine pleasure and surprise, "I get so many people

140

who, just out of thin air, write to tell me what a charming place this is and how much they enjoyed it."

The library, also known as the Club Room, where breakfast is laid out every morning, is a private retreat for inn guests. People use it all during the day for social meetings or relaxing or "sometimes homework," Bill says. "We give them a calculator, they sit down at a desk and go to work." The homey atmosphere made me feel like I was in my own living room, and I longed to have time to dig through the shelves of books, curl up in a lounge chair, and have a good "read."

The restaurant serves as a specialty dinner entrées grilled over the "wood-of-the-day," an interesting twist on the mesquite that is all the Texas rage. For lunch I had delicious chicken crêpes, a favorite dish of mine, and the sauce was exceptionally velvety. Late-evening suppers vie with a cup of Italian espresso in popularity.

Rooms are called suites because all have comfortable sitting areas, although the larger suites do have more than one room. The hotel was restored and opened one floor at a time, and the décor is traditional, with Queen Anne and other classic, English-period furniture and fabrics. I particularly loved the convenience of the serious-work desk and the color schemes of blue, green, mauve, burgundy, and rose combined with the deep, rich tones of the fine wood furniture.

How to get there: The inn is on the northwest corner of Main and Harwood in the heart of downtown Dallas.

✳

E: *I like the way Bill says that "innkeeping is a two-way street. We put forth this kind of effort and communication, and our guests give it right back to us; it's kind of contagious."*

Stockyards Hotel
Fort Worth, Texas
76106

Innkeeper: Jeff Landesberg
Address/Telephone: 109 East Exchange Avenue (mailing address: P.O. Box 4558); (817) 625–6427, outside Texas 800–423–8471
Rooms: 52,including 4 suites; all with private bath.
Rates: $85 to $135; suites, $160 to $350. Children welcome; no pets. All major credit cards accepted.
Open: All year.
Facilities and Activities: Restaurant, bar. Located in the Fort Worth Historical District with Cowtown Coliseum, Livestock Exchange Building (livestock auctions and rodeos), and Billy Bob's of Texas, world's largest honky-tonk. Fort Worth has outstanding museums and botanical gardens as well.

Fort Worth may be known as Cowtown, but this historic hotel isn't for just any wrangler coming in off the range. ☛ Elegant Western Opulence are the words for this hostelry, down the block from the horses and cattle of the exchange.

"Our style is 'Cattle Baron,' classic cowtown comfort," says Jeff. But I can't help wondering if cattle barons get ☛ a cowboy poem and a homemade praline on the pillow at home on the ranch like they do here at the hotel.

142

The hotel was built by Colonel Thomas Thannisch in 1907, when thousands of head of cattle were making Fort Worth rich. It exemplified fine western hospitality then, and the restored (in 1983) hotel is no less elegant and hospitable.

Most elegant is the lobby, with leather Chesterfield sofas and antique chairs upholstered in speckled hide. Bronzes and prints by Western artists Remington, Russell, and Jack White complement the mirrored baby-doe-hide mantel adorned with massive antlers. It's a real eye-catcher.

Most fun is Booger Red's Saloon, where I sat on the real saddle bar stools and nibbled on the happy hour (5:00 P.M. to 7:00 P.M.) chicken *fajitas,* nacho chips, and salsa to the tune of soft background country-western music.

Rooms have one of four decorating motifs: Western, Indian, Mountain Man, and Victorian. They each also have a view of either the historic shops and saloons of Main Street or of the indoor, skylighted atrium. I liked sitting in the wicker settee in the upstairs sitting area, surrounded by green plants and bathed in sunlight.

Yet more fun is to ride in the 1941 Cadillac limousine that the hotel has for local transportation, but you only have to step outside its door to be in the middle of the Wild West. You'll see ☛ horses being ridden up and down the street, and even the policemen are mounted.

How to get there: From Highway 820 take North Main exit 13 (Highway 81/287) south to Exchange Avenue. The hotel is on the northeast corner of Exchange and North Main.

Inn on the River
Glen Rose, Texas
76043

Innkeepers: Peggy and Steve Allman
Address/Telephone: 206 Barnard Street; (817) 897–2101
Rooms: 21 and 3 suites; all with private bath.
Rates: $60 to $115, Monday through Thursday; $70 to $125, Friday
through Sunday; full breakfast included. Complimentary cocktail
buffet Friday and Saturday evenings. 30 percent discount December 1 through March 1. No children; no pets. Smoking in public
areas only. MasterCard, Visa accepted.
Open: All year.
Facilities and Activities: Dinner by reservation. Dinosaur State Park,
with renowned dinosaur tracks, on edge of town; Fossil Rim Wildlife Park; historic small town square with boutiques and galleries.

The inn is on the river, all right—the beautiful Paluxy River—
and framed on its spacious back gardens by three famous old
oaks. The oaks are "The Singing Trees" of an Elvis Presley recording, and the lyrics were by a guest of the inn when it was the
Snyder Sanatarium.

This interesting building began life as a sanitarium for good
health—Glen Rose was known for its salubrious mineral waters
back in 1919, when the inn was built. A large square structure,

it has a wonderful spacious foyer, with the floor stylishly covered in large black and white tiles.

Two stairways, one on the right and one to the left, march up the rear lobby wall to rooms beautifully decorated, each one individually, by innkeeper Peggy, who for many years was a designer for the original Neiman-Marcus store in Dallas. Need I say more? You'll have as much trouble as I did choosing your favorite.

Breakfast means three to five courses, cooked by a chef who Steve says "is the only one we've had that can cook better than I." As you can tell from that, Steve considers himself quite a cook. During my visit, he had approved a menu of summer fruit and sunny sauces, a feast of fresh fruit in a liqueur sauce; parsleyed cottage eggs with honey-ginger ham; applejack pancakes; three-plum muffins; and for dessert, fresh peach blintzes. Coffee's ready for earlybirds.

Leisurely and casual is the style here. Peggy told me that a visitor from Scotland said: ☛ "This is run like a Scottish inn," which must be the right way because Peggy says that guests continue to return, bringing others.

I liked the small gift shop upstairs between the two staircases. The French doors opened onto a world of fancy needlework and toys. But best of all is the river. "It's always cool down here, even on the hottest nights," says Peggy. I sat outside and watched the moon rise over the tops of those three 250-year-old trees, and I could understand why the river and the trees were the reason the Allmans bought the property and opened an inn.

How to get there: The county courthouse on the square faces Barnard Street. With the courthouse on your right, go on down Barnard two blocks, and the inn will be on your left.

❧

E: *Miss Picasso, the cat, has her face marked by a black mask; it's two-tone, like the face in Pablo Picasso's* Seated Woman *(1927). Aldo, "mostly poodle," loves to be petted by guests "I call him mollycoddled," says Steve.*

The Nutt House
Granbury, Texas
76048

Innkeeper: Madge Peters
Address/Telephone: Town Square; (817) 573–5612
Rooms: 14; 9 (sharing 3 baths) and a 2-room suite with kitchen in the
main building; 4 (each with private bath) in the new annex.
Rates: $35 to $60 in the main building; $45 to $85 in the annex. Children welcome. No pets. American Express, MasterCard, Visa accepted.
Open: All year.
Facilities and Activities: Restaurant, open for lunch at noon every day
except Monday; dinner Friday and Saturday nights only. The
Granbury Opera House celebrated its 100th anniversary in 1986;
the entire town square is on the National Register of Historic Places;
water sports on nearby Lake Granbury.

Everybody loves to say that they've stayed at The Nutt House.
It's always good for a laugh as well as a good inn for dining
experience.

The house was built in 1893 for two blind brothers, Jesse
and Jacob Nutt. I could tell it was originally a store (a grocery) by
the storefront windows, now attractively hung with drapes and
plants. The building became a hotel in 1919, and it owes its

present fame to Mary Lou Watkins. A greatgranddaughter of one of the brothers, she opened The Nutt House Restaurant in 1970. Texans come from all over the state to dine here on such good country fare as chicken and dumplings, hot-water cornbread, fresh peach cobbler, and buttermilk pie. (There are also several good restaurants on the square.)

The inn's lobby has old-fashioned screen doors that lead to the restaurant, wooden floors, and the largest Norfolk pine that I've ever seen indoors. Madge told me that it is more than fifteen years old.

This is ☞ a real comfortable country place. Coffee's always in the pots in the lobby and in the upstairs hall of the annex. Whoever gets up first plugs them in.

"People just come out in their robes to sit and visit or play cards and dominoes," says Madge.

The rooms in the hotel, all upstairs, have screen doors and ceiling fans, reminders of an earlier time, although the hotel is now air-conditioned. They're ☞ furnished as though it's still 1919, and the upstairs parlor has old ledgers and such for browsing.

The new rooms in the annex are on the second floor, in what used to be the law offices of a Granbury lawyer who erected the building in the early 1890s. Four connecting offices form four guest suites, with their double transom doors left intact in case guests want connecting rooms. "The doors were just too lovely to remove," Madge says, and I agree with her.

Madge had a hand in the decorating of the rooms, and she is justly proud of them. She designed the window treatment for the nine-foot-tall windows: a combination of shutters and lace curtains, the latter all handmade by her.

How to get there: The inn is on the northeast corner of the square, directly across from the opera house.

*　❋

E: *The Nutt House is just like home. "If they're coming in late, we just leave their key in the mailbox, with their name on it, and they can let themselves in," says Madge.*

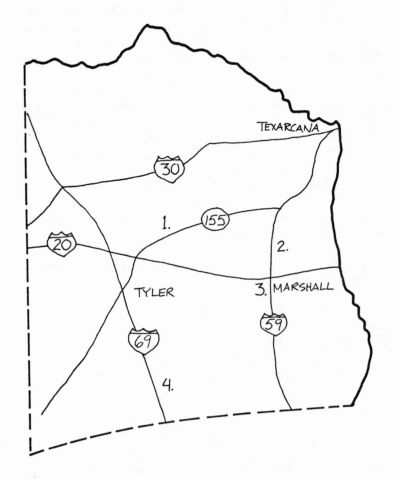

East Texas

Numbers on map refer to towns numbered below.

Annie's Bed & Breakfast
Big Sandy, Texas
75755

Innkeeper: Martha Jane and Dwayne Leslie (Les) Lane
Address/Telephone: Highway 155 North (mailing address: P.O. Box 928);
(214) 636–4355
Rooms: 13; 8 with private bath, some with lofts perfect for kids.
Rates: $48 to $173; includes continental breakfast Saturday, full breakfast rest of week. No pets. Smoking on outside porches only. American Express, MasterCard, Visa accepted.
Open: All year.
Facilities and Activities: Restaurant (closed Saturdays), gift shop,
needlecraft gallery. Needlecraft fair in July, quilt show in September, Annie's Pecan Festival in November.

This spanking gray-and-white dollhouse of an inn looks like
one that Queen Victoria might have played with in miniature.
The rooms, except for the Queen Anne Room downstairs, are
small, but I found them charming in every detail.

The walls, with striped or other floral wallpaper, are
wainscoted; lace curtains frame the windows; fluffy, frilled, and
lacy spreads and pillow shams cover the beds. Each room has a
copy of an antique safe. (It's really a refrigerator, for Saturdays

when the inn and restaurant staff have their day off. Then your breakfast is in the safe instead of in the tea room.)

I loved the atmosphere of camaraderie I found in the parlor when I arrived. It was early evening, and everybody was gathered around the television set, watching a vital football game. "Come join the party," they called out, waving glasses in the air.

"Looks pretty crowded to me," I answered. "There's always room for more," they said; sure enough, space was made for me on the antique sofa, and I joined them with a glass of wine.

I also loved the gourmet breakfast, served every day (except Saturday, when it's continental style). I had a terrible choice: should I indulge in the cream-cheese-and-pecan-stuffed French toast, or should I have the strawberry crêpes? Both begin with a muffin and either fresh-squeezed orange juice or a delicious cold strawberry soup.

The tea room, with its white picket fence and circular verandas, is in one of Big Sandy's oldest homes, built in 1905. It received the town's first official Texas Historical Marker in 1982. And yes ("Everyone always asks," says sales manager Robin Hamm), there really is an Annie; she founded a very successful needlecraft mail-order company, Annie's Attic, which operates right out of little Big Sandy.

How to get there: Big Sandy is on Highway 80 between Dallas and Longview. The inn is right in the middle of town, where Highway 155 crosses 80.

E: *I have stayed here several times, and it's always a treat to relax in a rocker on the porch or visit in the parlor with other guests, invariably interesting people.*

151

Excelsior House
Jefferson, Texas
75657

Innkeeper: Carole Wetsel
Address/Telephone: 211 West Austin Street; (214) 665–2513
Rooms: 14; 12 with private bath.
Rates: $30 to $55. Children welcome. No pets. No credit cards.
Open: All year.
Facilities and Activities: Breakfast served. Across the street from the Atalanta (Jay Gould's private railroad car) and next door to the Jefferson Historical Museum.

The Excelsior House has quite a reputation, especially since railroad magnate Jay Gould signed the register "End of Jefferson, Texas." He was angry because the town fathers wouldn't give him the right of way for his railroad.

Other, more contented guests, like Ulysses S. Grant, Oscar Wilde, Jacob Astor, and W. H. Vanderbilt, signed the register, too. If you're wondering what they were doing in this sleepy east Texas town, then you need to know that Jefferson was once Texas's second largest city.

But with the end of the steamboat and the absence of a railroad (shades of Gould), Jefferson metamorphosed into a small country town. It seemed likely to stay that way, too, until a group of local women raised enough money to restore the Excelsior House and to extol the historical aspects of the town. Today a stay at the Excelsior is a favorite tourist goal.

The hotel is lovely, a treasure of antiques. Oriental carpets cover the polished wood floors, heavy draperies grace the windows, and old portraits hang on the walls.

Many of the rooms have names, including—what else?—the Jay Gould Room. The Sleigh Bed Bedroom has a fine example of this piece of furniture; the Grant Room has ☞ a ceiling-high four-poster bed.

The lobby has exhibits of Jefferson memorabilia in glass cases and on the walls. The ballroom has a pressed-tin ceiling, large oriental rugs, a grand piano, and a crystal chandelier.

Breakfast is the only meal served, but it's a full one. Ham, eggs, grits, and the Excelsior's ☞ famous orange-blossom muffins are the hotel's notion of a proper plantation breakfast. And even dining can be historic in historic Jefferson. The Galley Pub on the next block, serving steaks, seafood, and chicken, with a salad bar and sinfully delicious desserts, is housed in an 1862 building. In the past, the premises housed law offices, cock fights, a Chinese laundry, and a bawdy house (upstairs).

How to get there: From Highway 49 (Broadway), take Polk or Line Street south to Austin. The hotel is equidistant from either.

Hale House
Jefferson, Texas
75657

Innkeepers: Linda and Mark Leonard
Address/Telephone: 702 Line Street; (214) 665–8877
Rooms: 6; 3 with private bath.
Rates: $45 to $65, including big Southern breakfast. Well-behaved children and pets. No smoking. MasterCard, Visa accepted.
Open: All year.
Facilities and Activities: Bicycles, tours in Model A Ford. Jefferson Historical Pilgrimage in May; historic-home tours; Jefferson Historical Museum; Jay Gould's private railroad car.

Whether you take your breakfast in the dining room, on the bright sun porch, or in the swing on the back porch, you'll agree that Linda Leonard is an artist with food as well as with the needle. Linda's talents as a cook are realized in the ham-and-cheese quiche, garlic-cheese grits, and homemade cherry pastries that she rightfully terms her big Southern breakfast.

Her talents as a needlewoman find expression in odd corners of the house; the results can be admired and, if you wish, purchased. Linda's specialty is beautifully smocked children's clothing, for sale both at hand or made to order.

Hale House is yet another example of the ☛ Victorian charm

of Jefferson, the east-Texas town that practically invented breakfast inns for Texas. Built circa 1865, the inn is furnished with antiques of oak and pine and made cozy with family heirlooms.

Coffee is ready at 7:00 A.M. on the sideboard in the upstairs hall for early risers, who may want to catch the first turn on the tandem bicycle. Line Street is a street of quiet residential homes, and a spin around City Park across the street is a fine way to start the day.

Jefferson was once Texas's second largest city, in case you were wondering about all the historical excitement in the air year-round. In 1873 Eastern financier and railroad magnate Jay Gould put a "curse" on Jefferson because city fathers refused to grant right of way for his rolling stock.

Believe the curse or not, Jefferson withered when the natural dam keeping Big Cypress Bayou at navigable level collapsed, putting a finish to the town's main source of prosperity: river shipping.

The Leonards are very helpful about guiding guests to Jefferson attractions, with pleas of "please do not let Priscilla and Abigail out the front door when you leave." As you probably guessed, Priscilla and Abigail are the inn cats. "We have two couples who return every Labor Day, and they say it's to see the cats." Well, they really are friendly, for cats. (Dogs are more my style.)

How to get there: Go east on Highway 49 (Broadway) and turn right on Line Street. The inn is on your left in the center of the block, across from City Park.

***

E: *Jefferson managed to keep* *Gould's elaborate, private railroad car, the Atalanta, and I had a lot of fun touring it and imagining what it's like to roll along the rails in supreme luxury!*

Hotel Jefferson
Jefferson, Texas
75657

Innkeepers: Tanya and Neely Plumb
Address/Telephone: 124 West Austin Street; (214) 665–2631
Rooms: 23; all with private bath.
Rates: $45 to $75, including continental breakfast. Children welcome.
No pets. MasterCard, Visa accepted.
Open: All year.
Facilities and Activities: Dinner for groups by reservation. Within walking distance of restaurants, antique shops, Jay Gould's railroad car, Jefferson Historical Museum, surrey rides through town, Bayou Queen Riverboat.

Before women could even vote, three ladies owned and ran this hotel, originally known by a diversity of names. Innkeeper Tanya feels strongly that this is an important historical fact.

The women were commemorated by three plantation breakfasts on the menu of the Cygnet Room, the inn's restaurant. Unfortunately at present you'll have to forgo choosing between Mrs. Grigsby's Favorite (1882), Mrs. Thompson's Delight (1872), and Mrs. Schluter's Treat (1902) because the restaurant is now closed, except for private parties by reservation. But there's hope that this will not be a permanent state of affairs.

The menu reflected the imaginative approach Tanya and Neely take towards innkeeping. "We named our restaurant Cygnet after the beautiful and delicate baby swan," says Tanya. On the next block, the Black Swan has taken over where the Cygnet left off; it's open Fridays through Mondays. Austin Street also has several other fine restaurants.

The lobby resounds (but softly) with honky-tonk or classical music. Comfortable couches and chairs are presided over by a huge bald-eagle sculpture by the door, and friendly townspeople come and go with cheerful greetings. (The Plumbs are well known in the area; they also own and operate the Gregg-Plumb Home in nearby Marshall.)

The building was built in 1861 as a warehouse to store cotton bales waiting to be shipped down the river, but when that trade died, along came Mrs. Thompson to turn it into a hotel.

The large hotel rooms have high ceilings and antique furniture, with some really fine old pieces in the wide hall. Bathrooms are modern, but there are tubs only, no showers.

My bedroom was huge, with two queen-sized brass bedsteads covered with light, fluffy quilts for spreads. There was one bathroom with tub and dressing-table basin and one with commode and dressing-table basin, both opening off the room. The view from beneath the flowered drapes and the scalloped window shades was of Jefferson's Austin (main) Street. The small town closes up early, and it was quiet as could be. I had a really restful night's sleep.

How to get there: Take Highway 49 to Polk, go south on Polk to Austin Street, then right on Austin. The inn will be on your left.

The Magnolias
Jefferson, Texas
75657

Innkeepers: Cheryl and Ken Kuesel
Address/Telephone: 209 East Broadway Street; (214) 665–2754
Rooms: 3; all with private bath.
Rates: $50, including afternoon tour of the historic house (fee charged to nonguests) and continental breakfast. No children. No pets. No credit cards.
Open: All year except Christmas.
Facilities and Activities: Jefferson Historical Pilgrimage in May; historic homes open all year; tour Jay Gould's railroad car; Carnegie Library has fine doll collection. Good fishing in nearby Caddo lake and Lake o' the Pines.

Built in 1867 by the cofounder of Jefferson, The Magnolias is a beautiful Greek Revival home. ☛ Stately magnolias shade the house, which the builder, Dan Nelson Alley, gave to his daughter Victoria as a dowry gift.

One of the loveliest guest rooms is called Victoria's Room. It's a blue room with a canopied bed and an antique dresser with a three-way mirror of beveled glass.

The house has been completely restored and is one of the stars of Jefferson's famous Historic Homes Tour. (The Magnolias has "Living History Tours" all year long, too, from 2:30 P.M. to 3:30 P.M. every afternoon.) The house is constructed of materials entirely from the Jefferson area and is viewed by Jeffersonians as a symbol of the Southern resilience and courage displayed immediately after the Civil War. The ☛ four white columns on the front porch were hand-hewn from solid trees. Nails were forged by hand, and framing timber and pine floors were cut by hand from local timber. Bricks were handmade, too.

All sorts of niceties add to a stay at The Magnolias. Decorator linens are on all the beds; coffee is served in an upstairs sitting area. Guests are free to make coffee in the kitchen and to use the microwave oven.

Particularly attractive is ☛ the garden room, filled with white wicker furniture, a contrast to the fine Victorian antiques that fill the rest of the home. Guests relax here, or in the double parlors, or on the wide, shady porches of The Magnolias.

Fine dining is to be had at the Stillwater Inn, The Magnolias' neighbor. The two share a single block, each surrounded by spacious green lawn.

How to get there: Highway 49 becomes Broadway as it enters into town. The inn is at Broadway and Friou streets.

McKay House
Jefferson, Texas
75657

Innkeepers: Peggy and Tom Taylor
Address/Telephone: 306 East Delta Street; (214) 665–7322 or 348–1929
Rooms: 6; 4 with private bath in main house, 2-bedroom suite with bath
    in guest house.
Rates: $50 to $70, breakfast included. No children under 12. No pets.
    No smoking. MasterCard, Visa accepted.
Open: Weekends only (Friday and Saturday nights).
Facilities and Activities: Jefferson Historic Pilgrimage in May; Jefferson
    Museum; Carnegie Library doll collection; historic homes.

Even though the McKay House is open only on weekends,
Peggy and Tom Taylor bring enough enthusiasm for a month, let
alone a week, every time they come. They live in Dallas and come
prepared with the spirit of old times, with Peggy dressing in
period costume to serve breakfast and Tom wielding hammer
and nails to continue renovating and rebuilding the historic
house.

"McKay House is one of the oldest houses in Jefferson,"
Peggy says, "and the oldest operating as a bed and breakfast, so
we want to be as authentic as possible. We want things to be as
they were back then."

This admirable attitude sounded like a hardship to me, but I couldn't have been more mistaken. Peggy and Tom travel extensively, and Peggy says she tries to take notes on ideas that will make *her* guests comfortable. Things like designer linens, Crabtree and Evelyn toiletries, fresh flowers in the rooms, and custom-made Amish quilts on the beds—and she sent wallpaper samples to Indiana to have them reproduced.

In matters that pertain to the old house and its authenticity, Taylor imagination continues to work. One of the rooms in the guest house resembles a one-room cabin, with utensils over the wood-burning rock fireplace.

The other has primitive pine furnishings that include the original wood shingles from a privy, complete with half-moon peephole. The Taylors have a great sense of humor, and Peggy just bubbles over with fun.

When I opened the clothes cupboard in my room and found two garments hanging there, I thought that perhaps previous guests had forgotten them. But no, ☛ each guest room is complete with a woman's Victorian nightgown and a man's nightshirt. Peggy hopes they are used.

"We want our guests to know how it was back in the 1850s," she says.

Peggy serves a "Gentlemen's Breakfast" of honey-cured ham, cheese biscuits, and homemade strawberry bread with cream cheese and strawberry preserves in the sunny glassed-in breakfast room. For dinner, she'll recommend several of Jefferson's great restaurants. Perhaps because this is only a part-time inn, the Taylors are able to keep such enthusiasm going. But somehow I doubt it. When they're ready for full-time hospitality, I bet the fun will still be here.

How to get there: From Highway 49 (Broadway), take Main Street south 5 blocks and turn right on Delta.

෴

E: *The ☛ antique music box in the entryway plays happy tunes, and BJ, the "schnoodle," comes to be petted. Peggy told me that he "adores coming here on weekends so he can be loved."*

Pride House
Jefferson, Texas
75657

Innkeeper: Ruthmary Jordan
Address/Telephone: 409 East Broadway Street; (214) 668–2675
Rooms: 8; 4 in main house, 4 in rear cabin, all with private bath.
Rates: $45 to $75, including continental breakfast. Children accepted in cabin. Pets discouraged. MasterCard, Visa accepted.
Open: All year.
Facilities and Activities: Front porches, swings, rocking chairs, and reading material everywhere. Jefferson is that part of Texas that seems most like the "Deep South"; historical homes to tour; Jefferson Museum and railroad baron Jay Gould's railroad car.

The hospitality of the Old South is what comes naturally to innkeeper Ruthmary Jordan. She finds innkeeping to be a life of "sharing, serving—and receiving.

"Wonderful people come through my life," she says. "They share with me their family, their insights, their interests—as I do in return."

They also share the inn that is one of the prides of Jefferson. In 1986 *Woman's Day* called it ☞ "one of the 23 most romantic spots in America." The Main House contains the Blue Room, the Green Room, the West Room, and the Bay Room, which Ruthmary calls her "lusty Victorian." It's furnished with East Lake–Victorian furniture, has stained-glass windows, and has gold stars on the ceiling.

The West Room is a wonderful Victorian red that really shows off the white iron bed. Here there are no less than ☞ four stained-glass windows, and the bath has a huge old claw-footed tub.

The cabin is really a misnomer; it's actually a saltbox house containing three large bedrooms and a suite. It's named Dependency, Ruthmary says, because it was the servant's quarters, and the folks in the main house were dependent on their work.

The Victorian parlor, I discovered, was a beautiful place to take my ease, although the porches, and the swing in the giant old pecan tree, were mighty tempting, too.

Breakfast is always one of Ruthmary's famous recipes. (For a while, she also had a restaurant downtown.) During my visit we had a delicious cinnamon pastry accompanied by honeydew melon, sausage, and croissants along with, of course, coffee, tea, and juice. Another morning you might be served either Ruthmary's special baked pear in French cream sauce or bread pudding with lemon sauce. For dinner, try the Stillwater Inn, two blocks down Broadway. Its restaurant is famous in east Texas.

How to get there: Highway 49 becomes Broadway as it heads east into town. The Pride House is on the northwest corner of Broadway and Alley streets.

Stillwater Inn
Jefferson, Texas
75657

Innkeepers: Sharon and Bill Stewart
Address/Telephone: 203 East Broadway Street; (214) 665–8415
Rooms: 3; all with private bath.
Rates: $50 to $65 weeknights, $55 to $70 weekends; continental break-
fast included. No small children. No pets. No smoking in guest
rooms. MasterCard, Visa accepted.
Open: All year.
Facilities and Activities: Dinner by reservation; restaurant open
Wednesday through Sunday; bar open all week. Jefferson Historical
Pilgrimage in May; Jefferson Museum; historical homes; antique
shops.

"It's very gratifying to have guests appreciate what we're
trying to do," Sharon Stewart says earnestly. She's speaking of
the new guest rooms upstairs as well as the restaurant, which
has become an east-Texas dining tradition. These innkeepers in
this 1890s Victorian–East Lake home have earned a reputation
for such fare as the menu during my stay.

Feature this: grilled breast of duck, wild rice or potatoes
puréed with garlic and cream, a carrot terrine, zucchini with
herbs, and, for dessert, Concord cake.

Sharon and Bill pride themselves on fancy desserts like the Concord cake, a tasty confection of chocolate meringue, chocolate mousse, whipped cream, and almonds, and on their homemade ice cream like cappuccino and macadamia nut. I had a big delicious dish of the macadamia while sitting on a scrubbed pine bench in front of the parlor fireplace.

The inn's color scheme is a restful pale blue and cream. Downstairs lie the bar and restaurant; upstairs, the guest quarters, newly constructed from light Salado pine, with their dramatically pitched ceilings, skylights, and a comfortable sitting place with books and Sharon's sewing machine.

Breakfast was hearty, in no way just plain vanilla croissants and coffee. Added were scrambled eggs with fresh chives and Pecos melon. ☛ "We've got an herb garden in the back," Bill says with typical enthusiasm, revealing the source of the fresh chives. Everything's from scratch, made by these two enthusiastic gourmets.

"Not to brag," says Sharon, "but we're the only restaurant in east Texas with two espresso machines!"

They also have ☛ a light and sunny inn—clean-cut is the word that comes to my mind, or maybe uncluttered. The few antiques, like the coffee table with old Dutch bellows and the scrubbed pine bed-benches in the parlor, all contribute to a getaway that helped unclutter my crowded mind!

How to get there: Highway 49 becomes Broadway as it enters town. The inn is on the northeast corner of Broadway and Owens.

Wm. Clark House
Jefferson, Texas
75657

Innkeeper: Suzanne Benefield
Address/Telephone: 201 West Henderson Street; (214) 665–8880
Rooms: 3; all with private bath.
Rates: $45 to $50, including continental breakfast. Children welcome
(cots and rollaways provided). No pets. MasterCard, Visa accepted.
Open: All year.
Facilities and Activities: Croquet, badminton. Within walking distance
of antique shops, other historic homes, restaurants.

"People love to sit out and have tea and coffee and visit,"
Suzanne says of the lovely, parklike inn grounds alongside the
Wm. Clark House. Huge old pecan trees provide plenty of shade,
there are park benches to sit on, and there's also an old-fashioned
rope swing.

The pretty pink-and-white Clark House is a Texas Medallion
home located in Jefferson's Historic District and one of the homes
Jefferson has become famous for, both as a bed and breakfast inn
and as a historical landmark. It sits on a corner, tidily enclosed in
its white picket fence.

The parlor, spacious the way they built them in Victorian
times, with high, high ceilings, large fireplaces, and bay win-

dows, is another favorite place to sit and visit. The grand piano adds a nice note.

The second parlor, across the hall, is now one of the inn's guest rooms, furnished with antiques from the 1800s. I loved the antique wash basin and ☛ the rope bed.

Another thing that took my fancy was the hand-painted Pennsylvania Dutch bed in another bedroom, unusual to see amid most of Jefferson's Victoriana.

Breakfast is served family style in the large dining room. Suzanne has two college-aged sons who help out in the kitchen and elsewhere when they're home from school.

"I use real butter," Suzanne says as she gives you the recipe for her delicious orange-blossom muffins. Her raisin-bran muffins are good, too. Coffee was enriched with half-and-half or cream: Suzanne is good for the dairy industry! In addition to orange juice, the fruit of the day was a refreshing mélange of peaches, bananas, and pineapple.

Staying at the Wm. Clark House is refreshing all the way. It's simple, quiet, and relaxing—a pleasant change. And for dining, there are a number of good restaurants on nearby Austin Street.

How to get there: From Highway 49, go south down Line Street and turn left onto Henderson.

Cotten's Patch
Bed and Breakfast Inn
Marshall, Texas
75670

Innkeeper: Jo Ann Cotten
Address/Telephone: 703 East Rusk Street; (214) 938–8756
Rooms: 3; share 1 bath upstairs, 1½ baths downstairs.
Rates: $55 to $65, including continental breakfast. No children. No
   pets. No credit cards accepted.
Open: All year.
Facilities and Activities: Marshall Pottery Company, Stagecoach Days
   in May, Fire Ant Festival in October, museums.

Cotten's Patch looks like an old farmhouse set somehow in
the middle of town. The white wooden house has the sort of tall,
narrow windows, peaked roof, and front screened porch that can
be seen in many a house on the prairie.

But inside—what a surprise! The home is packed with lovely
antique furniture, decorative *objets d'art,* and paintings. Everywhere I looked I discovered a new treasure, things like the old
ironing board and iron in the dining-room alcove or some of the
china that Jo Ann paints.

168

Innkeeper Jo Ann is an artist, and 🖙 she has painted delightful *trompe l'oeil* decorations on many walls: The front hall has a painted hall tree on the wall; the kitchen has a painted rug and a latticed apple tree. I really laughed at the broom and mop painted on the pantry door.

I had trouble picking a favorite room, a choice made difficult by Jo Ann's policy of first come, first choose. "The first one here gets to see all the rooms," she says. "I always let them tour the house before others get here."

Jo Ann finds that the gentlemen like to drink their coffee on the porch before the ladies get up, so the first one up gets to plug in the coffee. There are two pots, "one leaded, one unleaded," Jo Ann points out with a smile.

It's perfectly all right to eat in the lovely large dining room, but like most of Jo Ann's guests, I preferred to eat in the sunny country kitchen. "Most everybody just loves to eat in the kitchen," she says. Most likely to be closer to the fresh coffee cake, say I.

Touches like ice water and magazines in the rooms and bed turndown and candy on the pillow make Cotten's Patch a real treat. 🖙 Jo Ann also provides plastic "litter bags" filled with pamphlets describing what to do in historic Marshall.

The old Ginnocchio Hotel down at the historic train depot serves luncheon and dinner in its restaurant. Delicious luncheons can also be enjoyed at the tearoom on the grounds of the famed Marshall Pottery Company.

How to get there: From Highway 80 go south on Alamo to Rusk. Turn right and the inn will be on your left in the middle of the 700 block.

Gregg-Plumb Home
Marshall, Texas
75670

Innkeepers: Tanya and Neely Plumb
Address/Telephone: 1006 East Bowie Street; (214) 935–3366
Rooms: 3; one with private bath.
Rates: $55, including continental breakfast. Children over 7 OK. No
pets. Smoking in designated areas only. Cash and personal checks
accepted.
Open: All year.
Facilities and Activities: Historic homes, Stagecoach Days and Fire Ant
Festival, Marshall Pottery Company, Michelson-Reeves Museum of
Art.

"We like our guests to rock in our rockers and swing in our
porch swing, sipping lemonade and relaxing in our nineteenth-
century atmosphere," Tanya Plumb says. As an experienced innkeeper (she and Neely also own the Hotel Jefferson in nearby
Jefferson), Tanya knows what inn people like. And the Gregg-
Plumb Home has a 🖝 magnificent veranda to swing and rock
on. It covers the front of the house, going in a small circle around
the corner tower.

Though breakfast is simple—orange juice, a homemade
bread such as banana bread, coffee, and tea—the home is not. A

Queen Anne cottage, the house was built in 1893 by Mr. and Mrs. Edwin B. Gregg, Jr. "It was a happy home," Tanya says. Mrs. Gregg lived in it until her death in 1956.

The ten-room house has ☞ six beautiful ceramic-tile fireplaces. The mantels are of sawn oak, and over each is a beveled mirror. The hall is large enough to hold two organs, one contemporary and one antique.

More music continues in the parlor—it has a piano. The den has a television set ("If you simply must watch," as most of my innkeepers say), and the coffee pot is always out.

Other features of the house include stained-glass windows and original fixtures in the bathrooms.

Marshall is a wide-awake small town, with several fun festivals. Stagecoach Days in May bring parades, arts and crafts, sporting events, and stagecoach rides. The Annual Fire Ant Festival and Marketfest occurs in October, with a barrage of family-oriented activities.

Fishing and boating are fine on both moss-dripped Caddo Lake and Lake o' the Pines, both nearby.

Marshall is known for Sam's cheesecake, served at the tearoom at Marshall Pottery Company. Another place to dine is the restaurant of the Ginnocchio Hotel, a historic hostelry undergoing restoration.

How to get there: From Highway 80, turn south on South Washington to East Bowie. Go left, and the inn is on the corner of East Bowie and Doty.

La Maison Malfaçon
Marshall, Texas
75670

Innkeepers: Linda and Jim Gililland
Address/Telephone: 700 East Rusk Street; (214) 935–6039
Rooms: 3 with shared bath.
Rates: $55, including gourmet breakfast. Pets by prior arrangement. No
   smoking. No credit cards accepted.
Open: All year.
Facilities and Activities: Bicycles, children welcome to play with toys in
   young daughter's room. Historic-home tours, Marshall pottery, mu-
   seums.

At La Maison Malfaçon, you get to choose one of four interesting rooms, although no more than three are filled at a time
because of the single-bathroom situation; future plans, however,
include more renovation. In the meantime, each room is a treat,
with its own collection of memorabilia spread out around an antique trunk or piece of furniture. In the Four-poster Room, it's a
scented cedar chest.

The Blue Room has a gorgeous antique bed, a Victorian
chaise longue, and a quilt for a wall hanging. In the light, windowed Shakespeare Room, there's a chaise longue and another
unusual antique bed.

172

The Pink Room has rosy flowered drapes and spread, and I loved this room's marvelous old-fashioned dressing table with three oval, beveled mirrors that hinged so I could see myself at every angle!

But better not to look in the mirror after one of Linda's fancy breakfasts. The first morning, she serves bacon, her own herb-butter eggs, and her famous French toast topped with whipped cream and homemade fruit syrup.

"I love to use fresh strawberries when they're in season," she says.

If you stay an additional night, you'll feast the next morning on "eggs à la Maison Malfaçon," but it's no use begging for Linda's recipe. "They're my own private recipes," she answers with a smile.

In addition to the downstairs parlor and dining room, the upstairs hall has a pleasant sitting area with books and an antique secretary. Rockers are on the front porch, and a swing is in the backyard under a shady tree.

La Maison Malfaçon was once known locally as "the house of ill-gotten gains." Back in the Gay Nineties, the owner of this Greek Revival home (built in 1866) was reputed to have been a somewhat dishonest county official. Worse, rumor said that he did away with his wife and some of her relatives while amassing the fortune that bought him the house!

How to get there: From I–20 take 59 north into town. At the intersection of 59 and 80, turn west and proceed two blocks to Alamo. Turn south and the second street will be Rusk. Turn east and drive 1½ blocks. Inn will be on your right.

✳

E: *"We want our guests to feel welcome, to come and be at home," the Gilillands say.* *"Chrissy (age four) loves to have children come and play in her room."*

Meredith House
Marshall, Texas
75670

Innkeepers: Sandra and Michael Cason
Address/Telephone: 410 East Meredith Street; (214) 935–7147
Rooms: 4; all with private bath.
Rates: $55, including full breakfast; $10 per extra person. Children and
well-behaved small dogs welcome. Smoking on front porch only.
MasterCard, Visa accepted.
Open: All year.
Facilities and Activities: Caddo Lake State Park, Marshall pottery, his-
torical tour.

Comfort is the password at Meredith House, beginning with
the furnishings. "We brought together a lot of different styles,"
says Sandra. "We wanted comfort."

But they got more than comfort when they won ☞ the Historical Society's Dolly Bell Key Award in 1985 for historic-home
preservation.

This late Victorian (1910) cottage is a joy. I loved touches
like the enameled chandelier in the dining room, which picks up
the colors of the flowers in the wallpaper, and the bright orange
tub in one of the bathrooms.

The Sheraton Room contains fine reproductions of 1860s

English court-style furniture—a whole set, including a wonderful dressing table. (The room also has an outside door—in case you want to creep in quietly late at night!)

Furnishings in the Respess Room, named for Mike's grandmother, are eclectic, light, and airy, not heavy Victorian. I'd like to keep the French bed, gold with a bamboo motif.

The Duffy Room upstairs has colorful quilts on the beds and a sitting area. In the upstairs hall a refrigerator is for guest use. The mural over the stairs was painted by an uncle of Mike.

The 🖝 hearty breakfast, all you can eat, usually consists of buttermilk scrambled eggs, bacon, hot blueberry muffins, coffee, tea, and juice served in the dining room (early coffee on the front porch). It's a friendly meal that may last a while. "The other morning we had six for breakfast, and it was eleven [o'clock] before they finally got up!" Sandra told me. Sandra will keep you supplied with coffee as long as you want to sit.

For dinner, the Casons recommend several Marshall eateries. At nearby Caddo Lake "there's a wonderful seafood restaurant overlooking the lake, fifteen, twenty minutes away." Caddo Lake, its cypress trees dripping with Spanish moss, provides ample atmosphere.

Three cats, Catina, Abigail, and Sally, stay outside the inn, but Sandra will make one exception for cat lovers. "Catina, the blue-eyed one, is friendly, and she can come in if folks want."

How to get there: From Highway 80 take Washington south to East Meredith. Turn left and the inn will be on your right down the block. There's a sign in front.

⊷

E: *Meredith House has a lot to offer, not the least of which is the innkeeper's welcome. "We meet and greet our guests and do whatever we think necessary to make them feel like they're visiting friends."*

The Thomas J. Rusk Hotel
Rusk, Texas
75785

Innkeeper: Jim Perkins
Address/Telephone: 105 East Sixth Street; (214) 683–2556
Rooms: 38, including 2 suites; all with private bath.
Rates: $39, double-occupancy; $75, 2-bedroom suite. No pets. American
Express, MasterCard, Visa accepted.
Open: All year.
Facilities and Activities: Dining room and lounge closed Sundays.
Walking tour of historic Rusk; Texas State Railroad, a 3-hour,
round-trip steam ride through the narrowest state park in Texas;
Jim Hogg State Park and Museum. Golf, hunting, fishing. Fall Arts
and Crafts Festival.

The small town of Rusk sits atop ore-rich hills that once
upon a time almost turned the town into a metropolis. But history
decreed otherwise, and today the big attraction is the historic
Thomas J. Rusk Hotel, named after one of the signers of the
Texas Declaration of Independence.

I loved the sort of French-style entrance to this delightful
small two-story inn. A green scalloped awning shades the white-
painted French doors and windows, which really stand out against
the old red brick of the building.

Built in the 1920s, the hotel has since been restored into a little gem of a place to stay. What saved it from destruction perhaps is that it was built too well: It would have cost too much to tear it down!

The lobby lives up to the delicate elegance promised by the exterior. I was impressed by the oriental rug, the Queen Anne chairs, and the art nouveau chandelier.

The dining room, too—T.J.'s, it's called—has a hushed sort of elegance, with soft pink walls, pink tablecloths, and silver and crystal gleaming on the tables. In this setting even the countrified dish of chicken-fried steak takes on a new meaning. Served with a baked potato, green beans with bacon, tossed salad, hot rolls, and Texas pecan pie, it takes on an aura of haute cuisine.

Care was taken to preserve the 1920s feeling in the inn's rooms. Brass beds, traditional bureaus, and simple window treatment add up to very up-to-date renovations with a neat feeling of nostalgia.

How to get there: Rusk is situated at the intersection of highways 84 and 69 in East Texas. The hotel is on the town's main street.

❧

E: *Be sure to take a walk across the* *"longest footbridge in the country" in Footbridge Garden Park, built in 1861 for crossing the valley during rainy season.*

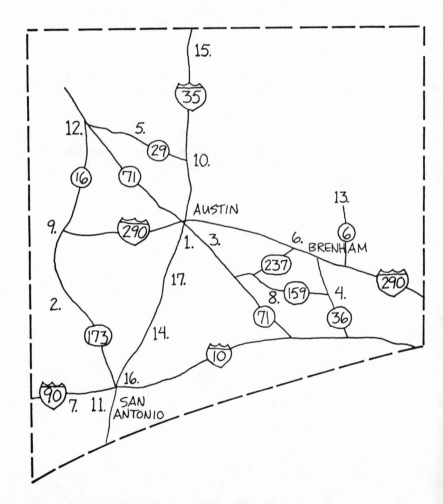

Central Texas

Numbers on map refer to towns numbered below.

The Brook House
Austin, Texas
78705

Innkeepers: Gwen and David Fullbrook
Address/Telephone: 609 West 33rd Street; (512) 459–0534
Rooms: 3 in main building; 1 with private bath, 2 share large hall bath. Carriage house and cottage can sleep 4, have private bath and efficiency-kitchen areas.
Rates: $50, $55, and $65, hearty continental breakfast included. (Rates negotiable depending upon length of stay.) Children welcome. No pets; no smoking. American Express, MasterCard, Visa accepted.
Open: All year.
Facilities and Activities: Located 4 blocks from University of Texas campus and close to the downtown-capitol area. Tennis courtesy of the Courtyard Tennis Club, hiking and jogging paths in parks nearby, canoeing on Town Lake.

Gwen, from Texas, and David, from England, are friendly, gregarious folk. The inn is a 1920s classic, with large square rooms and high ceilings, and the furnishings, comfortable country style, are in keeping with the inn's design.

"We don't want our guests to worry about valuable antiques, and we don't want to limit families with children, so long as they're well behaved," says David. ☛ "We've been lucky with children, but we don't have anything that we'd be devastated about if something happened."

Gwen has a background in design, and I love the way she has coordinated soft blues, greens, and rose into charming stencil patterns throughout the house. David, a builder, has added a lovely veranda along the back of the inn, where the landscaped yard leads to the carriage house and cottage, which also has a large porch. With hammocks, lounge chairs, and potted plants, I found these large areas, cool under shady trees, a delight to relax in.

Pocket doors divide the dining room from the lounge, which is particularly cozy in the winter with a roaring fire in the fireplace. The large bright dining room to the left of the spacious entryway is set for breakfast, but often guests take their coffee into the bright, modern kitchen, where Gwen prepares her hearty continental breakfast.

"Our guests won't go away hungry," she promises as she serves her specialty muffins (pecan, blueberry, heart-shaped beer biscuits, and sausage rolls) along with coffee, tea, juice, and often broiled grapefruit.

I had trouble choosing between the Blue Room, with its own front-view porch, the Rose Room, and the Green Room, all with tall ceilings, large windows, and small-patterned wallpaper. The house has lot of nooks and crannies, with ☞ good books to read (many I long to borrow) tucked into shelves in odd corners. ☞ Both the carriage house (above the garage) and the cottage make delightful private retreats.

How to get there: Exit Interstate 35 at 38th Street. Go west and turn left onto Guadalupe. Go 5 blocks to 33rd and turn right. The inn will be on the left.

❧

E: *Gwen has served breakfast at 4:30* A.M., *David waits up past midnight for late arrivals, and both go about their daily lives: "We go out if we need or want to; we let our guests be at home." And we are, exceedingly.*

Southard House
Austin, Texas
78703

Innkeepers: Regina and Jerry Southard and daughter Kara
Address/Telephone: 908 Blanco Street; (512) 474–4731
Rooms: 4 rooms, one suite; all with private bath.
Rates: $45 to $100, weeknights; $55 to $120, weekends; breakfast included. Usually no children under 13, but flexible for family reunions, and so on. No pets. Smoking permitted on upstairs and downstairs porches only. American Express, MasterCard, Visa accepted.
Open: All year.
Facilities and Activities: Located 12 blocks from Texas State Capitol, 4 blocks from restaurants, shops, and galleries.

A fascinating thing about the Southard House is that ☞ the second floor was once the first floor. In the entrance hall, there's a photograph taken in the 1890s showing how the home looked before the original owners hoisted the house and built another first floor underneath.

Regina and Kara showed me another fascinating thing in the office. It's a large world map, dotted with colored pins showing the many places in the world Southard guests have come from: Europe, throughout the United States, China, and New Zealand.

Southard House is a Victorian–Greek Revival home, built around 1890, with the present first floor added around 1906. In the lounge there's a player piano, and guests gather round in the evening convivially, wineglasses in hand.

The Southards have gathered antiques from all over. The Treaty Oaks room and suite, once the parlor, has a fireplace and a bathroom sink fitted into an antique washstand. White cutwork lace covers all the beds, and there are transoms over each bedroom door. I liked the antique-looking (though new) tile and original narrow-slatted wood walls in the bathrooms.

While weekday breakfasts are delicious ("I call them gourmet continental," says Kara, who fixes them, serving home-baked peanut-butter–orange bread or strawberry-yogurt muffins), it's the weekend breakfasts, prepared by Regina, that are spectacular. Mexican breakfast quiche, Belgian waffles, apple pancakes, or an especially wonderful egg-cheese grits are served with fresh-squeezed orange juice and just-ground coffee, taken in the shade of a green-bordered patio.

The Southard House offers airport pickup and special diets when requested. Calls are taken for business guests. One guest overslept; he was awakened by Jerry, who rushed him to the airport just in time for his plane. "He says we saved his life," Regina told me, "and he comes back to us every time he's in town."

Recommended restaurants for lunch and dinner are within walking distance—Sweetish Hill, an Austin classic, is just down the street on the corner of Blanco and 6th—and take-out food may be brought in. In the dining room, a nineteenth-century English-oak refectory table seems seven miles long.

How to get there: Take the 6th Street exit off Interstate 35, going west on 6th until you reach Blanco Street on your right. The inn will be on your left.

❋

E: You're apt to meet interesting people here: The University of Texas recommends the inn to visiting architects, lawyers, and those here to see the school's Huntington Art Gallery and its school of performing arts.

Stephen F. Austin Hotel
Austin, Texas
78701

Innkeeper: Jean Loubat
Address/Telephone: 701 Congress Avenue; (512) 476–1061
Rooms: 175, including suites; all with private bath.
Rates: $80 to $500.
Open: All year.
Facilities and Activities: Restaurant, coffee shop, bar; access to health
    club one block away. Off historic Pecan Street and within walking
    distance of the state capitol.

Afternoon tea in the English tradition, with cucumber sandwiches and a cart full of fancy cakes, is just one of the niceties at
the historic Stephen F. Austin, smack in the center of downtown
Austin. Named after the "father of Texas" when it was built in
1924, the hotel has undergone many changes in recent years,
including a short spell when it was called The Bradford. But that
didn't work, and the hotel is thriving once again under its rightful
Texas name.

Restored, refurbished, and renovated, the hotel is ☛ the
epitome of hushed elegance in a manner that I doubt its namesake ever experienced back in the days when Texas was a raw
republic. Rooms are furnished in a mixture of traditional and

modern, such as the Queen Anne desk chairs facing Chinese Chippendale desks. In all except the small standard rooms, the gold and white beds are draped in extensive canopies, their fabrics coordinated by a decorator. Plants thrive on tabletops or in planters on the floor, and chic magazines are ready for perusal on the glass-and-chrome coffee table, an amenity I always appreciate. Nothing to read sometimes can be worse than nothing to eat.

However, nothing to eat is hardly the case at this hotel. Innkeeper, Jean, a native of Paris, was first the food and beverage director of the hotel, coming from Maxim's in Paris and the Four Seasons Hotel in London. ☛ Both the Remington Room and the Austin Garden Room are rated three-and-a-half stars by the local newspaper. The former is elegantly formal, with etched glass and burgundy plush banquettes. Some of the tables have lovely cloisonné ashtrays instead of just the ordinary glass ones.

The Austin Garden Room is all white trellises and pink and green flowers—on the wallpaper and the tablecloths, that is. The Friday seafood brunch during my visit was extraordinary, a veritable feast for the eyes as well as the palate. Both the poached salmon, glazed with a port-wine aspic, and the bluefish, in a dill-and-Dijon sauce, were excellent. Dessert was a difficult choice, with a marbled, layered *genoise* winning out over blueberry mousse.

On your turned-down bed at night, you'll find a ☛ "gift from the kitchen," cookies, Danish, or cheese and crackers, to send you off to dreamland. You won't have any problem: Not only is the bed comfortable, downtown Austin closes up quietly at night.

How to get there: The hotel is on the northeast corner of Commerce and 7th Street. Take the 7th Street exit off I–35 and head west five blocks.

Dixie Dude Ranch
Bandera, Texas
78003

Innkeeper: Rose (Billie) Crowell
Address/Telephone: P.O. Box 548; (512) 796–4481
Rooms: 24 guest rooms and cottages; all with private bath.
Rates: $50 double occupancy to $65 single in guest rooms and cottages;
$55 double to $75 single in log cabin; children under 12 special
rates; weekly rates available, AP. No pets.
Open: All year.
Facilities and Activities: Horseback riding, hayrides, cookouts, swim-
ming, poolside parties, barbecues, other planned activities.

Mrs. Crowell has had the Dixie Dude for so long, she doesn't
need an address. The postman knows just where to find her.
"This is not a resort ranch," she says. "This is an old-time Western Stock Ranch that has, through 49 years, become a guest
ranch."

In fact, she likes to call the Dixie Dude ☛ "your home on
the range," and you get a warm welcome, like you're part of the
family. As I was driving over the cattle guard onto the ranch, Mrs.
Crowell passed by in her station wagon.

"I'm heading to town to get fresh vegetables for lunch," she
called out happily as she rolled down her car window. "You should

see the houseful we have today. ☞ Go on up; you can do just whatever you want to do at Dixie Dude."

One of the things I wanted to do was take the two daily trail rides. Bob Branahan is the Dixie Dude's personable wrangler— he teaches school in nearby Boerne when he's not wranglin'! The rides lead over truly scenic Hill Country; the ranch enjoys a beautiful view.

Back at the ranch, after a wonderful dinner of fried catfish, green garden beans with new potatoes, tossed salad, and cornbread, topped off with chocolate cake and ice cream, I was more than content to fall apart in front of the fireplace in the huge living room.

I let the other guests play the piano or the juke box or sit around playing card games. I completely relaxed, like Lobo the dog, who was content to lie under the cedar log bench on the front porch. As Mrs. Crowell told me to, I was doing just whatever I wanted to!

After a while, I went out back and inspected the ranch's vegetable garden. Then, I went and inspected the tack room, as though I know all about horses. Well, I knew enough to be impressed; Bob keeps the cleanest tack room I've ever seen. Last but not least, I took a cool swim in the underwater-lighted swimming pool, and then I sure slept like a top, what with all the fresh air and exercise.

How to get there: Dixie Dude is south of town, on FM (Farm Road) 1077 west of Highway 173 to Hondo. Drive approximately nine miles and the ranch entrance will be to your right. There are signs to guide you.

∽

E: *All the rooms are nice, but really interesting are Bayou Belles #1 and #2 in the log cabin. The rooms are huge, with cathedral ceilings, fireplaces, and antique furniture (like old sewing machines and needlepoint-covered ☞ rockers). What ☞ cozy places on a chilly fall or winter evening!*

Mayan Dude Ranch
Bandera, Texas
78003

Innkeepers: Judy and Don Hicks
Address/Telephone: Box 577; (512) 796–3312
Rooms: 60; all with private bath.
Rates: $70 per day per adult; 12 and under, $35; 13 to 17, $40; weekly
    rates available. No one-day stays. No pets. AP. All major credit cards
    accepted.
Open: Open all year.
Facilities and Activities: Cocktail lounge and television room. Horse-
    back riding, hayrides, cookouts, swimming in pool and Medina River,
    tubing in river, weight room, tennis. Daily activity schedule for
    adults and children.

Except that it's for real, Bandera's Mayan Ranch could fill in
for anybody's fantasy of a true Western dude ranch. Rock cottages, furnished with Western furniture right off the ranch, nes-
tle under old cedar trees. Down by the corral, wranglers (one of
them a Hicks son, Randy) saddle up the horses for trail rides
twice a day. The cool, clean Medina River winds along one
boundary of the ranch, begging for you to lie back on an inner
tube and just float along. . . .

Guests, says Judy, just can't believe the quiet. "They get on

188

the tubes and just float down the river." If you keep on going, maybe you won't have to go back to the same old grind!

The Mayan is run by an entire herd of Hicks—Judy and Don have thirteen children, several of whom have children themselves. The Hicks have been running the Mayan for more than thirty-five years, and they're experts at making you feel at home, 'cause they invite everyone to "join the family."

I love the cowboy breakfast (scrambled eggs, bacon, sausage, grits with butter, cottage-fried potatoes, biscuits and cream gravy, jellies, coffee) served on a bluff above the river—but you have to ride to it first. I signed up for a horse, but another option is the wagon, which goes faster—my horse kinda liked to lag behind. I guess she knew she wasn't going to get any of the delicious food that was busy sizzling on the fire for us.

Great fun was the softball game before dinner, between the "Cowboys" and "Indians." We were Indians, and our team won! Win or lose, all the players won a hearty appetite for the barbecue at the river and the Western sing-along. (But you still get to eat even if you prefer just to watch the game.)

From the large glass-windowed dining room, the view is of miles and miles of Hill Country. Watching the sunset from the deck outside the dining room and bar is a renewing experience. So is just sitting there, with a drink in your hand, enjoying the cool breezes blowing over the trees. One of the best things I got at the Mayan was "lots and lots of loafing."

How to get there: From Hwy 16 turn north onto Main Street, west onto Pecan, and then follow the Mayan signs to the ranch, which is 1½ miles northwest of Bandera.

✳

E: *The Mayan is world famous, and I loved meeting folks from such faraway parts as England and Japan.*

Twin Elm Guest Ranch
Bandera, Texas
78003

Innkeepers: Mary and Frank Anderwald
Address/Telephone: P.O. Box 117; (512) 796–3628
Rooms: 21; 17 with private bath, 2 2-bedroom suites with bath.
Rates: $55 double occupancy, $65 single; children $15 to $45 depend-
ing upon age; AP. Minimum stay three days, with some exceptions.
No pets. Check-in 4:00 P.M.
Open: March 1 to Labor Day.
Facilities and Activities: Horseback riding, hayrides, swimming, tub-
ing, fishing.

Twin Elm, a genuine Western guest ranch, is named for the
twin elm trees entwined in front of the lodge. ☛ An old chuck
wagon is in front, too, and it gives a great air of the Old West to
the premises. More to the point, several times a week meals are
served from it, just like the old days on the range.

Twin Elm is a family place, and there's ☛ lots of good em-
phasis on seeing that the kids have a good time. "We have camp-
fires around the pool," says Mary, "and have the kids toast
marshmallows. It's a nice gathering place. That is, if it's not too
hot," she adds with a laugh.

It's entirely possible that it won't be, not even in midsummer— ☞ Twin Elm is located on one of the highest peaks in the Bandera Hills, and I really enjoyed the breeze. The ranch overlooks the beautiful Medina River, and that's a refreshing sight, too.

After a trail ride through the beautiful scenery, both the river and the pool were great places to be, whether splashing in the pool or fishing in the river. The river yields bass and catfish, and, says Mary, "the kids love it."

Not only the kids loved being in the great outdoors. I thought it was pretty exciting seeing the deer wandering around making out like they lived there, too. And the rabbits, out there in the woods, gave the children at the ranch quite a chase. As Mary says, they have a good time out there trying to catch those little whitetails.

All this nature lovin' works up a good appetite, and meals were hearty enough for any ranch hand. We had good things like scrambled eggs with grits and cream gravy for breakfast, hamburger on the grill with beans and chips for lunch, and good old Texas chicken-fried steak for dinner.

Rooms, small but comfortable, have Western names like "Gunslinger" and the "Outlaws' Room." There's a television on the screened-in recreation porch, as well as both ping-pong and pool tables. There's a wooden pew from an old church to sit on and watch the game players, too.

How to get there: Twin Elm Guest Ranch is on FM (Farm Road) 470, which begins off Highway 16 west of Bandera. The ranch will be on your right just a short distance after you turn off onto 470.

The Pink Lady
Bastrop, Texas
78602

Innkeeper: Tina Wright
Address/Telephone: 1307 Main Street; (512) 321–6273
Rooms: 4 with private bath; cottage room with private bath.
Rates: $35 to $55, weeknights; $55 to $70 weekends, full breakfast
   included. No children under 12. No pets. MasterCard, Visa accepted.
Open: All year.
Facilities and Activities: Walking tours of historic buildings; Lock's
   Drugs with an old-fashioned soda fountain; restored opera house
   with dinner-performance on Friday and Saturday nights and a Sun-
   day matinee (in season). Bastrop State Park with the Lost Pines on
   outskirts of town.

"Lady" is the perfect name for this fancy pink-and-white
Victorian cottage whose large and airy rooms are fitted with
beautiful antique furniture. Each spacious room is named for a
founding father of Bastrop, a Texas town that was named for
Baron Bastrop, an engaging scoundrel who entitled himself.
   My favorite is the Orgain Room, pink and mauve, with a
fireplace and a beautiful antique loveseat. But it's hard to choose
between it and the white-eyelet Sayers Room, the blue Wilbarger
room with its outside door and porch, and the large front Godin

Room, which has a charming, antique round black stove. The stove is useful, too—it helps heat the room if the central-Texas winter is less mild than usual.

Then there's the Crocheron Cottage, an adorable room-and-bath along the side of the large corner property. It has its ☛ original wood floor, stenciled with a Texas motif design that matches that stenciled around the walls below the ceiling. The little front porch has a swing. You can have the place all to yourself, but when you want company, you just walk up the brick path to the common room.

This lovely large room, which stretches all along the back of the house and has huge windows overlooking a veranda and the shady green expanse of lawn, has a television, game table, and open bar, where I helped myself to some liquid refreshment before going out for dinner. Innkeeper Tina has a drawerful of menus from six nearby restaurants recommended by the inn.

☛ Tina performs culinary miracles for breakfast—no mere coffee and croissants for this former restaurateur from Michigan. Each morning brought a surprise: eggs Benedict, pigs in a blanket, cheese soufflé and bran muffins, or creamed sausage and eggs over homemade biscuits. Along with fruit, juice, and coffee to look forward to, I had no trouble at all getting up in the morning.

How to get there: From Highway 71 turn north at the caution light, cross the bridge over the Colorado River, and turn left at the second stop sign; that'll be Main Street. Go 3 blocks and the inn will be on the right.

❦

E: *Tina loves to tell about "Sidewalk," the town dog, who wears a bandana and some mornings wakes up the bank, other mornings the drug store. "He was arrested once, for getting into garbage, but the townspeople bailed him out," she recalled.*

High Cotton Inn
Bellville, Texas
77418

Innkeepers: Anna and George Horton
Address/Telephone; 214 Live Oak Street; (409) 865–9796
Rooms: 5, sharing 2½ baths.
Rates: $50, Sunday through Thursday; $65, Friday and Saturday. Includes country breakfast. No pets, no smoking. No credit cards.
Open: All year.
Facilities and Activities: Small swimming pool in back yard. Friday and Saturday Supper, Sunday brunch. Special Thanksgiving and New Year's Eve dinners for inn guests only. Spring and Fall festivals; historic-home tour in April; antique show in October; Austin County Fair.

Anna Horton says, "We're not pretentious," but the house itself is a *grande dame,* a beautiful home in the best Victorian manner. It's the largest house in town and was built by a very successful cotton broker back in 1906, when cotton was king. The name "High Cotton" comes from a colloquial Southern expression meaning everything's rosy.

Check-in time, Anna told me, is "when you get here," and check-out time is "when you leave." If there'a wait, well, guests can relax by the small backyard swimming pool.

I loved the informality of choosing my own room—guests, on arrival, get a choice of the rooms that aren't spoken for yet. ☞ This is a great way to have a tour of the inn. The rooms are named for old family friends as well as Horton antecedents (George Horton IV is fourth generation from Houston, sixty-five miles away). I chose Uncle Buster's Room, a large corner room with lace curtains, an antique wardrobe, and two gilt-framed portraits of a stern-looking Victorian man and woman.

There's a lovely formal parlor downstairs, and by the door to the upstairs wrap-around porch (there's one downstairs, too), ☞ a cheerful sitting area always has a cookie jar filled with the Hortons' famous cookies.

The furniture is all family antiques, and Anna amused me when I asked her about it. "Lots of it is dead relatives'," she said with a laugh. "George and I got married just when all the aunts started dying."

The dining-room table, however, is a back East item from Lancaster, Pennsylvania, a real conversation piece sixty-six inches wide, with twelve leaves. It vies for attention with the built-in china cabinet with its huge plate-glass door that slides up the wall and probably overhead as well, it's so large.

Breakfast is real country, with grits along with bacon, scrambled eggs and bran muffins, biscuits or rum-soaked cake, and always Anna's special blackberry preserves, which she puts up herself. Summer dinner was a treat, with chilled cucumber soup, marinated-chicken salad, fresh rolls, and Snow Pudding with custard sauce for dessert. Winters it's apt to be roast beef and Yorkshire pudding.

How to get there: The inn is on Highway 36 South, on the edge of Bellville.

❋

E: Peaches is a very shy lady Boxer; two striped ginger-marmalade cats, Butch and Sundance, usually are expelled from the house. If you want to see them or IB (short for Iddy Biddy), the striped gray tabby, just ask young Anna Campbell Horton.

The Knittel House
Buchanan Dam, Texas
78639

Innkeepers: Beverly and Bob Knittel
Address/Telephone: P.O. Box 261; (512) 793–6408
Rooms: 3; all with private bath.
Rates: March through November, $65; December through February,
$55; breakfast always included. Discount for booking all three
rooms; children permitted then, otherwise no. No pets. No smoking
in bedrooms. MasterCard, Visa accepted.
Open: All year.
Facilities and Activities: Pool, patio, spacious waterfront grounds; use of
modern kitchen with all amenities. Boating, water-skiing, fishing,
golf. Vanishing Texan River Cruise.

Beverly Knittel bubbles with Texas hospitality. She also loves
to cook. She told me about a couple from Germany who came for
a night and stayed a week. "We invited them to dinner, and we
taught them how to play dominoes."

The Knittel House 🖙 fronts on beautiful Buchanan Lake,
largest of central Texas's chain of Highland Lakes. Bob and
Beverly have a twenty-three-foot deep-sea cruiser, and summers
they take guests along for fishing and water-skiing. Guests also
have 🖙 golf privileges at Horseshoe Bay Resort.

"We enjoy sharing what we have with other people, and besides, we enjoy meeting people," Beverly says. What they have is a beautiful home on the lake, with three guest rooms in a separate wing, each with a bath and dressing room behind louvered doors. The house is on a steep hill, and the guest wing, with plenty of lights but no windows, is built into the side of the hill.

"People tell me, 'Oh, we get up at six.' " Beverly says with a laugh. "But here, they s-l-e-e-p!"

The bathrooms have showers only, but, says Beverly, "if guests really want a bath, they can come soak in mine," hers being a pink sunken oval tub in their luxurious upstairs quarters. The house was built by Bob's folks as a family getaway, but nobody was using it. Bob and Beverly, who has a catering background, have turned it into a posh getaway on the lake.

"We want people to become familiar with Lake Buchanan, too," Beverly says. "It's large and lovely, thirty-two miles long and eighteen miles wide, and more people ought to know about it."

Well, whether you like water or not, you ought to know about The Knittel House. I haven't yet mentioned the huge living-and-dining area with an entire glass wall fronting the lake, the large native-stone fireplace (with a tall wood-owl sculpture beside it), and the spacious dream kitchen that Beverly will turn you loose in (you have a choice here: Cook or have Beverly cook for you). "We recommend several good local restaurants, but you know, when people stay a few days, they get tired of eating out."

How to get there: From Marble Falls take Highway 1431 through Granite Shoals and Kingsland to Highway 29. Go east on 29 about 2½ miles. Turn left on a dead-end road right behind a People's Savings and Loan. Crest the hill, and the Knittel House is on the right down by the lake. (There's a "Knittel" sign beneath the dead-end sign.)

E: If you want Beverly to cook for you, you will get either something Mexican or a surprise. "I like to look in the cookbook and pick out something I've never made before!" she says.

Long Point Inn
Burton, Texas
77835

Innkeepers: Jeannine and Bill Neinast
Address/Telephone: Route 1, Box 86-A; (409) 289–3171
Rooms: 3; one with private bath, one shares bath with innkeepers, one
    a suite with sunken tub.
Rates: $45 to $60; $15 extra for children. Full breakfast included. No
    credit cards. No smoking in bedrooms.
Open: All year.
Facilities and Activities: Hide-a-beds all over the house for extra guests.
    Guests fish in five ponds stocked with catfish and bass and feed the
    cattle on 175 acres of ranchland. Close to Festival Hill at Round
    Top; Star of the Republic Museum at Washington-on-the-Brazos
    State Park.

"We're so pleased. We never expected to be so busy and to
have so many happy guests," says innkeeper Jeannine. The
Neinasts opened their lovely 🖝 chalet-style home to guests because they wanted to share the wonderful lifestyle they have
created for themselves out on the land.

· "Come and feed the cows, fish the ponds, traipse the woods,
listen to the quiet," they say enticingly.

This is hard to resist, especially as you return from the cows, the ponds, and the woods to the lap of luxury in the form of a large story-and-a-half house that is completely and wholeheart-edly turned over to guests. There's a piano in the parlor—may guests play it? But of course.

"In fact, we would love it if they would come and play. But so far nobody has," mourns Jeannine.

She compensates by lavishing on her guests such marvelous breakfasts as eggs Newport (with sour cream and bacon) or a casserole of cottage cheese, spiced ham, Monterey Jack cheese, mushrooms, and chili peppers, all with biscuits and homemade wild-plum jam. The baths are stocked with such amenities as fancy soaps and shampoos; the rooms are filled with fresh roses; and 🖝 pie, cookies, and coffee are served in the evening. The Neinasts believe in Texas hospitality with a capital H, and Long Point Inn is an ideal hideaway from the hectic pace of city living.

🖝 The view is remarkable: The ranch is set high on a hill on one of the Bluebonnet Trails of historic Washington County. In spring, says Bill, 🖝 the whole front yard is covered with bluebonnets and Indian paintbrushes.

There's always cool air, too, no matter how warm the day. Breezes sweep up the hill and through the wide-open breezeway to refresh and relax. No wonder that was my favorite spot to sit and sip a cold drink.

How to get there: From US Highway 290, take FM (Farm Road) 2679 to FM 390. Turn right, and Long Point Inn will be on your left on a hill not far from the intersection.

Landmark Inn
Castroville, Texas
78009

Innkeeper: Superintendent Shirley Walser
Address/Telephone: P.O. Box 577; (512) 538–2133
Rooms: 8; 4 with private bath, 4 share 2 baths.
Rates: $25 to $30. Children by prior arrangement. No pets. No smoking.
Cash and personal checks accepted.
Open: All year.
Facilities and Activities: Fishing, walking around historic town. Antique shows twice a year, St. Louis Day celebration in August, Old-Fashioned Christmas 2nd weekend in December.

Landmark Inn is a Texas State Historic Site, and as such it's administered by the Parks and Wildlife Department. The white-washed building has provided shelter for weary travelers for more than a century, and it might be the last bargain east of the Pecos River.

The inn is on one of Texas's prettiest rivers, the Medina. The old grist mill over the underground mill race, both built in 1854, is the place to catch lots of perch, catfish, and carp if you're an angler. (You'll need a license, Shirley says.)

The inn's rooms are furnished with authentic period pieces

200

that, while being perfectly comfortable, gave me the nicest feeling of early Texas and pioneer days.

If you're lucky, you might get the room Robert E. Lee slept in or the upstairs or downstairs room of the tiny bath house. Before the Civil War it was the only place to bathe between San Antonio and Eagle Pass. It gave up that valuable function when the lead lining the upstairs (which served as a cistern) was melted down for the Confederates.

One ell of the inn lobby is a museum, with artifacts and exhibits telling the story not only of the inn but of the town as well. Castroville, which calls itself the "Little Alsace of Texas," was colonized in 1844 by Henri Castro, a French Jew of Portuguese descent. The resulting mixture of French, German, Spanish, and English cultures has never obscured the ambience brought by Castro's first 2,134 homesick Alsatians. No food is served here at the inn, but you'll find great bakeries, sausage houses, and restaurants in this "little Alsace."

Inn grounds are quiet and serene, with shady oaks and soft green lawns broken only by steppingstones that lead to the original kitchen (now an ice-and-telephone facility) and the grist mill.

A wonderfully old and oddly shaped pecan tree stands near the river. One of the Famous Trees of Texas, it marks the approximate location of Castor's encampment back in 1844. Legend has it that Geronimo was chained to the tree overnight on the way from Mexico to imprisonment in San Antonio. His captors spent the night comfortably in the inn.

How to get there: The inn is on the south side of Highway 90, just after you cross the Medina River traveling west.

✹

E: *Each room has an Alsatian motto (along with its translation) on the wall: "Quio tient a sa tranquillite sait respecter celles d'autres . . . he who values his own tranquility knows to respect that of others."*

The Lickskillet Inn
Fayetteville, Texas
78940

Innkeepers: Jeanette and Steve Donaldson
Address/Telephone: Fayette Street (mailing address: P.O. Box 85); (409) 378–2846
Rooms: 4, with one community bathroom at the end of the hall.
Rates: $40 double occupancy, continental breakfast included. No children or pets. No smoking indoors, but permitted on the front porch. American Express, MasterCard, Visa accepted.
Open: All year by reservation only.
Facilities and Activities: Nearby Lake Fayette is famed for trophy-bass fishing.

The Lickskillet Inn is authentically old-fashioned. It's a simple dogtrot cabin (so called because of the hall running front to back with rooms opening off each side), much like the ones Texans lived in during the days of the republic. Its four rooms have been turned into guest rooms, and staying here is like visiting great-grandma and great-grandpa in the 1850s when the house was built.

Even the name harks back to earlier times, when settlers helped each other out in a neighborly way, whether building barns or harvesting crops. Afterwards everyone got fed, and latecomers were told to "lick the skillet clean" to get any dinner at all. Fayetteville was even named "Lickskillet" then because the expression was coined here.

The wide dog-run central hall of the small house is furnished with the antiques of four generations; there are memorabilia everywhere. Bedrooms have antique double beds with folksy quilts; dressers have crocheted doilies. The front bedroom, originally the front parlor, has a four-poster that belonged to Jeanette's great-grandmother.

Evidences of bygone days are everywhere. ☛ Each bedroom still has its wood-burning stove, with the chimney reaching up to the ceiling. The bathroom at the end of the run has green tin walls and ceiling, a footed tub, and house rules dictating "clean the tub after you use it." Rooms are named after the town fathers who founded Lickskillet in the 1820s. It didn't become Fayetteville until 1847.

☛ Jeanette and Steve are both chefs—Steve once served on the personal staff of a three-star general—and they cater private dinner parties for groups that book the entire inn. But individual guests get treated to Jeanette's special beer bread for breakfast. I particularly savored Jeanette's delicious homemade liqueur, which she sets out on a tray every evening—it was mellow to the last drop.

The Donaldsons have a pizza business on the side, literally— the public uses a side entrance, and it's solely take-out for them. But inn guests may order pizza to eat in the small dining room.

Guests take their ease on the front porch, where there are rockers and a swing, or relax in their rooms or the dining room. From the porch I could see over the white picket fence to the corner of the street, where the town square begins. Nothing much was happening there.

☛ "We nurture this atmosphere," Jeanette Donaldson says. "Peace and quiet." And friendship, too. "People may come as strangers, but they always leave as friends."

How to get there: From Highway 71 either Highway 159 or Farm Road 599 North will take you to Fayetteville. The Lickskillet Inn is halfway down the block from the square.

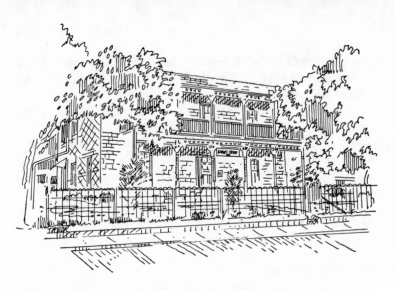

Baron's Creek Inn
Fredericksburg, Texas
78624

Innkeepers: Jean, Cord, and Bert Switzer
Address/Telephone: 110 East Creek Street; (512) 997–9398
Rooms: 2 suites in the main house; room and bath in the cottage. Refrigerators and microwave ovens in all three accommodations.
Rates: $65 to $75, continental breakfast included. Children over 13 OK. No pets. Smoking only on outside porches. No credit cards.
Open: All year.
Facilities and Activities: Pioneer Museum plus historic "Sunday houses" and almost-monthly celebrations in historic Fredericksburg.

The two big suites upstairs in the main house are named "Sunrise" and "Sunset," but "you can tell morning and evening without looking at the names," says innkeeper Bert, because each suite is absolutely and gloriously flooded with light at the right time of day. The luxury suites are composed of a parlor, bedroom, kitchen, and bath, and their combination of antique and rattan furniture makes an eclectic mix. Bathrooms have brass fixtures and claw-footed tubs.

☛ The most fun is to stay in the cottage, which in Fredericksburg is called a "Sunday house." The historic town is known for these little houses, which were built by prosperous

German-immigrant farmers for use when the family came into town for the weekends. On Saturday night they'd polka and play; on Sunday it was off to church; and on Monday, back to the farm.

Breakfast is brought to your door from 8:00 A.M. to 10:00 A.M., but "we've done it earlier and we've done it later," says Bert. He's the baker, and he was busy baking carrot-nut bread and apple-nut bread, both deliciously warm from the oven and accompanied by an artistic fresh-fruit plate, coffee, and orange juice.

The other meals are up to you; that's what the fridges are for. Fredericksburg is famous for German sausages and strudel, and most folks like to stock up in the delectable delicatessens. But the Switzers also operate Oma Kook's, one of the town's best-loved restaurants. German sauerbraten is a daily special, and Paprika Schnitzel is the fare for Sunday dinner.

"One time we tried to change the menu," says Bert, "and we had a local rebellion." So they didn't chance it with the desserts; ☞ the chocolate-pecan pie, apple-crunch pie, and cheesecake continue to please delighted diners.

Baron's Creek Inn is half-hidden by large old pecan trees, but I found it by its jaunty windmill, turning high above the leafy boughs. Then I sat on the porch and ☞ watched the squirrels play in the pecan trees. It was great country entertainment.

How to get there: Highway 290 goes through town, becoming Main Street. The inn is one block east and two blocks south of the Court House on Main.

205

Country Cottage Inn
Fredericksburg, Texas
78624

Innkeeper: Darlene Schneidewent
Address/Telephone: 405 East Main Street; (512) 997–8549
Rooms: 5 suites—4 bedroom–sitting-room suites and 1 2-bedroom suite;
　　all with private bath.
Rates: $85 to $150, continental breakfast and wine included. No pets.
　　Smoking on porches only. MasterCard, Visa accepted.
Open: All year.
Facilities and Activities: All rooms have microwave oven and cof-
　　feemaker. Fully equipped kitchen available. Admiral Nimitz Center,
　　Pioneer Museum, almost-monthly celebrations in historic Freder-
　　icksburg.

　　This cottage was built in 1850, just four years after
Fredericksburg was founded, and it was the only two-story house
in town. Cool stone walls are over twenty-four inches thick, and
the hardware was forged in the owner's smithy. The walls are
whitewashed, and exposed rafters are hand-cut. Most of the antique furniture was made in town in the mid-1800s.

　　☛ One of the rooms is furnished with antiques from the
birthplace of Admiral Chester W. Nimitz, hero of the Pacific

Theater during World War II. He was born just two blocks away from the cottage.

The Pecan Room has a Nimitz night table, a chuck-wagon-pie safe, an Amish quilt on the wall, and an eighteenth-century man trap (like an animal trap, but designed for humans) over the sofa. The coffee table is an 1825 wooden bellows from France. ☞ The whole inn is packed with such treasures; I didn't know what to look at first!

The Oak Suite has its original fireplace, and guests are permitted to build a fire, but I love Darlene's admonition: "Please build only small fires!"

The inn may be charmingly historic, but its bathrooms are beautifully modern—some of them have ☞ large whirlpool tubs! I was completely restored in one, after a wonderful day taking in all the small-town sights.

Breakfast is hot chocolate, coffee or tea, and sweet rolls from one of Fredericksburg's famous bakeries. ☞ Two of them, Dietz's and the Fredericksburg Bakery, have been in business since the town began, and I really recommend a sweet visit!

The old building is beautifully restored and scrupulously clean, and the simple structure is enhanced by ☞ Laura Ashley fabrics and bed linens. Soft terrycloth robes and ice water in each room made me feel like a fraudulent pioneer—it wasn't like this just a little over a hundred years ago, when hostile Indians were near and the living was pretty tough! Today, though, I could take my ease, along with a delicious paprika-schnitzel dinner down the street at Oma Kook's Restaurant.

How to get there: Highway 290 goes through town, becoming Main Street, and the inn is right there in the 400 block.

River View Farm
Fredericksburg, Texas
78624

Innkeeper: Helen K. Taylor
Address/Telephone: Highway 16 South; (512) 997–8555
Rooms: 2 suites upstairs accommodating up to 8, shared bath; 1 suite downstairs accommodating 4, private bath.
Rates: $45 to $55, full country breakfast included. Pets at discretion of innkeeper.
Open: All year.
Facilities and Activities: One mile to Lady Bird Johnson Municipal Park with swimming pool and 9-hole golf course, 18 miles to Kerrville and the Cowboy Museum.

Breezy is the word for River View Farm. It's set on a hill in the Hill Country and has a breezeway that catches a round-the-clock cool wind. I could just sit here for hours, cooling off and taking in the sweep of the green hills and ☞ listening to the lowing of the longhorns and the buffalo that Helen's neighbors raise.

Helen herself raises Texas herbs and plants as a business, so you can buy yourself some Texas cactus if you want. She also collects bird pictures, so the walls are hung with prints of feathered friends.

The downstairs bedroom has a beautiful quilt draped over a handmade cedar chest. The furniture is 1920s Queen Anne reproduction: dressing table, dresser, bureau, bed, and chair. ☛ The bathroom tub has a Jacuzzi, a nice luxury to find out in ranch country!

☛ Helen's breakfast is hearty enough for a rancher, too. Fresh, local German sausage, scrambled eggs with *jalapeños* (but not too hot, says Helen), cheese, biscuits, fresh peach cobbler, and jellies and jams, including Helen's specialty, blackberry jam.

It's all topped off by the centerpiece, fresh fruit in season, which everybody proceeds to eat. "Everybody always lingers," says Helen, "having more coffee and munching on the centerpiece." I can taste why: The county is known for blackberries, nectarines, peaches, strawberries, mangoes, and melons—watermelon, honeydew, and Persian.

Helen's guests practically have the run of the house. The kitchen; the large and comfortably furnished living room with its large stone fireplace; the glass-enclosed sun porch; and the breakfast room with its china cabinet full of heirloom china, framed German mottos, and the bird collection (mostly hummingbirds, which are Helen's favorite)—all conspire to make guests feel truly at home.

How to get there: The farm is 4 miles south of Fredericksburg on Highway 16, 1 mile south of Lady Bird Johnson Park. To the left you'll see a white fence and a cattle guard. Drive over it and there you are.

∽

E: *If guests aren't munching fruit or sitting on the breezeway, they'll be on the porches, rocking or swinging on the dogwood glider and waiting for the cows to come home.*

Lone Star Inn
Georgetown, Texas
78626

Innkeepers: Patty Thomas and Carol Gafford
Address/Telephone: Rt. 3, Box 1895; (512) 863–7527
Rooms: 4; 2 with private bath, 2 share.
Rates: $38 to $68, including full breakfast. Children over 12 OK. No
  pets. No smoking. No credit cards.
Open: All year.
Facilities and Activities: Lunch served on Fridays, dinner by reserva-
  tion. Georgetown's historic town square restored with restaurants
  and shops. Municipal golf course just down the road. Candle fac-
  tory, Inner Space Caverns. Fishing and boating nearby on
  Georgetown Lake.

Lone Star Inn is on three acres of central-Texas farm land
down the road from the small town of Georgetown. It's peaceful
and quiet. "Most everybody kind of comes and sits on the front
porch and swings or rocks in rocking chairs," Patty says. The
prairie-style house, built circa 1910, is a Georgetown classic. "You
can drive through Georgetown and pick out homes built by Belford
Lumber Company," Carol says. "Back then, if you wanted a good,
solid house that would last, you had Belford build it. In a sense,
there's a sort of snobbish pride in owning one in town." How

about one in the country? I asked. "Well, ours is the only rock one," both women said with a laugh.

Each of the inn's rooms is named for a Texas river, and there's a spare sort of cleanliness and tidiness that I like. The largest, San Gabriel, for the river that runs through Georgetown, was ahead of its time: It had a half-bath, to which Patty and Carol have added a shower. It also has mirrored his-and-hers closets, a fireplace, an old oak bed, and an unusual princess dresser.

The Rio Grande Room has an elk-skin rug on the polished wood floor and a doe-eyed deer head mounted in the bathroom! The Brazos Room, unlike the river, is pretty small, but it's a corner room with two lace-curtained windows letting in a lot of light and air.

Patty and Carol lodge a lot of wedding guests, and sooner or later either the bride's mother or the groom's, depending on which side is the out-of-town one, "needs someone to talk to," Carol says. "Then afterwards everyone comes and relaxes, whether they're staying here or not. Perhaps some of our most interesting weekends have been wedding ones."

Each and every evening you get to choose one of three breakfasts for the morrow; and on Fridays, lunches of soups, salads, and sandwiches are served and are open to the public. Homemade pies are a specialty—how can you make a choice between chocolate, buttermilk, or rum pecan? "We have a strange neurosis," Carol jokes. "We generally use old-fashioned recipes that go with the era of the house."

How to get there: Take Highway 29 from I–35 and go east 2.7 miles. When you pass the municipal golf course on your left, turn left onto the unpaved road to the inn. There are signs.

＊

E: *Schnauzers Poppy and Toppy can't quite understand why Patty won't let them greet everyone. "I have to hold them back—they like people." They want to jump on you is why, but how big is a schnauzer?*

City Hotel
Lacoste, Texas
78039

Innkeepers: Jaye and Gene Sherrer
Address/Telephone: North Front Street and FM (Farm Road) 471 (mailing address: P.O. Box 446); (512) 762–3742
Rooms: 3; all with private bath.
Rates: $37.50 to $45, full breakfast included. No children. No pets. Smoking in designated areas only. No credit cards accepted.
Open: All year.
Facilities and Activities: Pool. Sunday lunch; dinner (by reservation only) on Thursday, Friday, Saturday, Sunday. Near historic Castroville.

It's been more than forty years since the last train whistled past the City Hotel in little Lacoste, but this historic hostelry has a new lease on life. Jaye and Gene drove out from San Antonio one day in 1978 and took a look at the faded but structurally sound old hotel and made a momentous decision.

"This is our retirement thing," Jaye says, radiating a very youthful enthusiasm. "We lived in Europe for a few years and loved the cozy, homey inn atmosphere over there. We wanted to have a place like that of our own."

The hotel was built sometime between 1888 and 1913, quite

a time span, but so far the Sherrers have been unable to narrow it down. That the builder, a Mr. Schmidt, had wonderful taste is all that Jaye knows, and this she learned by discovering that "he put in nothing but the best."

Bathrooms, however, had to be added, with brass and porcelain fixtures and thick, padded carpet installed underfoot. Gold and white iron beds, covered with quilts, work with the Sherrer collection of antiques to create a Victorian feeling in the upstairs bedrooms. I liked it that ☛ each room has a door to the upstairs porch.

Downstairs in the restaurant and the tea room the décor is French and German, reflecting the Sherrers' love affair with Europe, and the cuisine follows the same vein.

"I love to cook," says Jaye as she bustles off to begin shrimp creole to be served that evening. Another specialty is chicken cordon bleu, served with German fried potatoes, mixed salad, and broccoli. Before and after dinner, guests lounge around the fireplace in the main dining room, eagerly anticipating or supremely content.

"We cook everything ourselves," Jaye says. ☛ Her desserts are spectacular: lemon–sour cream or fudge-nut pie or Italian cream cake. When they bought the hotel in 1978, Jaye envisioned a place where people could come and relax, enjoy a good dinner in a lovely atmosphere, and spend the night. She and Gene have succeeded beyond their fondest expectations.

"We wanted to have a European inn of our own," Jaye concluded, "and it's a dream realized. In addition, this historic old place deserved to be restored, and we feel fortunate to be the ones to do it."

How to get there: From I–10 South just east of Castroville, take FM 471 south to Lacoste. The inn is on the northeast corner of FM 471 and North Front Street.

The Badu House
Llano, Texas
78643

Innkeepers: Kathy and Lance Moran
Address/Telephone: 601 Bessemer Street; (915) 247–4304
Rooms: 6, plus one suite; all with private bath.
Rates: $45 to $85, continental breakfast included. Children over 13 OK.
   No pets. MasterCard, Visa accepted.
Open: All year.
Facilities and Activities: Lunch and dinner Thursday, Friday, Saturday;
   lunch, 11:00 A.M. to 2:00 P.M.; dinner, 6:00 P.M. to 10:00 P.M. Bar,
   Tuesday through Saturday, 11:00 A.M. until closing. Hunting in the
   "deer capital of the world," fishing. The area, on the Llano Uplift, is
   a bonanza for gem and rock collectors.

The Badu House is an inn in a million, because it began life
as a small-town bank. Built in 1891 for the First National of
Llano, this Italian-Renaissance palace housed the bank hand-
somely until the latter failed in 1898. Then the inn was bought at
auction by Professor N. J. Badu, a French minerologist who,
along with his descendants, actually used the imposing red-brick
and checkerboard-gray-granite building as home for more than
eighty years. And it is strong enough to have survived a 1900

tornado and a fire that destroyed the iron-boom town of North Llano.

"This building sure doesn't look like an inn" was my thought as I climbed the wide granite steps to the front door. But the stained-glass windows of the doors, one emblazoned with the letter *B*, the other an *H*, opened onto another world.

The doors opened onto a wide flight of polished wood steps leading to a landing furnished with an antique desk, love seat, chairs, and a jewel-tone antique rug. I walked up a few more steps around the corner to a sitting room with more Victorian settees and an antique sewing machine abandoned—a century ago?—in the midst of stitching.

Back downstairs, I found the Llanite Club, which is the bar and lounge where everyone gathers when not dining or sleeping. There I was welcomed heartily and invited to inspect the bar itself: ☛ a huge slab of llanite, the rare opaline stone discovered by Professor Badu and found nowhere else in the world.

The restaurant floors are the white marble of the bank. Solid brass hardware is decorated with an intricate flower motif reflected in the bright floral wallpaper, and I loved the three-part shutters that slide up and down to shade the large old-fashioned windows.

Kathy and Lance serve a simple coffee, juice, and homemade-Danish breakfast but really shine for lunch and dinner. The chef's selection at lunch was chunky fresh crab, on a bed of lettuce, tomatoes, and bell peppers, topped with a white orange-marmalade dressing. Dinner was veal Française, lightly breaded and sautéed with butter and garlic and topped with two jumbo shrimp. I have to confess. I ended with the most sinfully luscious dessert: ☛ apple supreme pie, chunks of apple-and-cream-cheese filling topped by a crushed-pecan-and-brown-sugar glaze.

How to get there: Llano is on Highway 16, northwest of Austin. Drive right through town, over the bridge, and the inn will be on your left at the corner of Highway 16 and Bessemer.

The Castle Inn
Navasota, Texas
77868

Innkeepers: Helen and Tim Urquehart
Address/Telephone: 1403 East Washington Street; (409) 825–8051
Rooms: 4; all with private bath.
Rates: $60, double occupancy; extra persons, $20. Includes continental breakfast, evening snack. No children under 13. No pets. No credit cards.
Open: All year.
Facilities and Activities: Dinners by reservation. Historic town with 14-foot statue of the French explorer LaSalle, who came to an untimely end near here in 1687, 150 years before town was formed; museum; Navasota Nostalgia Days Festival in May; main-street restoration project.

This majestic Queen Anne house is well named The Castle. It is ☞ too gorgeous to describe adequately. Local craftsmen built the mansion in 1893 as a wedding present from a local businessman to his bride. Of now-extinct curly pine, decorated with ornamental brass and beveled glass, with ☞ a sun porch enclosed by 110 panes of this glass, it is outstanding.

I love the turret on one corner, a tower that makes the house stand out among the leafy trees outside and provides circular window seats inside on the almost room-sized stair landings. There's also a twenty-foot stained-glass window in the stairwell.

The inn is furnished with antiques collected for more than thirty years by Helen and Tim. The music room has a player piano, a handcranked Columbia Grafanola, and a carved wooden head of Tim in an aviator's helmet. (Tim is a retired airline pilot.) The collection is so complete that private tours are often arranged just to show off this magnificent property. (Tours by reservation only.)

Breakfast can be served in your room or in the upstairs sitting room next to the upstairs porch. Delicious fresh-baked muffins, juice and coffee, and fresh fruit in season taste especially good in such baronial surroundings, and you can have it any time between 6:00 A.M. and the 11:00 A.M.—checkout time. Wine and cheese, with individual loaves of bread, is often served on the upstairs balcony, the better to enjoy the evening breezes.

"A lot of times when people go out to dinner, we don't know when they're coming home," says Helen, "so we leave a note telling them that their wine and cheese is waiting for them in the fridge." It's in the large upstairs hall, and stocked with soft drinks, which are consumed "on the honor system."

Each bedroom has a fantastic antique bed, one more amazing than the next. Another thing to marvel at is ☛ Helen's doll collection.

Helen and Tim will provide dinner if four couples want it, and it might consist of Cornish hens with wild rice, broccoli hollandaise, Mediterranean salad, and a peach cobbler à la mode. Delicious!

How to get there: The inn is four blocks west of the Highway 6 bypass on Highway 105, which becomes Washington, Navasota's main street.

Prince Solms Inn
New Braunfels, Texas
78130

Innkeeper: Ruth Wood
Address/Telephone: 295 East San Antonio Street; (512) 625–9169
Rooms: Three suites on the first floor, eight rooms on the second; all
　with private bath.
Rates: $50 to $70, double occupancy; suites $60, $85, and $95. Conti-
　nental breakfast included. No children under 12. No pets.
　MasterCard, Visa accepted.
Open: All year.
Facilities and Activities: Restaurant, bar. Tubing and rafting in nearby
　Comal River. Historic museums.

The Prince Solms Inn, a famous Texas landmark, has
been ☞ in continuous operation since immigrant German craftsmen built the handsome building in 1898. What's more, families
of its first patrons keep returning to this elegant, warm, and
welcoming inn. The beautifully restored building has front-entry
doors that are ten feet high, with panes of exquisitely detailed
etched glass. The inn shines with antique fittings gathered from
all over the world. Bronzes are from Europe, solid brass door-
knobs from old Lake Shore mansions in Chicago, and doors and
carriage lights from old San Antonio homes. It's more than an

inn; staying here makes me feel like I must be in a mansion back in the days of the Astor, Rockefeller, and Jay Gould railroad barons.

Guest rooms are furnished with beautiful, but sturdy, antiques, unusual light fixtures, and well-chosen, tasteful paintings and prints. Each room is named for the gloriously patterned wallpaper that decorates the walls.

Wolfgang's Keller is in the cellar, ☛ but what a cellar! With old brick walls and a fireplace—and Wolfgang Amadeus Mozart's portrait—setting the tone, the atmosphere is wonderfully old-world to match the delicious continental cuisine.

I had Wolfgang's wonderful weiner schnitzel and sampled the special linguine in a rich cream sauce, so I had to forgo the sinfully rich desserts until another time. ☛ Everything served here is made fresh daily. Mixed drinks, wine, and champagne are readily available from the bar.

The inn has a picturesque brick-paved courtyard in the rear, a shady garden spot filled with plants and flowers for guests to relax in and enjoy. It's also a great place for a reception or a meeting, and Ruth can arrange a *mariachi* band as easily as she can cater a special meal for your group.

I enjoyed the complimentary breakfast of home-baked pastries, breads, and muffins wheeled into my room on a tea cart and served beautifully. Elegant as it is, the Prince Solms Inn provides the Hill-Country friendliness that makes you feel truly at home.

How to get there: From Interstate 35 take Exit 187 to Seguin Street, then turn right around the circle to San Antonio Street. The inn will be on your left.

⚘

E: *Bill Knight, who presides over Wolfgang's, is a renowned pianist. Every night during dinner, he sits down at the grand piano in the center of the restaurant and entertains guests, drawing everyone into his magic circle. I hated to think of leaving the next morning.*

The Inn at Salado
Salado, Texas
76371

Innkeepers: Cathy and Larry Sands
Address/Telephone: North Main Street; (817) 947–8200
Rooms: 5; 2 share bath, 3 are suites with private bath.
Rates: $45 to $85; $10 extra for use of sleeper sofas in suites. Breakfast
    included. Children over 10 only. Smoking in designated areas only.
    No pets. MasterCard, Visa accepted.
Open: All year.
Facilities and Activities: Microwave and refrigerator in kitchen for guest
    use. Swing-set playground for children; bicycles. A driving-tour tape
    of historic Salado; historic-home tours; Central Texas Museum;
    Pace Park and Salado Creek; antique shops and boutiques.

    Stagecoaches used to rumble down the Old Chisholm Trail
to ford Salado Creek and stop at the old Stagecoach Inn in Salado.
That inn today is a historic restaurant, but you can still get the
flavor of those past days by staying at The Inn at Salado, in the
center of this historic village in central Texas, and dining at
the Stagecoach Inn Restaurant, just down the road a piece. You
can enjoy such regional dishes as chicken-fried steak and gravy
and peach cobbler. (For continental fare, the Tyler House is across
the road and down the block.)

The Inn at Salado is the happy work of Cathy and Larry Sands, who live just 300 feet behind the inn in a house built in 1855. The inn is newer—it was built in 1873. The rooms are named for influential people who helped found Salado.

"The Reverend Baines Room is in honor of LBJ's great-great-grandfather," says Larry. The antique bed there came from the Governor Hogg estate.

The General Custer Suite, Larry confessed, is named after the general because "he did camp out on the banks of Salado Creek." Whomever they're named after, the rooms are large and comfortable. A favorite is the L. Tenney Room, bright and cheerful with lots of windows and now the new addition of bookshelves.

"People like to have books to read," says Larry. "We want them to make themselves at home, to use the common room, to feel free to go into the fridge for their cold drinks and wine. This is a dry county, so they have to bring whatever they want to drink."

Guests make themselves so much at home with the games provided in the lobby that "some evenings we get into a real mean game of Trivial Pursuit," the Sands told me.

Pace Park across the street has a pavilion with picnic tables and grills for cookouts; and a favorite pastime, when the creek is running, is to roll up your cuffs and go wading. The water is cool and clear and oh! so refreshing.

How to get there: Take the Salado exit from Interstate 35 and drive right into town—that's Main Street. The inn is across from Pace Park and a stone's throw from Salado Creek.

Tyler House
Salado, Texas
76571

Innkeeper: Becky Bunte
Address/Telephone: North Main Street (mailing address: Box 571); (817) 947–5157
Rooms: 2 suites; each with private bath.
Rates: $65 to $75, continental breakfast included. No pets. Smoking in designated areas only. American Express, MasterCard, Visa accepted.
Open: All year.
Facilities and Activities: Lunch daily except Monday. Dinner daily except Sunday and Monday. The Central Texas Museum; Salado Square, a quaint and colorful shopping area.

The Tyler House may have just two suites, but they make wonderful retreats from the hectic pace of most of our lives. Salado is a green and lovely town on the Salado River with an interesting history. The town was settled predominantly by people of Scottish descent, and every November there's a "gathering of the clans," with Highland games and other diversions. I loved visiting the museum to see the many colorful tartan banners hanging there, waiting for the fall event.

The Tyler House is one of Salado's pioneer mansions. It was

built in 1857 by one of the founders of Salado College, which is just a ruin today. Salado is a very small town, but its past glories include the brief hope that it would be the capital of Texas!

The house sits high on a hill on Main Street, and ☛ the restaurant has been famous far longer than the guest rooms. People drive in from as far away as Dallas just for lunch. A very disappointed mother with two young sons arrived too late, and I could sympathize with her—the very same thing happened to me one time. But lunch is over at 2:00 P.M., and nothing can shake innkeeper Becky's rule. She explains it charmingly. "The ovens get shut off, and it takes way too long to get them going again."

Too bad, because one of the fine dishes I was glad not to miss was the bushes Normandy, a puff pastry stuffed with crab and shrimp in cream sauce. And for dessert: Amaretto mousse. The fare at Tyler House is truly gourmet. I strongly recommend the cream of artichoke soup if you're lucky enough to find it on the menu.

The two suites are named Dalby and Tyler, and both are exquisitely furnished with antiques. Fresh fruit, juices, home-made pastries, and hot coffee or tea are ready for you in the morning "whenever you wish," says Becky, who has been in charge of the Tyler House for three years and glows when she says how much she loves it.

There's a large lounge in a wing of the house with a fireplace and a piano. On Friday and Saturday evenings, ☛ Salado musician Sharon Murrah will play anything you want from the 1940s to the present.

How to get there: Salado is directly east of Interstate 35, just bordering the highway. You can't miss the signs. Tyler House is on Main Street, just north of Salado Creek.

Bullis House Inn
San Antonio, Texas
78208

Innkeepers: Christine Underwood and Anna and Steve Cross
Address/Telephone: 621 Pierce Street; (512) 223–9426
Rooms: 6; 1 with private bath, others share 2 baths.
Rates: $19 without breakfast to $45 with breakfast and private bath.
    Children under 3 no charge; over 3, $4. American Express,
    MasterCard, Visa accepted.
Open: All year.
Facilities and Activities: Affiliated with American Youth Hostels, with
    hostel on premises. The Alamo, Paseo del Rio (River Walk), shop-
    ping at La Villita, Institute of Texan Cultures, Hertzberg Circus
    Museum, Brackenridge Park and Zoo, Spanish missions, fiestas.

    Bullis House Inn and San Antonio International Hostel make
an unusual experience because it offers the best of two worlds.
While staying in the historic home of Civil War General John
Bullis, you get to mix with travelers from all over the world.
    Inn guests interact with hostel guests, and ☛ I felt like I
was taking an international voyage. Guests come to the inn and
the hostel from France, England, Australia, Germany, Japan—all
over. Innkeeper Christine fosters this action.
    "I love it," she says. "I've been in all sorts of jobs that deal

with the public, but a certain sort of person stays at an inn, more warm, more open. I love to sit in the evening over a cup of tea: the lost art of conversation revives at an inn."

Bullis House, a large white Neo-Classical mansion, was built by the general when he came to town from New York in 1865. But he didn't settle down. He fought hostile Indians in Texas and saw action in the Spanish–American War.

The colorful general, called "Thunderbolt" by the Indians and "Friend of the Frontier" by the settlers, earned formal thanks from the Texas Legislature.

Large white columns support the front portico. Inside, parquet floors, marble fireplaces, and chandeliers attest to early Texas elegance. Guest rooms are large, with high ceilings decorated with bead, billet, and other Romanesque ornamental moldings. The largest guest room has a bed, dresser, and mahogany desk that are Hepplewhite copies. Most of the rooms have fireplaces ☛ (there are ten altogether!), and I particularly loved the French doors in the rooms opening off the upstairs porch.

Breakfast is cold cereal; hot apple, cinnamon, or orange muffins; orange juice; and coffee, tea, or hot chocolate. San Antonio abounds in fine restaurants, and Christine has many recommendations. Mi Tierra, in the Mercado (market), is a special regional favorite.

Christine, who's keen on San Antonio, told me there is always some kind of parade or festival going on.

"I've never been in a city that parties so much," she says. "There are no strangers here!" This is high praise from an innkeeper who hails from California!

How to get there: Take the New Braunfels–Ft. Sam Houston exit off I–35 or the Grayson Street exit off Highway 281. The inn is on the corner of Grayson and Pierce, adjacent to Fort Sam Houston.

The Crockett Hotel
San Antonio, Texas
78205

Innkeeper: Dave Muth
Address/Telephone: 320 Bonham Street; (512) 225–6500
Rooms: 138 in original building; 65 in courtyard area, including suites;
all with private bath.
Rates: $59 to $450. No pets. All major credit cards accepted.
Open: All year.
Facilities and Activities: Two restaurants, cocktail lounge; swimming
pool, Jacuzzi. The Alamo; Paseo Del Rio (River Walk); shopping.

The Crockett is one of San Antonio's historic hotels, except
that it's the building that is historic, and not as a hotel. It was
built in 1909 to serve as both offices for the International Order
of Oddfellows and as a retreat for the lodge's traveling members.

Today, all that remains of the past is the exterior. In 1982 the
historical property was completely renovated, and the result is a
super-deluxe hotel with the warmth of an inn.

The new Crockett entrance is off a large atrium, newly created; but the old entrance, where the building angles at Bonham
and Crockett streets, is what I use. It puts me right at Lady Bird
Johnson Fountain and, down the street, Alamo Plaza.

The building's original cornerstone is outside this old main entrance, and in 1909 a time capsule was placed behind it. It was opened in November 1984, with its contents placed in a hotel safe-deposit box. Personnel Director Lisa Pardo has the key, if you want to discover what was in it. (An updated 1985 one replaced it.)

☛ My room overlooked the gardens of the Alamo just below, and the hotel's pool, in a courtyard with a waterfall, copies pretty faithfully the Alamo grounds just across the road. It's supposed to be a Texas-style "swimming hole," but that doesn't mean that it has sacrificed such new-fangled modernities as a Jacuzzi.

(There's an adults-only Jacuzzi up on the rooftop sundeck, too. I highly recommend it at dusk. ☛ The view of San Antonio from the Crockett roof is spectacular.)

The Crockett's eating places have cozy names, although the atmosphere of Lela B's proved to be one of elegant evening dining. ☛ Formal service of American cuisine is accompanied by waiters and waitresses singing Broadway melodies, very entertaining and, needless to say, very popular. I had American chicken bounty, breast of chicken stuffed with shrimp, scallops, and mushrooms baked in a mustard sauce, and for dessert Alamo creme, a mousse-like confection flavored with liqueurs and strawberries.

Peggy's Pantry serves breakfast and light lunches, and Ernie's Bar provides snacks as well as drinks.

How to get there: East Bonham intersects Crockett right at the rear of the Alamo Gardens. The hotel is angled at the intersection, just in front of the Lady Bird Johnson Fountain.

The Menger Hotel
San Antonio, Texas
78205

Innkeeper: Art Abbot
Address/Telephone: 204 Alamo Plaza; (512) 223–4361
Rooms: 196; all with private bath.
Rates: $50 to $105. Pets accepted. All major credit cards accepted.
Open: All year.
Facilities and Activities: Coffee shop, restaurant, lounge, gift shop; swimming pool. The Alamo; Paseo Del Rio (River Walk); 5 golf courses within 20 minutes.

Talk about illustrious neighbors! The Menger has the Alamo for its next-door neighbor. This classic San Antonio hostelry has been operating continuously since 1859, barely twenty-three years after the battle that turned a mission into a Texas shrine.

Called the finest hotel west of the Mississippi, The Menger was a bastion of refinement when there wasn't much of that on the rough Texas frontier. Even in my youth, when plenty of refinement had come to Texas, staying at the Menger was a treat I looked forward to when we went to San Antonio.

It was one of my first exposures to really beautiful and authentic antique furniture, and I thrilled to the list of famous people who had stayed there. Names like Sarah Bernhardt, O. Henry, General Sam Houston, and Theodore Roosevelt made the hotel ring with history.

Although the façade—long, flat, and business-looking—is rather plain, you can recognize the hotel by its white brick and the New Orleans–type iron work over the sheltered entrance.

The lobby is large and L-shaped. To your right as you enter, you'll get a glimpse of the really impressive two-tiered mezzanine, surmounted by a rotunda whose stained-glass ceiling is supported by white and gold Corinthian columns. (Some kids I know ran round and round the tiers until they got caught and caught it!)

Another eye-catcher, through the lobby's large glass wall, is the lush, tropical patio sheltering the pool. The hotel restaurant overlooks this Garden of Eden. Food is heavenly, too. Try the veal à l'Anglais, sautéed in white wine and topped with a demi-glaze sauce. For dessert, the mango ice cream is a Menger specialty.

It was ☛ in the Menger Bar in 1898 that Teddy Roosevelt enlisted his Rough Riders, and it hasn't changed much since that day. Lots of pictures of the president hang on the dark oak-paneled walls. There's usually live entertainment offered here in the evenings.

Next to the Alamo, The Menger is one of the glories of San Antonio.

How to get there: The Menger is on the corner of Alamo Plaza and Crockett Street, right next to the Alamo.

Norton-Brackenridge House
San Antonio, Texas
78204

Innkeeper: Carolyn Cole
Address/Telephone: 230 Madison Street; (512) 490–3285
Rooms: 4 with private bath (2 have kitchenettes); plus an upstairs suite
with living room, bedroom, kitchen, and bath.
Rates: $50 to $105, including continental breakfast. No pets. Smoking
in designated areas only. American Express, MasterCard, Visa ac-
cepted.
Open: All year.
Facilities and Activities: The Alamo, the Paseo del Rio (river walk), and
the Mercado are nearby San Antonio attractions.

Innkeeper Carolyn Cole has furnished her inn with such
treasured pieces of her past as her grandmother's rocking chair
and her very own small one from when she was a child. The room
she likes to put honeymooners in has a white iron bed covered
with a family quilt; her grandmother's chest; and palms, "because they're a Victorian-looking plant."

The bathroom has a stained-glass window, and Carolyn
leaves magazines and catalogues "and razors and little bottles of
shampoo" for her guests' convenience. Another nice touch is

the ☞ dish of chocolate mints and the cookies when you check in—it makes for a sweet visit.

A relatively new innkeeper, Carolyn likes to do things right. ☞ "My idea is to do the simple, since I'm just starting out, but to do the simple well!" she says enthusiastically.

The Norton-Brackenridge House was built in 1906. The handsome two-story home, with white Corinthian columns and spanking-white porch railings, began life on another street. Somewhere along the way, it was remodeled into four apartments.

It was moved to its present location in San Antonio's historic King William district in 1985. Carolyn acquired it a few months later, restored it completely, but retained the kitchens in each suite. Each kitchenette now has a microwave oven and a small refrigerator.

Breakfast, served buffet style, is set out on the second-floor foyer and available whenever you're ready for it. "People can mingle with other guests or go back to their rooms if they prefer," Carolyn says. But most inn people like to mingle, right? Breakfast might be Meunster cheese melted in croissants, cinnamon rolls, fruited butter (with grated orange rind or strawberries), Neufchatel cheese with pineapple, and a bowl of grapes or apples—"Granny Smith and Delicious, with skin on they're so colorful," says Carolyn, who has decorated her inn using her sense of color.

How to get there: Take I–35 south to the Alamo exit, then go left past Pioneer Flour Mills to Beauregarde. Take a left and then right on Madison, and the inn will be the 4th house on the right.

Terrell Castle
San Antonio, Texas
78208

Innkeepers: Nancy Haley and Katherine Poulis
Address/Telephone: 950 East Grayson Street; (512) 271–9145
Rooms: 2 rooms sharing a bath; one suite with private bath.
Rates: $59 to $69; suite $79; breakfast included. Pets permitted. Smoking in designated areas only. MasterCard, Visa accepted.
Open: All year.
Facilities and Activities: There are dog runs in the rear. San Antonio is the home of the Alamo and several Spanish missions. The River Walk downtown is lined with restaurants, bars, and boutiques.

Katherine and her daughter Nancy Haley have combined considerable talent in creating Terrell Castle. The magnificent stone mansion, built in 1894, is full of marvelous possibilities, with the existing guest rooms being only the beginning. Different wings of the four-story home are constantly being restored, with signs bearing the message "feel free to look around" posted for curious guests like me!

Open and ready for guests are a magnificent entrance hall with a red-brick fireplace and built-in seats in a "coffin" niche, as well as a parlor, library, music room, dining room, breakfast room, and an enclosed porch.

The home was built by Edwin Terrell, a San Antonio lawyer and statesman who served under President Benjamin Harrison as ambassador and plenipotentiary to Belgium in the early 1890s. He fancied a castle like those he saw in Europe, and as soon as he returned home, he commissioned a local architect to build one.

Well, while the Terrell Castle doesn't particularly remind me of a European castle, it does impress me as a very stately mansion. The front staircase is extraordinary. Antique furniture and lace curtains set off the fine parquet floors and curved windows in the parlor. The dining room has a huge fireplace and a wood-paneled ceiling, the first like it I've seen.

Rooms are named for their colors, and I had a hard time deciding whether I preferred the Blue Room or the Yellow; both are lovely. The suite has a fireplace, dressing room, small sitting room, and arched windows enclosing the porch.

All the fireplaces in the house are functional, including one with a green-tiled mantel in the meeting room on the third floor. The top floor, awaiting completion, has windows facing all four directions and a grand view of San Antonio.

Breakfast is a feast of ham, bacon, or sausage, eggs however you want them (I like mine poached or "over-easy"), muffins, raisin bread, biscuits, preserves, dry cereal, juice, coffee, tea, and milk.

There's a television in the large library-office, and guests can watch whenever they want. ☛ "The whole house is open to you," say Katherine and Nancy, who also have many good suggestions on where to dine in San Antonio, a fiesta city.

How to get there: Grayson Street is between Broadway and New Braunfels streets, adjacent to Fort Sam Houston.

TAYLOR

Aquarena Springs Inn
San Marcos, Texas
78666

Innkeeper: Rich Westfall
Address/Telephone: 1 Aquarena Springs Drive; (512) 396–8901
Rooms: 25; all with private bath.
Rates: $35 to $55; $8 per additional person over 4; $5 roll-away or baby
bed. No pets. All major credit cards accepted.
Open: All year.
Facilities and Activities: Restaurant on the grounds and at Peppers at
the Falls 1 mile away. Swimming pool; golf; Aquarena Springs Park
with glass-bottom boats, submarine theater, cliffside gardens and
aviary, sky ride, frontier village, Olympic-size pool, and other attractions.

Aquarena Springs Inn is ☞ built on the site of the oldest
permanent Indian encampment in North America. I'll bet that's
a surprise; it sure was for me! ☞ Archaeologists have found the
remains of Clovis Man, the hunter-gatherer who lived on the San
Marcos River over 12,000 years ago.

Another surprise— ☞ you can see where they lived if you
peer down from your glass-bottom boat. The site is covered by
Spring Lake, and I also saw some of the one-hundred varieties of
aquatic life swimming or growing down below.

Over 150 million gallons of Texas's purest water filters through honeycomb limestone to make Spring Lake, and on its shores is perched the prettiest white-and-aqua Mediterranean villa, Aquarena Springs Inn. It's been here since 1927, and nineteen of its rooms overlook the lake. Ducks and swans swim along, waiting to be fed bread crumbs—generations of inn guests have spoiled them rotten.

The back hall of the inn has huge glass windows so you can see the flora growing up the steep cliff immediately behind the inn. I also got a thrill from riding the Swiss Sky Ride and catching ☛ the Texas-Hill-Country view from the 300-foot-high Sky Spiral.

"It can be quiet here even in a crowd," said long-time innkeeper Paul Trottman, who retired to rest and write his memoirs. "The only noise we hear are ducks and trains—everybody mentions it." New innkeeper Rich Westfall agrees. "Even on the busiest days, it never seems crowded."

That's because there's plenty of room for everyone to spread out in this beautiful green parkland full of both fun and relaxing things to do. I munched on a plate of king-size nachos outdoors by the river at Peppers and took deep breaths of the fresh air alongside the crystal-clear water. Then, at the restaurant, I feasted on huge fried shrimp and a plateful of wonderful selections from the salad bar. Later, I sat on the inn veranda overlooking the lake and watched little children feeding the ducks. All I could hear was the laughter of the children and the quacking of ducks.

How to get there: From Interstate 35 take Exit 206 and go ½ mile west to Aquarena Springs Drive. There are signs—you can't miss it.

Crystal River Inn
San Marcos, Texas
78666

Innkeepers: Cathy and Mike Dillon
Address/Telephone: 326 West Hopkins Street; (512) 396–3739
Rooms: 8; 2 with private bath, 2 with shared bath, and a 2-room suite in main house, 3 rooms with private bath in The Innlet across the street.
Rates: $40 to $45 weekdays, continental breakfast included; $60 to $65 weekends, 3-course brunch included. No toddlers. No pets. Smoking in public areas only. MasterCard, Visa accepted.
Open: All year.
Facilities and Activities: San Marcos River, crystal clear, is great for water sports, and the Dillons will show you the ropes. Southwest State University, LBJ's alma mater, is nearby.

Crystal River Inn aims for a California feeling, says Cathy, and the colors and much of the inn décor carry out this idea most refreshingly. Cathy and Mike are "river rats" as well, and the inn rooms are named for three famous Texas rivers and reflect their personalities.

The Colorado Room has a distinctly Southwest flavor, with a rope-canopy bed and cactus in the window boxes. The Frio Room is sky blue, and the Pedernales Room is peach and navy blue.

236

The honeymoon suite is named for the beautiful Medina. The house, designer decorated, is clean and uncluttered.

"Last night I came up and just sat on the veranda," Tena Ward, visiting from Arlington, up near "Big D," told me. "It's a treat to stay here; it's so homelike."

Cathy says 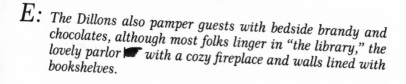 the veranda upstairs is the "happy hour" porch. "Usually our guests come breezing in here from Houston or Dallas, and they're all tightly wound. We put them up on the veranda with a drink in their hands, and in an hour the change is just amazing."

Crystal River Inn is also known for its knockout weekend brunch. I feasted on fruit-filled cantaloupe ring, beer biscuits that Cathy calls "beerscuits," sausage, and the *pièce de résistance*, bananas Foster crêpes topped with crême fraiche and toasted, slivered almonds. Cathy invented the recipe, and when she made the crêpes for a chamber-of-commerce fund-raiser, people were lined up and winding out the door waiting for them.

During the week, breakfast consists of fruit, sausage, coffee, tea, juice, and a whole assortment of homemade breads like zucchini and apple-fritter. Nothing wrong with that, either.

How to get there: Take exit 205 off Interstate 35. This is Highway 80, which becomes Hopkins in town. The inn will be on your right, just before you come to Rural Route 12 to Wimberley.

❀

E: *The Dillons also pamper guests with bedside brandy and chocolates, although most folks linger in "the library," the lovely parlor* with *a cozy fireplace and walls lined with bookshelves.*

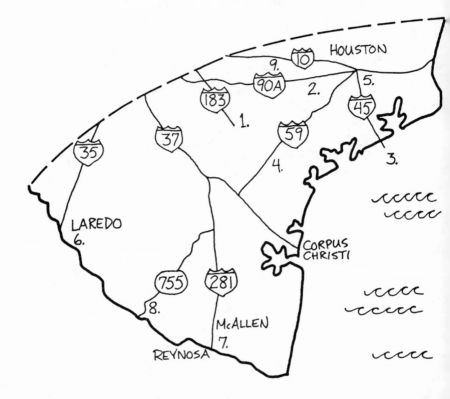

Gulf Coast/Border Texas

Numbers on map refer to towns numbered below.

Reiffert-Mugge Inn
Cuero, Texas
77954

Innkeepers: Lisa and Gil Becker
Address/Telephone: 304 Prairie Street; (512) 275–2626
Rooms: 6; all with private bath.
Rates: $40 to $45, weekdays; $45 to $55, Friday and Saturday; includes
continental breakfast. No children under 12 except by prior arrangement. No pets. Smoking outside building only. Cash and personal checks accepted.
Open: All year.
Facilities and Activities: Lunch and dinner by reservation. Two historic-
home tours a year (first Sunday in April; Christmas season). 54
holes of golf within a half-hour drive.

The Reiffert-Mugge Inn is a transplant. "Cuero inherited the
entire village of Indianola, once the finest port on the Gulf of
Mexico," says innkeeper Gil Becker, who also manages Karnak,
Cuero's cable-television system. "It was destroyed by the hurri-
canes of 1875 and 1886. Over a thousand salvageable buildings
were moved to Cuero."

One of them was the Reiffert-Mugge House, built by a retired Confederate general and president of the first chartered
bank in Texas. Restoring and opening it as a bed and breakfast

inn was a Becker project to save the handsome house from ruin. "We fell in love with it the minute we saw it!" says Lisa.

I can understand why. The lovely L-shaped home has two beautiful bay windows in front (now the side) and verandas that bend around the L. The acre of patios, gardens, and oak groves is neatly bordered by an ornate wrought-iron fence. In the large parlor and sitting room, I found the ☞ original wallpaper, installed in 1887, fireplaces, and parquet floors. Memorabilia that Lisa and Gil found in the attic are on exhibit.

Emil's Room is blue, and The Nursery has twin beds, quilts, and stuffed toys. Hilda's Room is reached by going outside onto the veranda. Framed on the wall is the love story of Hilda and Fred Mugge: He proposed to her on his company stationery!

I found some fascinating buildings on the grounds. In addition to the garage, the servants' quarters, the bath house, and the laundry, there's ☞ the Radio House, now the sixth guest room. "It was built for Fred's radio," says Gil. "When he wanted to play his new-fangled radio, the first one in town, he had his own small house to retire to—nobody else wanted to hear it!"

The Mugges also had the first steam heat and the first electricity in town. "The Mugges were great on firsts," Gil says with a twinkle.

Breakfasts, Lisa's specialty, often include apple or lemon loaf, cornbread with bacon and cheese, fresh fruit or spiced peaches, orange juice, and coffee, milk, or tea. A special dinner menu might include rolled chicken breast with crabmeat stuffing, broccoli and mushroom stir-fry, glazed carrots and pineapple, and Caesar salad, all topped by "Gooey Butter Cake," an inn secret.

"At five o'clock we like to have a glass of wine with our guests," Gil says. "We make ourselves accessible without being in the way."

How to get there: From Highway 183 into town, take Esplanade Street west. The inn will be two blocks in on the corner of Esplanade and Prairie.

The Farris 1912
Eagle Lake, Texas
77434

Innkeepers: Helen and William Farris; Keith Popp, assistant
Address/Telephone: 201 North McCarty Street; (409) 234–2546
Rooms: 16 share 4 baths; 4 suites with private bath.
Rates: $85 to $95 per person, AP, during hunting season (Nov./Dec./ Jan.); $40 single, $48 double out of season; continental breakfast included. Set-ups for drinks included all year. No children under 12. No pets in hotel (there are two dog kennels in rear). Smoking in rooms and other designated areas only. American Express, Master-Card, Visa accepted.
Open: All year.
Facilities and Activities: Excellent duck, deer, and goose hunting; golf and tennis courts nearby; National Wildlife Refuge, 6 miles.

The Farris 1912 is on the town corner where Eagle Lake began in 1857; before that, the site held a cowboy stage stop. Helen and William Farris bought and renovated the hotel in 1974, and Victorian and turn-of-the-century antiques reflect the 1912-to-1930s era that was Eagle Lake's Golden Age.

Today The Farris 1912 revels in the Hunting Age: Its rooms are at a premium during the winter, and it caters to the nostalgia buffs the rest of the year. Bedrooms upstairs open off a huge, square mezzanine, where hunters can relax after a sumptuous meal and play cards or dominoes in the cozy, family atmosphere. There's a 10:00 P.M. curfew, though, because all mighty Nimrods rise early.

But the downstairs Drummers Room, with a bar set-up and game tables amid the stuffed game birds decorating the walls, stays open all evening.

The meals are really something to write home about, and assistant innkeeper Keith told me why Helen finally had to write a cookbook: "After the many years of hunters trying to sneak recipes, Helen has everything all spelled out!"

The family-style buffet is a groaning board. A plate full of Polynesian chicken, scalloped potatoes, and fresh green beans smothered in onions and tomatoes shared space with both carrot and apple salad, eaten by candlelight on a lace tablecloth. Whether you're out hunting all day or not, dinner means time to clean up and relax. And have fun trying to choose between Helen's famous bread pudding and her chocolate mousse for dessert!

Room #1 still has the original 1912 hotel furnishings—dark Mission Oak dresser, rocker, and even a hat rack. Every room has a washstand. The entire lobby is a florist, gift, jewelry, and antique shop, and many of the antiques throughout the hotel are for sale.

How to get there: Eagle Lake is one hour west of Houston via US59 and 2½ hours east of San Antonio via I–10 or US90A. The Farris 1912 is two minutes from the town square.

≥

E: *Helen Farris says: "No gratuities are charged, expected, or permitted at any time for lodging or food services." How about that for service?*

The Gilded Thistle
Galveston, Texas
77550

Innkeepers: Helen and Pat Hanemann
Address/Telephone: 1805 Broadway; (409) 763–0194
Rooms: 3; 1 with private bath, 2 share bath; ½ bath downstairs.
Rates: $100 to $125, with full breakfast and snack tray in evening. Children over 7 accepted Monday through Thursday. No pets. No smoking in bedrooms. MasterCard, Visa accepted.
Open: All year.
Facilities and Activities: Historic Ashton Villa and the Bishop's Palace are just down the street on Broadway; the historic Strand, just five minutes away. The Seawall and Gulf beaches are nearby.

I asked innkeeper Helen Hanemann to explain The Gilded Thistle's name, because it seemed to me to be a contradiction. Helen, very much into Galveston's history, said that, like native thistle, sturdy Texas pioneer stock sank deep and lasting roots into the sandy island soil, building a Galveston that flowered into a gilded age of culture and wealth.

Her home was part of those people and their times—in the late 1800s, Galveston's Strand was known as "the Wall Street of the West"—and The Gilded Thistle is a lovely memorial to Galveston's past.

The ☛ beautiful antiques throughout the house make it an exceptionally elegant place to stay, ☛ but the atmosphere is so homey that my awe melted away to pure admiration. Helen is on duty at all times, and I joined the other guests in her kitchen, watching her arrange the fresh flowers that fill the rooms.

It wasn't hard to get used to being served on fine china, with coffee or tea from a family silver service. Breakfast, Helen says, is "whenever you want," and I took mine on the L-shaped screened porch around the dining room, especially enjoying Helen's specialty, "nut chewies." There's always a bowl filled with apples or other fruit on the sideboard.

Tea and coffee are available at all times, and I loved it when my morning began with orange juice and a pot of boiling water for coffee or tea at my bedroom door.

The evening snack tray could almost take the place of dinner, what with its strawberries and grapes and other fruit in season, at least four kinds of cheese, and wine. "It's my gift to you for coming," Helen says. For dining, she helps guests choose from the town's many fine restaurants, from Gaido's (famous for seafood) on the Seawall to the Wentletrap (continental fare) on The Strand.

Helen loves company and is in her element when two of Galveston's big hotels send her their overflow. She'll even trade her bedroom with those guests who prefer her twin beds to the guest rooms' doubles. But I reveled in the master bedroom, with its four-poster facing a bay window, which made a cozy setting for the antique sofa and chairs surrounding the mantelpiece.

☛ The Gilded Thistle is also gilded horticulturally. The inn's landscaping won two prizes in 1986: the Springtime Broadway Beauty Contest and a second-place award for a business in a historic building.

How to get there: Stay on Highway 45 south, which becomes Broadway as soon as you cross the causeway onto Galveston Island. The inn will be just beyond 18th Street, on your right.

The Matali
Galveston, Texas
77550

Innkeeper: Dan Dyer
Address/Telephone: 1727 Sealy Street; (409) 763–4526
Rooms: 3; 1 with private bath, 2 share bath.
Rates: $85 the first night, $75 subsequent nights, breakfast and evening
wine and cheese included. Children over 12. No pets No smoking.
American Express. MasterCard, Visa accepted.
Open: All year.
Facilities and Activities: Rates include passes for swimming pool at
nearby resort hotel and for transportation on the Galveston Trolley
Car, which stops at the inn's front door on its way to the historic
Strand and to the beach.

Innkeeper Dan Dyer chose to name his inn after Amadeo
Matali, who lived in this pretty Victorian mansion from 1928
until his death in 1981 (he was in his nineties). But old-timers in
Galveston still call it the Isabella Offenbach Maas House. That's
because Isabella Maas, the sister of the famous French composer
Jacques Offenbach, built the home in 1886 with her ship-
chandler husband, Samul Maas. I loved the old photographs of
the Maas–Offenbach family hung on the walls; they made me
feel as if I were really staying at a family home as a guest.

The house has ☛ an elaborate gingerbread exterior, with stained-glass windows, an iron fence, and even a hitching post. Inside, four wood-burning fireplaces are beautifully crafted in cherry wood, mahogany, and oak. ☛ The one in the parlor is unique—it has twin flues, one on each side of the stained-glass window, which is over the mantel!

☛ Each of the guest rooms has a private veranda, and I loved the stenciled floors in the Maas Room. The Offenbach Room has twin beds and a sitting area with wicker furniture.

Besides a large formal parlor and large dining room, The Matali has a music room, complete with upright piano and a ☛ 1917 Victrola, both of which guests are welcome to play. Cozy furniture is pulled up to the cherry-wood fireplace, there's a game table waiting, and an interesting spoon collection under glass begs for inspection.

Actually, the whole atmosphere at the Matali is one of play. Dan is a great one for getting his guests laughing and joking. He's the perfect innkeeper, believing that when you stay at an inn, "you actually become a part of where you stay, instead of being a tourist spending money."

Dan restored the beautiful house with tender, loving care, spending fifteen months stripping and refinishing the woodwork. A now-extinct curly pine was used for wainscoting in the dining room and up the fine carved cypress staircase. The staircase and the jeweled stained-glass windows above it are the first striking thing you see when you enter.

There's a wet bar in an alcove off the dining room and coffee set out for early birds. Breakfast consists of such hearty treats as pancakes, sausage, eggs, and fresh fruit in addition to coffee, tea, and orange juice. For evening meals, Dan will suggest one of Galveston's fine seafood restaurants.

How to get there: Take Interstate 45 south, which becomes Broadway after you cross the causeway into Galveston. Turn left at 18th Street, and proceed one block to Sealy. The inn is on the corner of 18th and Sealy, just on your left.

Tremont House
Galveston, Texas
77550

Innkeeper: Roy Chen
Address/Telephone: 2300 Ship's Mechanic Row; (409) 763–0300
Rooms: 108; all with private bath.
Rates: $80 to $110, depending upon season. No pets. Some non-smoking
   rooms. All major credit cards accepted.
Open: All year.
Facilities and Activities: Dining room open for breakfast and lunch;
   Wentletrap Restaurant open for dinner; lobby bar open for tea and
   cocktails. Shuttle to Hotel San Luis for use of swimming pool. Shops,
   galleries, restaurants on The Strand historical district; the 1877
   sailing ship *Elissa;* Victorian homes in nearby silk-stocking district.

   The Tremont is the elegant transformation of one of
Galveston's historic drygoods buildings, the Leon Blum Building,
into a first-class luxury hotel.
   The long, narrow four-story building has handsome Neo-
Renaissance details, dormer windows, and a mansard roof. But it
doesn't look much like a hotel, as it has the elegant appearance
of business buildings in European capitals like Paris and Geneva.
The entrance is marked by potted plants on each side, and a

friendly uniformed doorman is quick to open the door with a smile.

Once I stepped inside, I was entranced. The color scheme of the entire hotel, guest rooms included, is black and white, softened by the gold of gleaming brass and the green of potted palms. The white stucco, black-and-white-tiled atrium/lobby is shaded by tall, flourishing trees dappled, daytimes, with sunlight from the skylights four stories above. I rode up through the light in one of the 🖝 two bird-cage elevators, but not before I was welcomed by innkeeper Roy and the friendly desk personnel.

"We try to the best of our ability to provide a warm and friendly service," Roy says. "We always call our guests by name, and we enjoy providing those special extra touches, like Godiva chocolates at nightly turn-down and complimentary shoeshine, with your shoes returned to you wrapped."

My black-and-white room had fourteen-foot celings and eleven-foot windows. I would have felt dwarfed if not for the warm Victorian furnishings: the white-and-brass bed, the white-eyelet ruffled spread, and the lush black carpet (with a small white pattern woven into it) on the richly polished wood floor.

The original Tremont House, built in 1839, burned in 1865. In its time it was the largest hotel in the Republic of Texas, and Sam Houston made his headquarters there. The second Tremont, built in 1872, had its share of glory, too, with Edwin Booth, W. H. Vanderbilt, Buffalo Bill, two Sioux chiefs, and Anna Pavlova among its guests. So you can see that today's Tremont House has quite a tradition to follow.

The Merchant Prince, an attractive small restaurant off the atrium, serves light repasts. Between times, guests gather in the atrium for afternoon tea or cocktails. The white wicker furniture sets just the right mood.

A walkway joins the atrium to the Wentletrap, named for a rare seashell and serving fine continental food. I had breast of chicken in a light creamed artichoke-heart sauce, and my companion said the red snapper Pontchartrain was delicious. We finished off with a scintillating Grand Marnier soufflé.

How to get there: Drive south on I–45, which becomes Broadway on the island. Turn left on 23rd, and Ship's Mechanic Row is 7 blocks down.

The Victorian Inn
Galveston, Texas
77550

Innkeeper: Yvonne Daniel
Address/Telephone: 511 17th Street; (409) 762–3235
Rooms: 4 sharing 2 baths; 3rd-floor suite with private bath.
Rates: Summer: $75, Sunday through Thursday; $85, Friday and Saturday; suite, $100 weekdays, $110 weekends. Check for winter rates. Hearty continental breakfast included. No children under 12. No pets. American Express, Diners Club, MasterCard, Visa accepted.
Open: All year.
Facilities and Activities: Close to The Strand historical district, the historic sailing ship *Elissa,* the Railroad Museum; the Seawall, beaches.

Isaac Heffron, who built the first sewer systems for both Houston and Galveston, built his family a beautiful red-brick residence with a wraparound veranda and a gorgeous circular porch upstairs off the master bedroom. That room is named Mauney's Room, and it was the one for me. Green and yellow, two of my favorite colors, decorate the big room, which is filled with brass, wicker, and antiques. It shares a bath with Isaac's Room, which is brown and blue with patterned wallpaper.

This house is so lovely, there's not room here to describe all

250

the beautiful things in it. The entry hall is immense. It has a hand-carved wooden settee by the fireplace and two more facing each other at the end of the room, with a checkerboard set up for guests on the table between them.

The parlor has a floor done in a hand-cut-and-laid maple design, a hand-carved mantel, and its original crystal chandelier. But the best part of this elegant inn is the welcome that Yvonne offers to guests—I just know she loves her job.

Her enthusiasm is catching as she tells about the work she's done looking up Heffron family history. She even has some 1915 newspapers with items about the Heffrons for guests to read.

In addition to local history lessons, guests get fresh flowers in their rooms, coffee and tea anytime they want in the sunny, yellow butler's pantry, and, for repeat guests, a bottle of wine. Breakfast is orange juice, coffee, tea, milk, fruit in season, cold cereals, a variety of breads—"energy stuff," says Yvonne—and either croissants or her wonderful applesauce-oatmeal bread stuffed with raisins. I started out with just half of the thick piece Yvonne cut but soon went back for the other half.

I sat on the curved upstairs porch with a refreshing glass of iced tea in my hand and rocked in the fresh breeze sweeping in off the Gulf. Ryan's Room has a balcony, and Amy's Room has an open porch, so I wasn't the only one savoring the breeze. And of course, there's always the veranda that wraps around the house, with its view of shady green trees and other grand old houses.

Galveston is synonymous with seafood. The Captain's Table offers a "whale of a flounder" as well as shrimp, oysters, and crabs. Angelo's Fisherman's Reef serves super seafood, too, along with a panoramic view of trading ships from all over the world.

How to get there: Drive south on Interstate 45 into Galveston; the highway becomes Broadway. Turn left at 17th; the inn will be on your left when you reach the 500 block.

❋

E: *If Yvonne knows it's a special occasion, she just loves to surprise you with a special tray of wine coolers and cheese or some other treat.*

The Virginia Point Inn
Galveston, Texas
77550

Innkeepers: Eleanor and Tom Catlow
Address/Telephone: 2327 Avenue K; (409) 763–3760
Rooms: 5; 4 double, one single; one with private bath, others share.
Rates: $60 to $125, with full breakfast and snack tray in evening. Children over 12 OK. No pets. No smoking in bedrooms or dining room. American Express, MasterCard, Visa, Diners Club accepted.
Open: All year.
Facilities and Activities: Excursions on a 40-foot sailboat are offered to guests if the Catlows are going sailing. Bicycles are furnished.

The Virginia Point Inn, towering above the garden on its corner lot, is a grayed, white-stucco Neo-Mediterranean house, foursquare with huge screened porches both upstairs and down. And as large as the inn is the welcome extended by innkeeper Eleanor Catlow, who eagerly gives tours of the house.

When I asked about the inn's name, she gave me a copy of a letter written in 1864 by Tom's great-grandfather, R. S. Guy. He was stationed in a Confederate Army fort on Virginia Point, a spit of land in Galveston Bay overlooking Galveston Island, and the letter makes fascinating reading.

The small, single room, named the R. S. Guy Room, was the

sewing room when the house was built. It still has an ironing board built into the wall and a wonderful old oval washbasin in working condition.

The big bedrooms open off porches, and the shared bathrooms can be entered without leaving your bedroom. I was fascinated by all the built-in wall cupboards surrounding each room's quite-modern closet. Even more, I loved the 🖝 thoughtfulness of terry wraps and sun hats in guest closets.

Early morning coffee and juice, brought on trays complete with tiny vases of fresh flowers, are followed by a hearty breakfast of melon, cold ham and cheese, cereal, and hot breads served from 8:00 A.M. to 10:00 A.M. in the dining room.

At 6:00 P.M. a wine-and-cheese tray appears in the parlor, where Eleanor and Tom like to join their guests, answer questions, and give advice about what to see and where to go in historic Galveston. They also keep a collection of menus and are happy to recommend one, or all, of Galveston's fine restaurants.

When I came in from sightseeing on a warm summer day, I was really pleased to find a filled cookie jar, as well as the makings of tea and coffee, in the large, square butler's pantry off the kitchen. 🖝 An old fridge is there for guests to store soda and beer in, too.

What guests like most of all, says Eleanor, is to go sightseeing for a while, and then "they return and sit on a porch all afternoon and read." The inn's breezy, screened verandas are so delightful that they've been used as settings for fashion-magazine photography shoots.

How to get there: Go south on Interstate 45, which becomes Broadway as soon as you cross the causeway onto Galveston Island. Turn right at 24th Street and the inn is one block in to your left on the corner of 24th and Avenue K.

⌒

E: *There's a wonderful old Art Deco jigsaw puzzle on the parlor table. It's a circle puzzle called "The Seven Deadly Sins," and whoever wants to can rock on the porch—I'd rather work the puzzle!*

The Dial House
Goliad, Texas
77963

Innkeeper: Dolores Clarke
Address/Telephone: 306 West Oak Street; (512) 645–3366
Rooms: 4; share 3 baths.
Rates: $40 to $45, single; $50 to $55, double occupancy; price depends
on whether private bath is requested. Full breakfast and large
evening snack included. No pets. No smoking. MasterCard, Visa
accepted.
Open: All year.
Facilities and Activities: Goliad State Park has Spanish missions and
the Presidio La Bahia, a fort infamous in Texas history.

The first thing you'll notice about The Dial House is its
landscaping, which is lush and green and bountiful. Dolores is a
passionate gardener, and you may have to hunt for her somewhere on her grounds.

"Everything out here, including trees, has been planted by
these gnarled old hands," she says with great good humor. Dolores
is also passionate about The Dial House, which is a family home
furnished with pieces that were in the house "before I was born."

Dolores grew up during the Great Depression. Her parents

went from one place to another looking for work, and they often sent young Dolores to her Aunt Dial in Goliad.

"This was my refuge. I loved it here, and my aunt gave me the house before she died." Dolores's refuge was my delight; it is a real treat to stay here. Dolores does things like sheets with pink roses in the room that has pink roses all over the wallpaper. She laughs about what she calls the "vile green" wallpaper in the dining room, which she papered years ago when her aunt asked her to redo those walls.

"I don't know why I picked it—guess because I liked green. It's quite a conversation piece!"

So are breakfast and the evening snack tray, both evidence of Dolores's supreme hospitality. Her breakfasts always have two kinds of meat and several main choices, such as scrambled eggs, quiche, and sausage rolls. "In case people don't like one thing, they can have another," says Dolores.

There's always a big plate of fresh fruit (I recommend particularly a bowl of Dolores's home-frozen peaches) and hot biscuits. "They're full when they leave my table," Dolores can well boast.

What Dolores calls her "evening snack tray" filled me up: finger sandwiches along with an old family recipe called "waxed pecan squares," old-time bread pudding with warm peach sauce, a banana-cream cake with whipped cream and fresh bananas, and brownies besides. Dolores is an innkeeper who truly loves her calling and loves to see you eat.

She has two kinds of oatmeal cookies "I keep ready to pull out at any time, German chocolate cake, cheesecake . . ." I had to cry halt—at least until the next day.

How to get there: The inn is located east of Highway 77A/183 and three blocks north of US 59.

✳

E: *I loved relaxing in Dolores's "Plant Room," which she built to house her plants and her collections of dolls that she played with when she was a little girl.*

The White House Inn
Goliad, Texas
77963

Innkeepers: Janet and Mert Rawson
Address/Telephone: 203 North Commercial Street; (512) 645–2701
Rooms: 3; all with private bath.
Rates: $35 to $45, double occupancy; $5 for extra person in room; full
   breakfast included. Playpen for babies. No pets. Smoking accepted
   but not encouraged. MasterCard, Visa accepted.
Open: All year.
Facilities and Activities: Dove, duck, quail, turkey, and deer hunting
   September and October; quarterhorse racing March, July, Septem-
   ber. (No pari-mutuel betting in Texas, but picture may change
   because of recent bills in state legislature.) Goliad is a historic Texas
   town with many mementos of Texas's War of Independence from
   Mexico.

"I like to serve as though I'm still entertaining in my own
home," says Janet as she toasts another piece of her wonderful
homemade bread and pushes the pot of homemade apricot mar-
malade closer to me. The Rawsons treat all their guests the same,
royally, on silver and china, and it's no wonder that they have a
lot of repeat business.

"They come for the breakfast," Janet says with a modest

laugh, and I believe it. In addition to juice and fruit in season, we had special scrambled eggs, sausage, and homemade bran muffins as well as Janet's marvelous bread, but I could just as well have arrived on a quiche day.

The ☞ atmosphere of the inn is of colonial New England, not surprising since the Rawsons are from back East. There's even ☞ an old spinning wheel in the parlor, and it fits cozily alongside the tiled hearth and the warm wood-paneled walls.

There are lots of interesting antiques in the inn. One of the more unusual is ☞ the 1800s rosewood Melodian, an air-pumped organ, in the dining room.

The Blue Room has a king-sized brass bed and a blue washbasin, which make it seem very European. (The bathroom has the commode and a shower.) Both the Blue Room and the Yellow Room (with twin beds) are very large corner rooms.

The Green Room, in a separate wing at the side of the house, is almost a suite, it's so large. It also has a different feeling from that of the main house—it's almost oriental in its furnishings, with bamboo furniture and oriental art. With its sleeper sofa in the sitting area, this room is perfect for a family.

Janet keeps ☞ fresh flowers in each room, as well as ice water and yummy brownies, which are my undoing! Menus are handy for determining where to dine when going out on the town.

The Rawsons, transplanted Easterners as they are, have become enthusiastic Texans. "We believe in Goliad!" Janet says. Her eyes shine as she tells about the original Goliad County Court House with a "hanging tree" on the grounds, the square with antique shops, and the Spanish missions, each full of history, just south of town.

How to get there: The inn is one block north of Highway 59 and three blocks west of Highway 183/77A, which puts it right in the center of town.

La Colombe d'Or
Houston, Texas
77006

Innkeeper: Steve Zimmerman
Address/Telephone: 3410 Montrose Boulevard; (713) 524–7999
Rooms: 6 suites; all with private bath.
Rates: $150 to $200, with continental breakfast. No pets American
   Express, MasterCard, Visa, Diners Club accepted.
Open: All year.
Facilities and Activities: Restaurant, bar. Located just five minutes from
   Houston central business district, the Astrodome, Houston Museum
   of Fine Arts, Rice University, and Menil Art Foundation.

It's no surprise to find this exquisite inn so close to two art
collections: ☛ The inn is patterned after its namesake in St.
Paul de Vence, France, where many of that country's famous
painters traded their work for lodging. Houston's Colombe (the
dove) is hung with fine art, too, and each suite has a name I
certainly recognized.

I stayed in the Van Gogh Suite, named for one of my favorite
Impressionist painters. Others are named for Degas, Cézanne,
Monet, and Renoir; the largest suite, up at the top, is called
simply The Penthouse. ☛ The suites are decorated with fine art,
although there are no original works of their namesakes.

But I didn't miss them, so swathed in beauty and luxury was I in this prince of an inn. On my coffee table I found fruit, Perrier water, and wine glasses waiting to be filled from my complimentary bottle of the inn's own imported French wine.

Owner Steve Zimmerman has succeeded in bringing to Houston's Colombe d'Or the casual elegance of the French Riviera. ☛ European and American antiques, as well as his own collection of prominent artists' works, are set in the luxurious house that was once the home of Exxon-oil founder Walter Fondren and his family.

The twenty-one-room mansion, built in 1923, is divided into suites, each boasting a huge bedroom with sitting area and ☛ a glass-enclosed dining room with Queen Anne furniture, china plates, linen napkins, and cutlery in readiness for breakfast. As soon as I telephoned in the morning, a waiter arrived with a tea cart from which he served a very French-style plate of sliced kiwi fruit, raspberries, and strawberries, in addition to orange juice, coffee, and croissants with butter and jam. I ate this artistic offering surrounded by the green leafy boughs waving outside my glass room.

You may have luncheon or dinner served in your room, too, but I feasted downstairs on meunière of shrimp and lobster, cream-of-potato-and-leek soup, the inn's Caesar salad, and capon Daniel; and as if that weren't enough, I ended with creme Bruleé! ☛ French chef Hervé Glin even came to my table (and others) to see that the food met with my approval!

How to get there: 3410 Montrose is between Westheimer and Alabama, both Houston thoroughfares.

❧

E: *If you long to visit France, you may decide you don't have to once you've visited La Colombe d'Or. The inn is a member of "Relais et Chateau," a French organization that guarantees excellence, and I absolutely soaked up the hospitality, tranquility, and luxury!*

The Lancaster Hotel
Houston, Texas
77002

Innkeeper: Roberta Sroka
Address/Telephone: 701 Texas Avenue; (713) 228–9500
Rooms: 93 (including 8 suites); all with private bath.
Rates: $125 to $450. Pets permitted with deposit (refundable if there's
  no damage). One nonsmoking floor. All major credit cards accepted.
Open: All year.
Facilities and Activities: Restaurant, afternoon tea in lobby, lounge,
  24-hour room service; access to health club. Adjacent to Jones Hall
  and Alley Theater, close to Music Hall and Wortham Lyric Center.

"We're known as the Theater Hotel in town," says Roberta.
"We're across the street from Jones Hall and the Alley Theater
and just blocks from the Music Hall and the new Wortham Lyric
Center." Which makes the Lancaster Grille a popular pre- and
post-theater eating spot. Its specialties are the cream-of-onion
soup and broiled-rib lamb chops. I had a time, too, deciding
whether I wanted the white- or the dark-chocolate mousse for
dessert! For breakfast, my mushroom omelet was very good.

Often the performers themselves, especially singers, are hotel guests, Roberta told me. The reason is insightful.

"Our windows open, which is very popular with opera stars.

They open them all; air conditioning is bad for their throats." Also popular, certainly with me, were all the special touches that make this elegant hotel so charming. Each room has a sitting area. Fresh flowers, turn-down service, and ☛ truffles on my pillow at night, as well as a terrycloth robe, complimentary morning and evening newspapers, a bathroom scale, and an umbrella!, made me feel like someone cared.

"We pride ourselves on personal service and attention," Roberta says. "We have a complete guest-history report, and we try to include favorite champagne and flowers in guests' rooms."

Hotel décor, traditional country English, includes flowered chintzes and dark polished wood. Furniture is all authentic reproduction, and bathrooms are extra large, complete with special toiletries and bottles of Evian and Artesia waters. The lobby has a living-room atmosphere, comfortable and relaxing for cocktails.

I can see why The Lancaster also has a reputation for being very romantic. It's hard to believe that you're in the center of downtown Houston, that relatively new metropolis of modern, avant-garde buildings, and not in the heart of London, where this sort of quiet elegance is traditional.

"We have a lot of people who spend their wedding night with us," says Roberta, "and they return for anniversaries and birthdays."

It is a wonderful way to celebrate.

How to get there: The Lancaster is in the heart of downtown Houston, on the northeast corner of Texas Avenue and Louisiana.

Sara's
Bed & Breakfast Inn
Houston, Texas
77008

Innkeepers: Donna and Tillman Arledge
Address/Telephone: 941 Heights Boulevard; (713) 868–3533
Rooms: 12; one with private bath, one 2-bedroom suite with 2 baths; 9 share 5½ baths.
Rates: $46 to $96, including continental breakfast. Children over 12 only. No pets. Smoking in outside areas only. American Express, MasterCard, Visa accepted.
Open: All year.
Facilities and Activities: Spa on large sun deck, sun balcony, and widow's walk; television room and games. Houston Heights area of historic interest. Near Farmers Market.

Sara's is named for the Arledges' young daughter, who loves having an inn so much that she's become a parent's dream. "Whatever I ask, she'll do," Donna says. "She loves the idea, she loves the place, she loves to help!"

This ☞ pretty-as-a-picture Victorian is easy to love. Bright bedrooms are furnished with antiques and collectibles. A circular stairway leads up to the third-floor ☞ widow's walk and view of the Houston skyline. Viewing sunrise from the front balcony cheers early risers. The Heights neighborhood has a small town feeling, great to walk (or jog) around in, in spite of the big city less than four miles away.

But it wasn't always so. "To give you an idea," Donna says, "the house had no front door, no back door, all the wood had been pulled out." It was Tillman who fell in love with the house, and in conversations every day, he would tell Donna, "Just look what we could do with it."

Donna gave in. "I finally said anybody who would want something that bad ought to have it."

Each charming room is named after a Texas town, with décor to suit that mood. The Galveston Room has nautical beds, the Tyler Room is white wicker, the San Antonio Room is Spanish. I was intrigued by the plate collection on the dining-room walls. "That's my grandmother's collection," Donna said. "We keep adding to it."

Rooms have books and luggage racks. Downstairs bedrooms have washbasins. The ☞ garden sitting area on the second floor is furnished with white wicker, and the four windows of the cupola shower the entire house with light.

Breakfast is a friendly gathering in the dining room, with the plate collection for an ice-breaker if need be. But many guests are repeaters, which makes them old friends.

Donna has the menu for her favorite dining place, Danna's Restaurant, about five miles away and the nearest good place to eat. Chicken Danna is a super choice: breast of chicken stuffed with mozzarella cheese and prosciutto, all smothered with a brandy-cream sauce. For dessert, have the "Mountainous Cream Puff," huge and filled with delicious vanilla custard.

If you tell Donna it's a special occasion, there will be champagne and a small cake waiting. "If I know about these things, I love to do it," Donna says. One guest surprised his wife by telling her they were going to Austin (the city) for the weekend, and she was certainly surprised by the Austin Room at Sara's! (She loved it!)

How to get there: From east on I–10, drive to Shepherd Drive, turn left onto 11th, then right onto Heights Boulevard. Proceed 1½ blocks; the inn will be on your left. From west on I–10, take Heights Boulevard exit and drive to 941.

Warwick Hotel
Houston, Texas
77251

Innkeeper: Ben Hendrick
Address/Telephone: 5701 Main Street; (713) 526–1991
Rooms: 310 rooms and suites; all with private bath.
Rates: $90 to $125 to $1,100 for the presidential suite. No charge for children (under 18). All major credit cards accepted.
Open: All year.
Facilities and Activities: Restaurant, café, private club open to guests. Swimming pool, saunas, beauty salon, use of fitness club one block away. Gift shop. Valet parking. Both Houston Fine Arts and Contemporary Art museums; Hermann Park with city zoo; golf, tennis; Astrodome, Astroworld.

More than a first-class hotel, Houston's Warwick is 🖙 an art museum in the bargain. When it opened in 1964, it was hailed as a "jewel in a perfect setting." Owner John Mecom set the scene for his fabled private collection of priceless European antiques and *objets d'art.* 🖙 Works of art are placed in every nook and cranny of this elegant hostelry for guests to enjoy.

Staying here, I felt like royalty. The statues at the front entrance are from an eighteenth-century Viennese palace. The 🖙 tapestry of the goddess Diana hanging on the rear wall of the lobby is a priceless Aubusson woven in France in the early 1700s.

Much of the beautiful, satiny wood paneling throughout the hotel came from the palace of Napoleon's brother-in-law, Prince Murat. So you see what I mean.

But it's not just the art; the hotel personnel helps to make you feel royal. Everyone leaps to attention with a genuine smile, however slight your wish. "We exist to provide a suitable background for particular people," says innkeeper Ben. "We try to blend traditional European elegance with Southern hospitality."

Guests also get to enjoy what Houstonians have been impressed by for years, the famed Warwick Club with its own glass elevator rising to the top of the building. Lunch, cocktails, and dinner can be savored while taking in an all-round view of the spectacular Houston skyline. And the food in the Warwick compels you to send your compliments to the chef.

I especially recommend the veal Parmesan, the supreme of hen, or the blackened red snapper. Dessert poses the ultimate test: The pastry cart holds such delicacies as Black Forest cake, Irish cream cake, Sacher torte, and cheesecake, not to mention assorted French pastries.

Rooms, as you can imagine, are supremely elegant in the continental manner. The furniture was custom designed in Louis XV and Louis XVI style, perfect background for Mecom's authentic antique accessories. (I could see why the presidential suite is so expensive: a goodly amount of Prince Murat's panels cover the walls here.)

The Warwick is both a Houston legend and a Houston landmark. Everyone should feel like royalty at least once in a lifetime!

How to get there: The hotel is situated on south Main Street on the north edge of Hermann Park, between the Texas Medical Center and the central business district.

La Posada
Laredo, Texas
78040

Innkeeper: Charles Jensen
Address/Telephone: 1000 Zaragosa Street; (512) 722–1701 and (800) 292–5659
Rooms: 272; all with private bath.
Rates: $55 to $79. No pets. All major credit cards accepted.
Open: All year.
Facilities and Activities: Restaurant and bar, two swimming pools. One block from the International Bridge and Nuevo Laredo, Mexico. Museum of the Republic of the Rio Grande on the grounds.

La Posada's emblem is an eighteenth-century-Spanish gold piece, a 1736 Philip V original, which sets the scene for this very Latin place. Almost everyone at La Posada, in fact most everyone in Laredo, is bilingual, Spanish being spoken as freely as English.

Los Dos Laredos, as the sister cities of Laredo and Nuevo Laredo are called, are a blending of the two distinctly different cultures living together in harmony. Because of this, Los Dos Laredos have *ambiente,* says innkeeper Charles Jensen, and La Posada, right on the Mexican border, considers itself pretty special.

266

It's this friendly *ambiente* that makes inn guests consider La Posada pretty special, too, and I for one return again and again. The two courtyards around blue pools, the arched walkways among tropical flowers and shrubs, the tall palm trees, the friendly and helpful staff—all make going "down to the border" a fun weekend jaunt. First I walk over the International Bridge and shop for marvelous Mexican crafts at prices that are a dream. Then I return for a swim in the newer pool (it has a swim-up bar), a snack in the Import Lot, and dinner in the inn restaurant.

Both American and Mexican food are specialties. For lunch, I had chicken enchiladas; for dinner, the soup du jour (New England Clam Chowder), and thick, juicy prime rib. The salad of lettuce wedges had a delicious curried dressing, and for dessert I succumbed to a chocolate sundae.

La Posada is two buildings in one. The historic part is a white-stucco and red-roofed Spanish building, built in 1916 as a high school. ☛ It stands on the site of the 1755 Spanish village of San Augustine de Laredo, facing San Augustine Plaza with its statue of Mexican hero General Zaragoza. (The second half is an adjacent building remodeled to match perfectly the original Spanish structure.)

Forming the enclosure of the inn's east courtyard is what was once the capitol of the short-lived Republic of the Rio Grande. The Republic was formed in 1839, when local citizens felt neglected by both Mexico and the Texas Republic; but forming their own country soon brought more attention than was wanted! The town was split down the middle when the border question was finally settled, and Laredo folks had the choice of being either Texan or Mexican. The result is a bilingual, bi-social, bi-cultural, bi-economy border town with the best of both worlds and a wonderful inn.

How to get there: Follow I–35 south to Zaragosa Street just before the International Bridge. Turn left, and there's underground parking just past the inn entrance.

La Posada
McAllen, Texas
78501

Innkeeper: John Fischer
Address/Telephone: 100 North Main Street; (512) 686-5411
Rooms: 169 (plus 7 suites); all with private bath.
Rates: $55 to $79. No pets. All major credit cards accepted.
Open: All year.
Facilities and Activities: Restaurant, cafe-cabaret, lounge, pool, convention and meeting rooms; shuttle bus to Reynosa, Mexico. McAllen International Museum. Fishing, hunting, golf, tennis.

This official Texas Historical Landmark has been an inn since it was built in 1918. It was known then as Casa da las Palmas (House of the Palms), and ☞ beautiful green palms still sway over the Spanish Colonial building. The inn has been a center of the valley's social life ever since. (The valley is what this border area of Texas is known as.) McAllen, like most Texas border towns, has close ties with its sister city, Reynosa, and ☞ shopping over the border is a stellar attraction.

"I happen to love Mexico," John says. "Here at La Posada I like to feel that I'm in a Mexican inn, where they're cordial and caring about their guests. There's that one-to-one relationship.

Hopefully, to our staff, guests will always be just that, never a room number."

La Posada calls itself "A Special Place in Time," and I tuned into the special feeling John describes. "When I walk into the hotel each morning I feel like I'm in a different world. Easy-paced, relaxed, genteel and retiring, none of the hurly-burly . . ."

The white-stucco building is imposing, with its red-tiled roof and long arched walkway. The lobby, spacious and airy, looks onto a tropical garden surrounding the ☞ Mexican-tile swimming pool. Arched openings look down on the courtyard from the upper balcony.

☞ Rooms are very Spanish, with deep red carpeting, red-and-black bedspreads, and heavy Spanish furniture. My room had arched windows; I could have been in Spain.

The open circular stairway in the lobby allowed me to sweep down majestically (when I did not use the elevator) to the piano bar for a refreshing frozen margarita. Complimentary snacks added to the cherished feeling. Ruby Red's Café is a lively night spot; the cabaret is named for the valley's renowned ruby red grapefruit.

If you've never tried Mexican food for breakfast, here's your chance. Scrambled eggs with green chilies, Mexican pork sausages, and hot buttered flour tortillas in the coffee shop start the day right. At lunch I had *huachinango Veracruzano,* a delicious fish dish. Or, you might try oysters Tesoro, also an original recipe.

How to get there: Heading west on Business 83, turn north on Main. The inn will be on your left.

La Borde House
Rio Grande City, Texas
78582

Innkeeper: Che Guerra
Address/Telephone: 601 East Main Street; (512) 487–5101
Rooms: 21; all with private bath.
Rates: $40 to $59. No pets. American Express, MasterCard, Visa accepted.
Open: All year.
Facilities and Activities: Restaurant and lounge. Hunting, fishing, bird watching. International Bridge to Mexico; historic Fort Ringgold.

La Borde House is elegant, no doubt about it. Even though it was built on the Texas–Mexico border in 1899, it was designed by French architects in Paris (France, not Paris, Texas!). Leather merchant François La Borde had his inn designed at Paris's Beaux Arts School as a combined home, storehouse, and inn. Its guests were often either cattle barons who sold their herds on nearby Rio Grande River docks or military officers en route to California. La Borde brought to life his visions of European grandeur, and I reveled in its reconstruction. Actually the ambience is New Orleans Creole, and I felt like Scarlett O'Hara when Rhett took her there to wallow in luxury.

Restoration in 1982 was authentic, established from original records and photographs. The inn was built by both European and Rio Grande artisans originally, and replacement brick actually was found at the same brickyard in Camargo, Mexico, that was used originally.

I was entranced by opulence such as collector-quality oriental rugs and English Axminster carpets, and early ledgers record such purchases. Each posh bedroom, named for a local historical event, boasts antique furniture and wallpapers. Many of the papers and fabrics are duplicates of those used in the 1981 restoration of the Texas governor's mansion in Austin.

"It tells the whole history of the border, it's that simple," says Che. "I really get a joy out of the smiles I see on people's faces as they reminisce about old times here in the valley."

The cozy lounge adjoining the restaurant is the place for authentic margaritas (cool tequila drinks), and the restaurant is the place for special border cuisine. The regular Mexican plate of tacos, enchiladas, and tamales, beans, and rice has a special flavor, just right for lunch.

For dinner Che suggested I try the chicken cilentro, which is sautéed in butter, seasoned with that savory south-of-the-border herb, and served on a rice bed. It was delicious, and I topped it off with fried ice-cream, a neat treat of frozen cream dipped in batter and deep fried in a hurry.

How to get there: From Highway 281 take Highway 83 west, which becomes Main Street in town. The inn is on the corner of Main and Garza.

Weimar Country Inn
Weimar, Texas
78962

Innkeeper: Angela Teas
Address/Telephone: Jackson Square; (409) 725–8888
Rooms: 9; 7 with private bath.
Rates: $40 to $80, including continental breakfast. No children under
    12. No smoking. American Express, Visa, MasterCard accepted.
Open: All year.
Facilities and Activities: Restaurant and bar open for lunch Friday,
    Saturday, Sunday; dinner Thursday, Friday, Saturday, Sunday. Bar
    closed Mondays.

This lovely inn has been called "a treasure from what was little more than a shell." It began life in 1875 as a rough-hewn drummer's inn and had the bad luck to be burned down in 1900. Rebuilt, it was demolished by a hurricane in 1909, but today it's been restored as a lovely country inn and restaurant, an elegant hideaway for rest and relaxation and down-home country food.

Each room is furnished with English antiques, and ☛ the queen-sized beds are swathed in homemade quilts. The rooms are named for the ☛ Texas scenes and symbols that grace the stained-glass transoms over each door. I had the "Lone Star

Texas" room; its transom is a beautiful red, white, and blue Texas star.

Hardwood floors gleam throughout the inn, authentically copied pressed-tin ceilings are high overhead, and parlors with red plush furniture just beg to be lounged in.

Chef Pete Heiman is known for his blackened redfish and Hawaiian chicken. I had the chicken, which was terrific, followed by good old-fashioned cherry cobbler. Other choices for dessert were fresh peach or coconut-cream pie. Sunday lunch is a mouth-watering buffet.

Breakfast of juice, coffee, rolls, and blueberry muffins is spread out on a magnificent antique server on the upstairs landing, a roomy place to lounge. I mingled with other guests, but you could carry a tray to your room and loaf some more. ☛ The inn is designed to encourage self-indulgence.

The large lobby-lounge leads to the Texas Railroad Town Bar, named for the railroad tracks that run across the road from the inn. (The original hotel was named Jackson's. It was built when the old Galveston, Harrisburg and San Antonio Railroad finally reached D. W. Jackson's property.) Nowadays, the Weimar Country Inn guarantees that at least one train (a freight) will pass your hotel window each visit.

A porch, running around two sides of the inn, has potted plants and benches to loaf on. I sat down and gazed contentedly across the road to ☛ the old bandstand, the old train station (now the town library), and the relic of a caboose alongside, open for inspection.

How to get there: Weimar is on Interstate 10 between Houston and San Antonio. The hotel is on Jackson Square, one block south of the highway, across the railroad tracks.

❀

E: *Weimar Country Inn puts out a chatty monthly calendar telling of local events you can attend while visiting the inn. Write to get on the mailing list. (P.O. Box 782, Weimar, TX 78962.)*

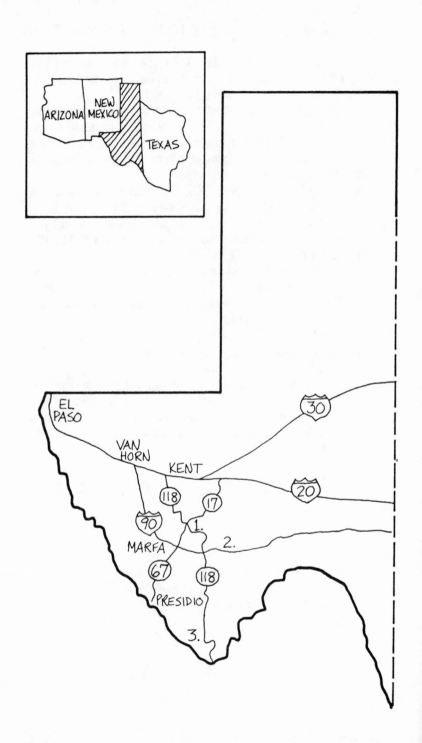

West Texas

Numbers on map refer to towns numbered below.

275

Indian Lodge
Fort Davis, Texas
78734

Innkeeper: Jane Russell
Address/Telephone: Box 786; (915) 426–3254
Rooms: 39; all with private bath.
Rates: $30 to $45; children under 6, free; from 6 to 12, $2. No pets. All major credit cards accepted.
Open: All year except on Christmas Day.
Facilities and Activities: Heated swimming pool. Restaurant. Fort Davis National Historic Site; McDonald Observatory. Nature and hiking trails in Davis Mountains State Park.

Indian Lodge is unique in several ways, all delightful. To begin with, it's set in a state park in the midst of the beautiful Davis Mountains and consequently is managed by the Texas Parks and Wildlife Department. Secondly, it was built by the C.C.C., the Civilian Conservation Corps, in the 1930s. Finally, it was built Indian-pueblo style, and it was built to last.

The lodge's ☞ adobe walls are more than eighteen inches thick. Still in use are many of the massive cedar beds, chests, dressers, and chairs the C.C.C. crew built. In 1967 a complete renovation added twenty-four rooms, a heated swimming pool, and the restaurant.

276

The restaurant serves a wide variety of food—seafood, steak, Mexican food, hamburgers, sandwiches—which is a good thing: The lodge is in an isolated, if beautiful, spot. "We fix box lunches for our guests who want to be out in the park all day," says Jane. Which is what most people want to do.

This part of trans-Pecos country (west of the Pecos River) is greener than I expected. It seems that the mountains surrounding the lodge catch moisture-filled winds, and consequently more rain falls. Added bonuses are the cool nights even in the middle of summer.

"Indian Lodge is so popular, you'll need to make reservations well in advance," says Jane. "Not only is the lodge a fine place in which to stay, but the surroundings are heaven for nature and wildlife buffs as well as for bonafide geologists, botanists, and other nature experts." ☞ All the rooms face the east, too, so everybody gets a gorgeous view of sunrise over the mountains.

The lodge lobby is huge, with massive cedar furniture around fireplaces at each end of the room. I joined most of the guests, however, outside on the verandas; we watched the great view of the landscape, with its prickly pear, yucca, and other desert plants marching up to the mountains.

Be sure to take in the many sights offered in the surrounding areas. McDonald Observatory, operated by the University of Texas, offers public information lectures and displays. (Visitors' viewing through the telescope, however, is limited to the last Wednesday night of each month.)

Fort Davis National Site has a sound re-creation of an 1870s military-retreat parade, with a present-day volunteer in period costume at attention. He sits silently on his horse, while the recording of bugles sounding the retreat mingles with the sounds of shouted orders and the jingle of horses' harnesses. It's vivid and haunting.

How to get there: The lodge is 4 miles northwest of Fort Davis, via Highway 118, in the Davis Mountains. Take 118 west 3 miles to the Park Road–3 entrance and follow the park road to the lodge.

Limpia Hotel
Fort Davis, Texas
79734

Innkeeper: Barbara Laughlin
Address/Telephone: P.O. Box 822; (915) 426–3237
Rooms: 11 in main building, 8 in annex; all with private bath.
Rates: $35 to $110 (for a 4-bed suite). Pets in one room in the annex or
    other rooms by prior arrangement. American Express, MasterCard,
    Visa accepted.
Open: All year.
Facilities and Activities: Fort Davis National Historic Site; McDonald
    Observatory; Overland Trail Museum; Neill Doll Museum; Davis
    Mountains State Park. Hiking trails.

The Limpia is ☞ a real old-timey Western hotel, the kind of
place that makes you expect to see a prospector or two, complete
with panning equipment. The big pink limestone building sits
solid and sturdy on the town square, along with the town's post
office and one bank.

Just around the corner on the side street, the sign hanging
in front of the old-fashioned drugstore boasts "the best Cokes in
Texas." Must be true—inside the large square store, folks are
sipping through straws at the round iron-and-marble tables, while
old-timers rally round the pool table at the rear.

Innkeeper Barbara likes to tell about town history. "Considering that my training was in the field of education and that I've taught adult education here in town, I really like this job." The hotel, she says, was built in 1912 to accommodate a sudden surge of tourists coming to take advantage of Fort Davis's healthy climate. The reason they didn't come earlier is the same reason the town is named Fort Davis: Indians.

Fort Davis was established in 1854 to protect both settlers and the Butterfield Overland Mail from the Apaches and Comanches. They were vanquished about 1886, but it took a while for local merchants to capitalize on the peace and safety.

The Limpia was considered quite elegant in the Fort Davis of 1912. It had prssed-metal ceilings and solid oak furniture and was illuminated by gaslight. Today, it still has pressed-tin ceilings and oak furniture; but the gas has of course been replaced by electricity and other new-fangled notions, such as private bathrooms and air conditioning.

But guest rooms still have transoms over the doors and ☛ a definite air of the Spartan West—no Victorian frills and flounces for the Limpia. The overstuffed furniture in the parlor, in front of the fireplace, almost seems out of place, but it's darn comfortable, especially on a chilly evening.

The hotel itself no longer operates Sutler's Boarding House Restaurant behind the building, but its new management serves the same good country dinners, salads, sandwiches, and pie à la mode. The Loft, above the restaurant, continues to offer good cheer from its bar under the wooden beams that support the building.

How to get there: Highway 118 goes right into town, and the hotel is on the town square across from the bank and the post office.

E: *Afternoons, I loved to sit on the old-fashioned glassed-in veranda, where I could rock under trailing wisps of potted fern and enjoy the bright geraniums while* ☛ *watching the sun set over the Davis Mountains.*

The Gage Hotel
Marathon, Texas
79842

Innkeeper: Giddings Brown
Address/Telephone: P.O. Box 46; (915) 386–4205
Rooms: 20; 19 in main building, 7 with private bath and 12 sharing
men's and women's facilities down the hall on each floor; 1 cottage
room with private bath.
Rates: $30 to $50, with senior-citizen discount. MasterCard, Visa accepted.
Open: All year.
Facilities and Activities: Restaurant serves breakfast and lunch weekends only, dinner 7 nights a week. Bar serves beer and wine only.
Guided tours through Big Bend National Park; Rio Grande River
canyons; horseback trips into mountains of Texas and Mexico; deer
and antelope hunting. The Post, a nearby county park on site of
1880–1893 Fort Pena Colorado, has spring that was a major gathering place for Comanches and is now dammed into a pleasant
pond.

The Gage Hotel was built in 1927 by prosperous banker-
rancher Alfred Gage, who really lived in San Antonio. He wanted
comfortable accommodations when he visited his west-Texas
holdings, so he built this two-story yellow brick to serve as his
headquarters.

The hotel was a true oasis then, more so even than now. Marathon (named by an obscure sea captain who claimed the land reminded him of Greece) and Alpine are the only towns in Brewster County, although it's the largest county in Texas.

I'm sure I wasn't the first visitor to be pleasantly surprised by the sight of this tidy, compact building with its arched doorway and its porch full of rocking chairs, just waiting by the road for a weary traveler.

The rooms, named for such Brewster-County sites as Persimmon Gap, are comfortable but Spartan, definitely more in the male mode, with ranch-style décor, pine floors, and Mexican colonial furniture mixing with English antiques. I was particularly interested in the lobby's original front desk and key box and the antique Chuso (primitive form of roulette) game in the bar.

Giddings shows off the hotel artifacts with enthusiasm. "I like meeting people," he says, "particularly people on a vacation who are having fun. It's a lot more fun working with people who are having fun," he says with a laugh.

The restaurant has some interesting specialties on the menu. I liked the breakfast egg enchiladas, which are eggs scrambled with green onion, rolled up, and liberally covered with ranchero sauce, and the dinner enchiladas pesto, "a cross-culture dish you won't get anywhere except at The Gage," says Giddings. You might think that having both dishes is too much of a good thing, so the menu also has standard west-Texas fare.

I really fell for ☛ the alligator pear pie, an amazing concoction of avocado, cream cheese, lemon, and sugar, but it's seasonal out here in Marathon, where avocados don't grow on trees.

How to get there: Highway 90, running straight through town, goes right by The Gage. I certainly recommend a stop!

Badlands Hotel
Terlingua, Texas
79852

Innkeeper: Regina Worster
Address/Telephone: Star Route 70, Box 400; (915) 424–3471
Rooms: 17; all with private bath.
Rates: $47 to $73. Children OK. Pets accepted. American Express,
MasterCard, Visa accepted.
Open: All year.
Facilities and Activities: Restaurant and bar; swimming pool, tennis,
9-hole golf course; shops, Lajitas Museum; hiking and dove hunt-
ing in Big Bend National Park, rafting on the Rio Grande.

☛ The Badlands Hotel looks just like the set for an Old
West movie. In fact, it looks so much like one that I was surprised
to see the building fronts really had backs!

But they do, and you'll find a hotel with real rooms and a
saloon and a string of Western shops sitting here in the middle of
the desert. And just across the road are the tennis courts and the
swimming pool. And the desert.

This may be confusing, but the whole resort area is called
Lajitas, and it's on the western edge of Big Bend National Park.
You could also stay at The Cavalry Post, built on the site of the
post where General Pershing and his troops tackled Pancho Villa

back in the early 1900s, or in the two motels, La Cuestra or the new Officer's Quarters.

The Badlands Hotel's rooms are all upstairs; the large ones are furnished in Early American, with French doors opening off the upstairs porches onto a great view of the wide-open spaces. On the ground floor you'll find the restaurant; the Badlands Saloon, a regular Western dance-hall kind of bar; and a row of interesting shops. There's the Frontier Drugstore, with an old-fashioned soda fountain; the Mercantile Western Wear (in case you left your boots at home); J. Paul's Liquor Store; and Angie's Flying Circus, a gift store where, among other things, you can buy a kite.

"There's good kite flying here," says Regina. "Surrounded by mountains as we are, you can always count on an airstream."

You can count on good food, too, traditional hearty western dependables. The chicken *fajitas* at lunch were excellent, and I enthusiastically agree with Regina when she says "our barbecue is extra special."

There's usually fun entertainment in the Badlands Saloon: a Mexican band or great country-western dancing. During Oktoberfest you'll probably find a German band merrily oompahing away. The hotel has special parties and dances regularly, Regina says. Almost any time you come, you'll get in on the fun.

How to get there: Take Highway 118 south from the intersection of I–10 and I–20. Lajitas is just west of the road, before you reach Big Bend National Park.

Indexes

Alphabetical Index to Inns

Inns with Restaurants

Inns Serving Dinner by Reservation Only

Inns with AP or MAP Available

Inns with Kitchen Facilities or Privileges

Inns with Meeting Facilities

Inns Near Water

Inns with or with Access to Swimming Pools

Inns with Golf or Tennis Facilities

Inns with Downhill or Cross-Country Skiing nearby

Pets Accepted (by Prior Arrangement and with Restrictions)

Inns That Do Not Accept Children or That Have Restrictions